PRAISE FOR ROBERT K. FITTS'S

Wally Yonamine: The Man Who Changed Japanese Baseball

"Fitts's expertise in Japanese baseball emerges throughout the narrative, as readers come to understand the evolution of baseball in Japan. . . . [*Wally Yonamine*] serves as a great primer on the general historical evolution of Japanese baseball, seen through the career of Wally Yonamine."
     —**ERIC B. SALO**, *NINE*

"Extensively researched, well-written, and endlessly informative and fascinating, this book makes an excellent addition to anyone's baseball library and is absolutely required reading for anyone interested in Japanese-American baseball relations."
     —**MICHAEL STREET**, *Baseball Daily Digest*

"This is a must-read and a must-add to the bookshelf for those with an interest in the history of Japanese baseball, and a worthwhile read for any baseball fan looking to broaden their knowledge of this great game that has spread around the globe."
     —**PAT LAGREID**, Baseballbookreview.com

"A great read about a Japanese baseball player who has been too long overlooked."
     —**L. A. HEAPY**, *CHOICE*

BANZAI BABE RUTH

BANZAI
BABE RUTH

Baseball, Espionage, &
Assassination during
the 1934 Tour of Japan

ROBERT K. FITTS

University of Nebraska Press • Lincoln and London

Library of Congress Cataloging-in-Publication Data

Fitts, Robert K., 1965–
Banzai Babe Ruth : baseball, espionage, and
assassination during the 1934 tour of Japan /
Robert K. Fitts.
    p. cm.
Includes bibliographical references and index.
    ISBN 978-0-8032-2984-6 (cloth : alk. paper)
1. Baseball—United States—History—20th
century. 2. Baseball—Japan—History—20th
century. 3. Ruth, Babe, 1895–1948. 4. Sports
and state—United States. 5. United States—
Foreign relations—20th century. 6. Civilization
—American influences. I. Title.
    GV863.A1F58 2012   796.357—dc23
    2011027373

SET IN CHAPARRAL PRO BY KIM ESSMAN
DESIGNED BY A. SHAHAN

In memory of Wally Yonamine, a
true gentleman who inspired all who
knew him to become better people

Contents

Illustrations

following p. 146

Recurring Japanese Characters

Aoshiba, Kenichi	Pitcher on All Nippon team
Araki, Sadao	Nationalistic general in Japanese Imperial Army
Atsuta, Sukeyasu	Founder of War Gods Society
Date, Masao	Top pitcher on All Nippon team
Fuma, Isamu	Outfielder on All Nippon team
Hamazaki, Shinji	Short pitcher on All Nippon team
Hirota, Koki	Foreign minister of Japan
Horio, Jimmy	Japanese American outfielder on All Nippon team
Ichioka, Tadao	General manager of All Nippon team
Ikeda, Shigenori	Newspaper writer at *Hochi Shimbun*, had idea to invite Babe Ruth to Japan
Inokawa, Toshiharu	Catcher on All Nippon team
Isobe, Asaichi	Member of the Young Officers in Imperial Army
Karita, Hisanori	Shortstop on All Nippon team
Kataoka, Taro	Member of the Young Officers in Imperial Army
Kita, Ikki	Political philosopher and intellectual inspiration for the Young Officers
Kudo, Raisuke	Member of the War Gods Society
Kuji, Jiro	Catcher on All Nippon team
Makino, Motonobu	Infielder on All Nippon team
Marunaka, Yasuichi	Newspaper editor of *Nichi Nichi* newspaper
Matsumoto, Takizo "Frank"	American-educated professor at Meiji University

Map of Japan with location and dates of the games.

Prologue

In early March 1944, Staff Sgt. Jeremiah O'Leary crouched in his muddy foxhole on Cape Gloucester in the South Pacific. Artillery pounded overhead. Visibility was poor in the mangrove swamps, but O'Leary knew that the enemy would come soon. They always did. So far, the invasion of New Breton had gone well. The First Marine Corps had landed at Cape Gloucester on December 26 and, aided by the new Sherman tanks, drove the Japanese back. As a war correspondent, O'Leary had been on the front lines the entire way with a rifle in one hand and a portable Remington in the other. With defeat eminent, the Japanese had begun their suicidal banzai charges. One would certainly come any minute. Sure enough, the artillery ceased. Off to his left, O'Leary heard, "They're coming!," and throaty yells came from the jungle ahead. But the expected banzai never came. Instead, O'Leary distinctly heard in broken English, "To hell with Babe Ruth!," as several dozen Japanese made a fatal charge across the intervening swamp.

A decade earlier, some of those Imperial soldiers may have been among the five hundred thousand Japanese lining the streets of Ginza to welcome Babe Ruth and the All American ballplayers to Japan. On November 2, 1934, a motorcade took the players from Tokyo Station to the Imperial Hotel, built in 1923 by Frank Lloyd Wright. Ruth, though no longer the best player in the league, rode in the first open limousine. At thirty-nine, he had grown rotund and just weeks before had agreed to part ways with the New York Yankees. His future in professional baseball was in doubt, but his godlike charisma remained intact. To the Japanese he still represented the pinnacle of the baseball world. Millions followed his exploits in baseball magazines such as *Yakyukai* and *Asahi Sports*. Sharing the car was his former teammate Lou Gehrig—the Iron Horse—now the world's greatest player. The two stars rarely made eye contact and did not converse despite the surrounding spectacle.

The rest of the entourage, distributed three or four per car, followed: Connie Mack, the venerated seventy-one-year-old manager and part-owner of the Philadelphia Athletics; Jimmie Foxx, the Athletics' burly third baseman known as "the Beast"; Earl Averill, the Snohomish, Washington, native who had been the first American Leaguer to homer in his first plate appearance—sportswriters called him the Earl of Snohomish when he played well and Big Ears on his off days; Detroit's Charlie Gehringer, the slick-fielding, power-hitting second baseman; Yankees goofy ace Lefty Gomez; former batting champion Lefty O'Doul, who had fallen in love with Japan during a 1931 tour; and a gaggle of lesser-known stars. Only one player didn't seem to belong—a journeyman catcher with a .238 career batting average named Moe Berg. Although he was not an all-star-caliber player, his off-the-field skills would explain his inclusion on the team. Berg was a Princeton and Columbia Law School graduate with a gift for languages who had already visited Japan in 1932. Berg would eventually become an operative for the Office of Strategic Services (OSS), the forerunner of the CIA, and many now believe that this trip was his first mission as a spy.

The motorcade headed east from Tokyo Station, away from the hotel, so that the visitors could parade through the wide streets of Tokyo's opulent Ginza shopping district, where rows of fans, often ten to twenty deep, crowded into the road to catch a glimpse of the Americans. The pressing crowd reduced the broad streets to narrow paths just wide enough for the limousines to pass. Confetti and streamers fluttered down from well-wishers leaning out of windows and over the wrought-iron balconies of the avenues' multistory office buildings. Thousands waved Japanese and American flags and cheered wildly. Cries of *"Banzai! Banzai*, Babe Ruth!" echoed through the neighborhood. Reveling in the attention, the Bambino plucked flags from the crowd and stood in the back of the car waving a Japanese flag in his left hand and an American in his right. Finally, the crowd couldn't contain itself and rushed into the street to be closer to the Babe. Downtown traffic stood still for hours as he shook hands with the multitude.

Ruth and his teammates stayed in Japan for a month, playing eighteen exhibition games against Japanese opponents in twelve cities. But there was more at stake than sport. Japan and the United States were slipping toward war as the two nations vied for control over China and naval supremacy in the Pacific. Politicians on both sides of the Pacific hoped that the goodwill generated by the tour and the two nations' shared love of the game could help heal their growing political differences. Many observers, therefore, considered the all-stars' joyous reception significant. The *New York Times*, for example, wrote, "The Babe's big bulk today blotted out such unimportant things as international squabbles over oil and navies." Connie Mack added that the tour was "one of the greatest peace measures in the history of nations."[1]

But the shared love for a sport would not be enough to overcome Japan's growing nationalism. Just two miles to the northwest of the parade at the Imperial Japanese Army Academy in Ichigaya, a group known as the Young Officers was planning a coup d'état against the government, an upheaval that would jeopardize the tour's success and put the players' lives at risk. In another section of Tokyo, the ultranationalist War Gods Society met at their dojo. Their actions would tarnish the tour with bloodshed.

Banzai Babe Ruth is the story of the doomed attempt to reconcile the United States and Japan through the tour of Major League all-stars in 1934. It will reveal how two groups of men from different cultures, temporarily united by their love for baseball, became tragically divided as their countries rushed toward war. It is a tale of international intrigue, espionage, attempted murder, and, of course, baseball.

We shall see how Babe Ruth, the jovial demigod of baseball, brought the two nations together and forestalled talks of war, before becoming a symbol in Japan of American decadence, cursed by the Imperial troops charging to their certain deaths. We shall also see how a seventeen-year-old pitcher named Eiji Sawamura became a national hero by playing against the Americans in friendship but died in the

South Pacific as their bitter enemy. We will follow Moe Berg's forays into espionage, the Young Officers' attempt to overthrow the Japanese government, the ultranationalist War Gods Society's attempt to murder tour organizer Matsutaro Shoriki, and the birth of Japanese professional baseball. The book will introduce the lesser-known tales of Victor Starffin, the Russian immigrant and player for Japan whose father was a convicted murderer, and Jimmy Horio, a Japanese American who played for the All Nippon team in an effort to gain a Major League contract. The 1934 All American tour of Japan was more than just a series of exhibition baseball games. It was an event that changed lives and influenced Japanese American relations, for better and worse, for decades.

BANZAI BABE RUTH

PART 1

"When I say I'll do something,
I bet my life on it."

MATSUTARO SHORIKI, 1929

1

Matsutaro Shoriki sorted through the papers on his desk, trying to finish his work before his next appointment. The third-largest newspaper in Japan generated a lot of paperwork, but that was a blessing in disguise. It had not always been that way. There were fewer papers five years earlier when Shoriki bought the struggling *Yomiuri Shimbun* in 1924. Even though he had no previous experience in the news or publishing industry, Shoriki was confident he could turn the company around. Once he focused on a task, he rarely failed. For example, he had become a judo master, Third Dan, by the time he had graduated Tokyo Imperial University—an accomplishment that required many years of dedication for most men. That particular skill had been useful in his previous career as a police inspector; it may have saved his life during the suffrage riots. In February 1920 nearly one hundred thousand protesters had snaked through Tokyo to the home of Prime Minister Kei Hara to demand his resignation. As they reached the minister's compound, a stocky figure blocked the small gate. Shoriki spread his arms wide, demanding that the crowd disperse. An agitator rushed forward. Seconds later, Shoriki had the attacker immobilized and arrested. The police inspector then scanned the crowd, spotted its organizer, plunged into the mob, and emerged with his target in an arm hold. After the arrest, the leaderless mob melted away.[1]

Shoriki had enjoyed his time as a policeman. His daring was celebrated within the department, but he usually relied on guile rather than physical force. Twice he quelled riots by withdrawing his officers and appealing to the crowds' leaders to respect decency. Shoriki rose through the ranks and, at thirty-six years old, became the director of the Secretariat of the Metropolitan Police Board—the chief of staff for Tokyo's police force. But his career had collapsed in just one day.

On December 27, 1923, Prince Regent (and future emperor) Hirohito along with his chief chamberlain, Viscount Tamemori Iriye, traveled by car from the Akasaka Palace to the Japanese parliament. At the Toranomon intersection, twenty-seven-year-old Daisuke Namba stepped out of the crowd, drew a pistol, and fired into the prince regent's car. The window shattered as the bullet narrowly missed Hirohito's head. The crowd detained Namba, who was later executed for the assassination attempt. That evening Prime Minister Gonbei Yamamoto and his cabinet submitted their resignations. Shoriki along with the patrolmen assigned to the Toranomon area were dismissed.

Only two months later Shoriki borrowed one hundred thousand yen (about fifty thousand dollars at the time) and purchased *Yomiuri*. The paper had a circulation of just forty thousand and was losing money through poor management. Shoriki reduced expenses by cutting waste, instituting rigid employee work hours, and collecting outstanding bills. He pushed himself hard, putting in long hours, and expected his employees to do likewise. He habitually told his staff, "I'm going to work five times as hard as the presidents of the other Tokyo newspapers. Therefore, the least you can do is work twice as hard as the other editors."[2] He increased circulation by adding household and entertainment sections, a religious column, and comics and focusing on sensational crime. By 1929 Yomiuri's circulation had jumped nearly fivefold, but Shoriki still searched for ways to surpass rival papers.

On this day, his old schoolmate Shigenori Ikeda arrived at the appointed time. The two friends could not have looked less alike. Ikeda, young looking for his thirty-seven years, had a thin, almost feminine face supporting a stylish haircut complete with a flip in front. The dour Shoriki looked older than forty-four. The remaining hair on his balding head was closely cropped, and his heavy-rimmed black glasses with his thick neck gave him an unmistakable turtlelike appearance. Photographs rarely show the uncompromising Shoriki smiling.

Ikeda was the father of the eugenics movement in Japan. He joined the newspaper staff at *Hochi Shimbun* soon after college and became their correspondent in Germany from 1919 to 1924. There, he became enthralled by the growing field of eugenics, gaining a doctorate from Jena University before returning to Japan. He founded the Japan Eugenic Exercise/Movement Association in 1926 and the journal *Eugenic Exercise/Movement* the following year. Unlike later practitioners in the field, who favored sterilizing individuals with genetic disabilities, Ikeda advocated building a stronger gene pool through physical exercise, hygiene, and marriages of compatible couples from distinct geographical and genealogical lines. He crusaded against cousin marriage—a common early-twentieth-century Japanese practice. To help individuals find suitable spouses, Ikeda set up eugenic marriage counseling and even matchmaking services at high-end department stores.[3]

The two sat in Shoriki's office, discussing the newspaper business while sipping coffee. Shoriki's coffee was notorious. Sold in cheap cups for five *sen* (about two cents) in the newspaper's cafeteria, it was as bitter as coffee could get. But Shoriki seemed to love it and had it brought to his office for guests. Eventually, the August heat and humidity became unbearable, and they climbed to the roof of the blocklike concrete building to cool off. The *Yomiuri* building was just three stories, but the high ceilings of its top two floors made it tower above the surrounding old-fashioned wooden shops.

Soon after the friends settled on the roof, Ikeda shifted the conversation to baseball—in particular Babe Ruth, the star of the New York Yankees. Shoriki had founded a baseball team while in middle school, but had abandoned the sport and now had little interest in the game. He barely listened.[4]

"How about it, Shoriki-san? If we brought Babe Ruth to Japan, he'd be a big hit."

"What? Babe Ruth . . . ?" Shoriki refocused his attention on Ikeda as his friend repeated the idea. Shoriki could promote his newspaper and attract new subscribers by bringing Babe Ruth and a team of American ballplayers to Japan. The newspaper owner remained quiet, then asked, "Why don't you do it over at your company?"

"It's no good," Ikeda said.

"You brought it up with them, Ikeda-kun?"

"Not just *Hochi*, but *Mainichi, Asahi, Jiji*. . . . None of them wants to take the risk."

"And why not?" asked Shoriki.

"The money."

"How much would such a thing take?"

"Two hundred and fifty thousand yen."

"I see," said Shoriki with a short intake of breath. "That's not cheap." In 1929 250,000 yen was equivalent to $115,000.

Shoriki considered the idea. Below, small wooden barges, laden with dry goods, glided down the rock-lined canal that had once formed the outer moat of medieval Edo castle. Men with long poles stood in the sterns, punting the boats along. Baseball was Japan's most popular spectator sport, with thousands attending top collegiate games. Perhaps there was money to be made there.

Although not a fan, Shoriki knew a little about baseball from publishing the newspaper. He probably knew that soon after Horace Wilson introduced the game to his students at Kaisei Gakko in 1872, Hiroshi Hiraoka created Japan's first adult team. In 1871 the Japanese government had sent the fifteen-year-old Hiraoka to the United States to study locomotive engineering. Hiraoka returned with a thorough understanding of railroads and helped set up Japan's extensive rail system, but the young man also brought back a ball, a wooden bat, and a love for baseball. In 1878 he created the Shimbashi Athletic Club and built Japan's first field in 1882. The game spread throughout the country, and by the late 1880s amateur leagues played in Tokyo.[5]

Shoriki certainly knew about the Ichiko high school team and their celebrated victory over the adult American players from the Yokohama Country Club in 1896—he was a baseball-playing eleven-year-old at the time, and the game was big news. He would have also watched the game spread to Tokyo's colleges at the turn of the century. By 1903 Waseda and Keio university teams had become the pinnacle of Japanese baseball, with games between the rival universities attracting thousands of fans and sometimes igniting riots.

To improve their game, Waseda's team traveled to the United States in 1905, beginning a long tradition of transpacific baseball tours. After stopping in Hawaii, Waseda traveled to the West Coast, playing college and amateur teams. They returned with up-to-date equipment and tactics. Two years later the St. Louis School of Honolulu became the first American team to tour Japan. American and Japanese universities soon began regular baseball exchanges. Between 1905 and 1929 sixteen American college teams came to the Land of the Rising Sun, while seventeen Japanese squads traveled to the U.S. mainland.

But these amateur exchanges did not interest Shoriki. Although Japanese fans had flocked to watch American collegians at the beginning of the century, the fans would no longer pay much to watch amateurs. Visiting professional and especially Major League teams, however, could fill the stadiums and help sell newspapers. The first pro team came to Japan in 1908, only a year after the St. Louis School tour. Hoping to gain an overseas market, the Reach Sporting Goods Company organized a team of Major and Minor Leaguers for seventeen games in Japan. The Reach All Americans contained no stars (the most recognizable names were Hall of Famer Ed Delahanty's little brother Jim of the Washington Senators and his teammate Bill Burns), but they won all of their games comfortably. Fans jammed the stadiums to watch the professionals. Against Keio University, the six-thousand-seat capacity stadium sold out, and fans had to be turned away.

The *Chicago Tribune* reported so favorably on the All Americans' reception that Japan was included on the 1913–14 Major League World Tour. The Chicago White Sox and New York Giants (both reinforced with players from other teams) traveled thirty thousand miles through thirteen countries over four and a half months to "transplant America's game in athletic and sport-loving countries."[6] The Major Leaguers stayed in Japan for four days, playing two games against each other and a third against Keio University. Once again, the rabid fans surprised the visiting ballplayers. The dock at the port of Yokohama was draped with banners and packed with supporters and sportswriters to welcome the teams. Crowds followed the players' cars as they traveled through Tokyo, while eighteen thousand attended the three games.[7] World War I, however, precluded further international baseball tours for the remainder of the decade.

In 1920 a Californian promoter named Gene Doyle formed a team of Minor Leaguers sprinkled with journeyman Major Leaguers to barnstorm in Japan. The squad included an outfielder from the San Francisco Seals named Herbert Hunter, who would become known as the "Baseball Ambassador to the Orient." Hunter had been a rookie with great promise when he joined the New York Giants in 1916, but in four big league seasons hit just .163 in thirty-nine games. During his brief time in the Majors and several subsequent seasons in the Pacific Coast League (PCL), Hunter became known as an eccentric who was the butt of almost every clubhouse joke. Although friendly, with a charming smile, the young man was so absentminded that his manager would escort him to the railroad station to ensure that he would not miss the team's road trips. Once in a tie game with bases loaded and one out, Hunter caught a fly ball in center field, stuffed it into his back pocket, and jogged to the dugout.[8]

Doyle's team played six games in Japan, winning five comfortably and one against Keio University by a 1–0 score. The players, however, managed to embarrass their hosts. The exact nature of their indiscretions is lost to time, as contemporary articles refer to them only as "regrettable features" and note that the inclusion of wives in future tours would curtail further undesirable behavior.[9] Hunter, alone, was exonerated. He adored Japan and returned the following winter to coach teams from Waseda and Keio universities and arrange a true Major League tour for the fall of 1922.

Embarrassed by the problems of the 1920 tour, Major League Baseball commissioner Judge Kenesaw Mountain Landis seized control of the 1922 affair. He first instructed Hunter to select players known "not only for playing skill but for good deportment" and then appointed umpire George Moriarty "with instructions to keep a sharp eye on the deportment of the tourists; and to report to the [Advisory] Council any infractions of the accepted rules of good behavior." Hunter put together the first all-star team to visit Japan. The team included future Hall of Famers Waite Hoyt, Herb Pennock, George Kelly, and Casey Stengel as well as lesser stars. Before the team departed from Vancouver, Landis sent the team an open letter. "The institution of baseball will be advanced by your individual and collective performances" and "is keenly interested in having the tour reflect credit upon our national game and its professional players.

Of course the players appreciate the necessity and importance of maintaining the high standards of play and sportsmanship and of personal conduct on and off the field which they observe during the regular championship season."[10] Considering the after-hours pastimes of many ballplayers during "the regular championship season," the behavior of Doyle's 1920 squad must have been particularly depraved.

The team played seventeen games, giving the Japanese their first extended look at how baseball was played at its highest level. As in the past, the Japanese reacted with unbridled enthusiasm. Between six and ten thousand fans attended each game, despite tickets priced between $0.50 and $2.50 each (during the same year, the average ticket price for all of Yankee Stadium's seats was just $0.70).[11]

Despite Landis's precautions, the '22 team nonetheless created a controversy. After the Americans won the first six games by a 58–1 combined score, attendance started to dwindle. In the seventh game, the All Stars faced off against a Keio University alumni team, known as the Mita Club. Stacked with the best former Keio players, including a slim left-handed pitcher named Michimaro Ono, Mita could field a stronger nine than their alma mater. To nearly everybody's surprise, Ono held the Americans to just three runs as the Japanese scored nine off Waite Hoyt to win the game. The upset made instant heroes of Ono and his teammates, but not all the local baseball pundits were pleased. Many claimed that the Americans had thrown the game to increase attendance in the remaining contests. In any case, Hoyt became the only Major Leaguer to lose to a Japanese team before World War II.[12]

The loss incensed Landis, and no other Major League team toured Japan during the remainder of the 1920s. Collegiate and semipro teams filled the gap until the Philadelphia Royal Giants, a squad of Negro League players that included Biz Mackey and Rap Dixon, came in 1927. The Royal Giants played twenty-four games, losing just one to Michimaro Ono, who was then pitching for Daimai. The Japanese victory, however, was tainted, as the umpires had mistakenly disallowed the Royal Giants' tying run. Although the umpires had made a clear error, the Royal Giants showed uncommon sportsmanship and accepted the blunder without complaint. Japanese players and scribes noted that the Negro Leaguers conducted themselves far better than their white counterparts. On the field they did not run up the score or employ demeaning plays, such as having the fielders sit down as the pitcher struck out the side. Off the field, the Royal Giants behaved themselves, unlike the sometimes-rowdy big leaguers.[13] Fans swarmed the stadiums to watch the Royal Giants play flawless defense and pound mammoth home runs, but at the same time keep the scores close enough to make the games interesting.

Based on the success of past Major League tours, Shoriki realized that Ikeda's plan had merit. Sponsoring an all-star team and covering the event in his paper would certainly lead to more sales, and if he could bring Ruth . . . It would be a gamble, but then all his life Shoriki had taken risks. The newspaper owner often reminisced about a lesson he learned in 1906—a lesson that colored his approach to life.

During Shoriki's senior year at the Fourth Higher School of Kanazawa, the school's athletic teams traveled to Kyoto for an interscholastic match. The Kyoto school beat Kanazawa at baseball, tennis, and fencing. Only judo remained, but Kyoto's top judo wrestler, Tomojiro Kojima, was a master—Second Dan—although still a schoolboy. Kojima, looking unbeatable, had already defeated four Kanazawa wrestlers when Shoriki stepped into the ring. Rather than opening with the standard move toward the opponent's sleeve and neck band, young Shoriki gambled. With a yell, he threw himself at Kojima and tried a desperate off-balance throw. If Kojima had maintained his composure, he could have pinned Shoriki within seconds. But he didn't. The surprise worked, and Shoriki knocked Kojima to the ground. Wrapping his hands around the Kyoto wrestler's throat, Shoriki held tight until the referee declared Kojima defeated. From that moment on, Shoriki knew he would have to gamble to succeed in life.

Shoriki looked back at Ikeda, "But do you think Ruth would really come?"

"Yes, he will. He certainly will. I've been in contact with Ruth's secretary," Ikeda lied.

"Ikeda-kun, if *Hochi* isn't going to do it, I will. Send a telegram in your name to Babe Ruth immediately."

Ikeda looked doubtful. He had not expected Shoriki to agree this quickly.

"Don't worry, Ikeda-kun. When I say I'll do something, I bet my life on it."[14]

Shoriki had no way of knowing the irony of this last statement. Bringing Ruth to Japan would nearly cost him his life.

2

In August 1929 the Babe had not felt better in a long time, but it had been a roller-coaster year. The new year began with devastating news. On January 11, Ruth's first wife, Helen Woodford, perished in a Watertown, Massachusetts, house fire. The Babe and Helen had been separated for about six years but as Catholics had not divorced. At the time of her death, Helen was passing as the wife of Dr. Edward Kinder, a dentist. Her true identity, revealed several days after her death, along with the suspicious nature of the fire had created a scandal. Was it a suicide? Was it murder? Stories filled newspapers in Boston and New York. Ruth held a press conference three days later. As he addressed the twenty reporters crowded into his suite at the Brunswick Hotel, the Babe sobbed. He abandoned his prepared statement and choked out, "Please let my wife alone. Let her stay dead." He added after a pause, "That's all I've got to say." The reporters slunk away. Several days later the medical examiner ruled out foul play, and the scandal evaporated.

On April 17 Ruth married Claire Hodgson at a 5:00 a.m. ceremony at St. Gregory's on Manhattan's West Side. Despite the early hour the supposedly secret wedding drew six thousand fans. The Babe had met the former showgirl beauty in early 1923 when a mutual friend introduced them before a game at Griffith Stadium in Washington DC. The next day he invited her to dinner. According to Helen, the affair grew out of friendship. She was probably the first, and only, woman the Babe viewed as an equal. By the end of the season she was his confidante and lover. As Mrs. Ruth, Claire vowed to end the Babe's self-destructive behavior. The overdrinking, the overeating, the overspending, the all-night parties, the women, they would all have to go. She gave her husband a 10:00 p.m. curfew, changed his diet, removed the hard liquor from the apartment, banned certain so-called friends, and put the Babe on an allowance. The Bambino did not protest, but instead nestled into domestic life. He adopted Claire's daughter, Julia, while Claire adopted his daughter, Dorothy. Although Dorothy would have a difficult relationship with her step-mother, Julia loved her new father, and the two became close.[1]

In late August 1929 Ruth received an unusual telegram from Japan. A fellow named Shigenori Ikeda was asking if he would barnstorm in the Land of the Rising Sun. The Bambino's initial reaction to the telegram is unknown. Ruth was probably unaware that they played baseball in Japan. In any case his agent, Christy Walsh, declined the offer, stating the Babe had other commitments. Walsh telegrammed his response to the *Hochi* newspaper, inadvertently alerting executives that Ikeda was arranging a business deal for a rival newspaper. Although Ikeda kept his job, he could no longer help Shoriki bring Ruth to Japan.

Shoriki pressed on without Ikeda. Knowing that he could not bring Ruth to Japan by himself, he contacted Gyoji Arai, a former schoolmate from both Kanazawa and Imperial University, at the newly formed division of tourism at the Ministry of Railways. It did not take long to convince Arai that inviting Ruth and a team of American players would be great publicity for the tourism division. Rail Minister Tasuke Egi, however, disagreed. Fearing that *Yomiuri* lacked the assets to avert financial disaster should the plan fail, Egi would not support the project.

Despite Egi's fears, the *Yomiuri* newspaper continued to grow, allowing Shoriki little time to focus on baseball. By late 1930 the newspaper owner realized that to bring Ruth to Japan, he would need able assistants. He went after the best. Waseda University's manager, Tadao Ichioka, was a national hero, pictured on magazine covers and baseball cards and covered in newspaper gossip columns. He had been Waseda's manager since 1926, leading them to a 73-34-1 record. Like all of the school's managers, Ichioka had played for the team, becoming the starting catcher in 1915 and the captain, under the famed manager Suishu Tobita, two years later. He undoubtedly enjoyed college life, as he remained captain until he graduated in 1921 at the age of twenty-nine. In September 1930 Shoriki told Ichioka of his plans to bring Ruth to Japan and asked if he would oversee the project as the head of *Yomiuri*'s sports department. Ichioka shocked his team and fans by abruptly leaving the university in midseason and joining *Yomiuri* on September 23.

Shoriki also needed a Japanese who knew Major League Baseball. While reading a newspaper called *Yokohama Boeki Shimpo*, the *Yomiuri* owner noticed an article about Major League Baseball written by Sotaro Suzuki, a Japanese businessman living in New York. The author was an amateur writer whose passion for the American game drove him to share his experiences with his hometown. Suzuki had briefly attended Waseda University but left after a year or two for the less prestigious Okura Shogyo (now Tokyo Keizai University). Upon graduation he joined the silk trading company Komatsu Shoten and was sent to Manhattan as Komatsu Shoten's representative. Sotaro loved New York and stayed from 1920 to 1929. When business slowed he attended cultural events, audited classes at Columbia University, and spent his afternoons at one of New York's three Major League ballparks. An affable man with a retreating hairline and round wire glasses, Suzuki soon became friendly with many players, including Giants outfielder Frank "Lefty" O'Doul. When silk sales fell after the 1929 stock market collapse, Komatsu Shoten terminated Suzuki's position. Sotaro returned home and was unemployed in September 1930 when Shoriki hired him as a special assistant and writer on Major League Baseball.[2]

Bolstered by Ichioka and Suzuki, Shoriki tried another tactic to lure Ruth to Japan during the fall of 1930. He approached Toshio Shiratori of the Ministry of Foreign Affairs and suggested that bringing a team of Major Leaguers with Ruth would help Japanese-American relations. Ticket sales, he explained, should cover the costs. Ties between the United States and Japan had been relatively strong during the 1920s. Politically, Japan had followed the United States toward democracy by creating universal male suffrage in 1926. Economically, the United States purchased 40 percent of the island nation's exports, and Wall Street investors, led by J. P. Morgan, had helped Japan rebuild after the devastating 1923 earthquake, thus cementing the economic ties. The market crash in 1929, however, weakened these bonds. The demand for Japanese luxury goods, such as silk and porcelain, crumbled. As an astonishing two of every five Japanese families earned income from the silk industry, unemployment rose by 47.5 percent between 1925 and 1930, bringing starvation to many rural families. The economic troubles soon ignited political unrest. Both radical and right-wing organizations flourished, and the military, believing that Japan's economic salvation lay in controlling Asian markets and raw materials, became overtly hostile toward their European rivals in the Pacific. As the anti-Western rhetoric rose, tensions between Japan and the United States grew, even though war seemed unlikely.[3] Relations worsened as a result of racist immigration laws in the United States, restricting migration from Asia.

Baseball exchanges between the two countries seemed to ease diplomatic tension—even if the goodwill was fleeting. After Herb Hunter's 1922 visit, a representative of Mariya Sporting Goods named M. Nishio told the *Sporting News*, "As long as Japan and the United States have something in common like baseball, there is bound to exist nothing but the best of feelings and relations between these two countries." The newspaper added, "It's the Gospel truth, too, that on the diamond peace is being made between these two countries that politicians and demagogues in general cannot break. All the so-called 'peace conferences' that may be held won't have as much real effect toward reaching an understanding as one season of baseball in which Americans and Japanese can meet on the common ground of the diamond."[4]

Shiratori and his superiors at the Ministry of Foreign Affairs agreed that bringing Ruth to Japan might help reconcile the nations. On November 20, 1930, the ministry telegrammed Renzo Sawada, the Japanese consul in New York. "Yomiuri Newspaper would like to invite 15 or 16 players in addition to Babe Ruth. . . . The newspaper would like to do something for the good relationship between Japan and America so please negotiate and telex a reply."[5] Sawada contacted Christy Walsh about Ruth's availability after the 1931 season but was told that the Babe already had a contract with Universal Pictures in Hollywood to shoot a series of instructional movies.

After two years of thwarted plans, most men would have given up, but patience and perseverance—Shoriki's trademarks as a police inspector—once again brought him what he desired. Soon after the

Ministry of Foreign Affairs informed Shoriki that Ruth was unavailable, they gave the *Yomiuri* president better news. Herb Hunter was planning to bring a Major League all-star team to Japan in November 1931. Perhaps, the ministry suggested, Shoriki could cooperate with Hunter.

Since the 1922 Major League tour, Hunter had returned to Japan five times as an adviser and coach, building strong friendships with university officials and players. In the fall of 1928 he brought the great Ty Cobb as well as recently retired catcher Fred Hofman and former Yankees star pitcher Bob Shawkey to instruct Japanese players. Ernie Quigley accompanied the players to teach umpiring techniques. Occasionally, the players joined university teams during scrimmages. "Cobb," Hunter told the *Sporting News*, "couldn't control his zest to win, even in those games. Wearing his uniform of a Japanese college, he wanted to win as badly as when he was with the Tigers. And pity the young Japanese player who didn't understand him and threw to the wrong base!"[6] For the Japanese, the visit was a resounding success, but the players parted on bitter terms, with Cobb claiming that Hunter owed him money.[7]

When Shoriki learned of Hunter's plans, the American was already en route to Japan, robbing Shoriki of the opportunity of telegramming him to set up an appointment. Not knowing Hunter personally, most Japanese would have found a mutual friend to introduce them and facilitate a business relationship, but Shoriki was not a typical Japanese. The newspaper owner ordered an employee to intercept Hunter as he disembarked at Yokohama and escort him to the *Yomiuri* office. Undoubtedly surprised, and probably a bit taken aback at the unexpected welcoming, Hunter refused to accompany the guide, citing fatigue after the long trip. He did, however, agree to meet Shoriki the following day.

Hunter had planned to ask the *Mainichi* newspaper to sponsor the forthcoming tour. *Mainichi* was the largest paper in Japan, with a 1.5 million daily circulation, and had sponsored Hunter's past coaching ventures. But the persuasive Shoriki convinced Hunter to let *Yomiuri* sponsor the games in Tokyo while conceding that *Mainichi* could control the Osaka-area matches. Unbeknownst to Hunter, *Yomiuri* lacked an Osaka office and had few business ties in the Kansai area. Allowing *Mainichi* to sponsor the Osaka games not only enabled Hunter to fulfill his obligations to his past sponsor but also helped Shoriki overcome a logistical headache. The parties agreed that *Yomiuri* would pay the visiting ballplayers' expenses plus one hundred thousand yen and all profits from ticket sales above fifteen thousand yen in estimated expenses.[8] Shoriki explained that the American squad needed to be a true all-star team. If he could not get Ruth, he at least wanted the next best. As in past tours, the Major Leaguers would play Japan's top college teams.

Hunter returned to the United States eager to recruit his team but immediately hit a snag. Commissioner Landis refused to sanction the tour and forbade players to sign with Hunter. Landis was convinced that Hunter had thrown the game during the 1922 tour and had cheated Cobb during the 1928 visit. To plead his case Hunter turned to baseball's premier writer, Fred Lieb, who was friendly with Landis and National League president John Heydler. Hunter offered Lieb 50 percent of the profits if he could convince Landis to sanction the tour. Lieb agreed and persuaded Heydler to back the trip for educational and diplomatic purposes. Landis, however, remained stubborn.

At first Landis insisted that Hunter could not be involved, despite Lieb's pleas that "it would break Herb's heart if he was left behind." Heydler finally convinced Landis to compromise. The commissioner would sanction the tour if Lieb, as Major League Baseball's official representative, would sign the players and run the team. Lieb would also be responsible for disciplining players who became "too far out of line, especially when it came to drinking and wenching." Hunter could accompany the team but could not play or "handle any money."[9]

Throughout the '31 season, Lieb recruited players and promoted the tour with articles in the *Sporting News* and other publications. His squad was impressive; seven of the fourteen players would later make the Hall of Fame in Cooperstown. The roster included Lou Gehrig, Frank Frisch, Rabbit Maranville, Mickey Cochrane, Al Simmons, Lefty Grove, George Kelly, and Frank "Lefty" O'Doul. Lieb spent the season trying to convince Ruth to join, but the Babe swore that he would remain true to his movie contract. In September Shoriki offered Ruth twenty-five thousand dollars to come to Japan. After

Ruth declined, Shoriki telegrammed Lieb: "Sign Ruth no matter what you have to pay him." Lieb showed the Babe the message, asking him to name his price, but once again Ruth rejected the generous offer.[10]

Not everybody within the *Yomiuri* newspaper supported Shoriki's plan to sponsor the tour. Many board members and employees believed that he was putting the newspaper at risk. If an unforeseen disaster occurred or even if ticket sales were low, the newspaper would take a devastating financial hit. In the midst of the Depression, critics wondered if the paper could survive such a loss. Then, in early fall, two potentially crippling events occurred. First, the *Mainichi* newspaper backed out. *Yomiuri* would now have to bear all the tour's expenses, be fully responsible for any financial losses, and coordinate the Kansai-area games. Shoriki was probably pleased to be the sole sponsor and pressed forward with his plans, but the news must have jolted his critics.

On September 18, 1931, less than a month before the Americans were due to leave the United States, the Japanese Kwantung Army began its invasion of Manchuria. At 10:20 p.m. Japanese soldiers blew up a small section of the Japanese-owned South Manchuria Railway near the Chinese-controlled town of Mukden. Claiming the explosion an act of Chinese aggression, the Kwantung Army attacked the Chinese garrison at Mukden and seized control of Manchuria without waiting for orders from Tokyo. Upon learning of the unauthorized military action, the Japanese government did little beyond a private reprimand. The invasion outraged the international community, and the League of Nations resolved that the Japanese should withdraw before November 16. As the Major League team left the United States on October 15, 1931, on board the *Tatsuta Maru*, the newspapers contained no platitudes about solving international differences through baseball. Many on both sides of the Pacific feared the countries would soon be at war.

Perhaps influenced by newspaper reports of Japanese aggression, the American players were less-than-ideal ambassadors. Traveling on board the *Tatsuta Maru* was a group of Japanese diplomats headed by an admiral, who were baseball fans and enjoyed talking with the all-stars.[11] The admiral especially liked the company of shortstop Rabbit Maranville, who nicknamed him Icky. Maranville was famous for his sophomoric humor, which included donning a pair of glasses when arguing with umpires, packing manager Bill McKechnie's hotel-room closet with live pigeons, and dousing sleeping teammates with water. One afternoon Maranville stumbled across the admiral fast asleep on a deck chair. The prankster fetched a bottle of black ink and promptly decorated the diplomat's bald crown with a smiley face.[12] The admiral's and his entourage's reaction to Maranville's artwork is unknown.

Arriving in Tokyo, the Major Leaguers were greeted with a tumultuous parade as tens of thousands of fans cheered the visitors with cries of "Banzai!" (May you live ten thousand years!). "The enthusiasm of the Japanese for baseball just about borders on the fanatical," Lou Gehrig told the *New York Times*. "Everywhere we played we packed them in and after the games thousands who had been locked out still would be standing in the streets waiting for us to come out. At times it would take hours for our cars to take us from the park to the hotel."[13]

The Americans played seventeen games against top collegiate teams and amateur all-star squads, winning all. The Japanese were overmatched, scoring just thirty runs as the Major Leaguers pounded out nearly five times that many. The consensus was that the Japanese were slick fielders and had some good pitchers but were poor hitters. Lefty Grove particularly dominated the Japanese, striking out fifty-five and not allowing an earned run in thirty-eight innings. Yet before he closed the second game by striking out six straight on just twenty pitches, the Japanese nearly took the game. Waseda's star right-hander hurler Masao Date and American starter Larry French of the Pittsburgh Pirates each gave up only one run in the first six innings. In the top of the seventh, a bases-loaded double by the right fielder, Isamu Fuma, put the Japanese up 3–1 and knocked out French. The embarrassed French lost his cool and threw a tantrum in the dugout, shouting curses and racial epithets at the opposition. Lieb tried to calm French down, but the pitcher continued despite the presence of a Japanese dignitary on the bench, a Harvard graduate who spoke fluent English. According to Lieb, the man "took French's tirade like a thoroughbred and never let his eyes stray from the field."[14] The Japanese lead was short-lived, however, as the Americans scored seven in the bottom of the eighth to take the game.

During the one-sided games the Americans showboated to amuse the fans. In the seventh game Lefty Grove fielded a ground ball on the mound and, instead of throwing the batter out at first, threw to third baseman Willie Kamm, who tossed it across the diamond in time to nip the batter. In another game left fielder Al Simmons laid on the ground while Grove pitched. Although showboating was common during American barnstorming games, it was unheard of in Japan. Some of the fans may have found it amusing, but the Japanese players and writers found it patronizing and deeply insulting. Having already injured their hosts' pride, the Americans began to bench jockey in the seventh game. Bench jockeying was a part of the Major League game, and the personal insults could get brutal—nearly anything went, including racial and sexual insults. The Japanese, however, were unfamiliar with the practice. As the Americans yelled at the opposition, most of the Japanese, perhaps not understanding the taunts, remained impassive. One player, however, understood and took exception.

The Americans had nicknamed him Nosey, but the Japanese knew the second baseman from Waseda as Osamu Mihara—a future member of the Japanese Hall of Fame. Mihara's hot temper would trouble him his entire career. In a game during his time at Waseda, Mihara stole home against a right-handed pitcher while a left-handed batter was up. After the game former Waseda manager-turned-commentator Suishu Tobita scolded the young second baseman for taking such a chance when the odds favored the Waseda batter. Tobita was a legend and more than forty years old, and Mihara should have humbly accepted the chastisement and apologized with a deep bow, but instead he violated Japanese social norms by shouting back at his senior.

Angered by the Americans' taunts, Mihara yelled back in English, getting quite acerbic. The bullying Americans decided to retaliate. Strangely enough it was the affable Lefty O'Doul, a future member of the Japanese Hall of Fame, who decided to put Mihara in his place. O'Doul told his teammates, "I'm going to bunt and force Nosey to cover first base. We'll have some fun!" The hulking O'Doul bunted down the first base line, drawing the first baseman toward the plate to field the ball. The diminutive Mihara raced over to cover the bag and take the throw. The two collided at full speed, with the big American going down hard. O'Doul staggered up, clutching his chest, two ribs broken. Mihara, having held onto the ball, smiled and addressed Lefty in Japanese. The Americans did not understand, but Mihara's teammates smiled and bit back laugher.[15]

O'Doul went to the hospital that night, had his ribs taped, and was ordered to refrain from playing baseball or golf for the remainder of the tour. He joined Lou Gehrig on the bench. The Iron Horse, who would set a Major League record of playing in 2,130 straight games, had broken two fingers the previous day and was also forced to watch the remaining games. He would, of course, recover before the start of the 1932 season.

During nongame days the players toured cultural sites, including the temples of Nikko, the ancient capital of Nara, Meiji Shrine, and a sumo match. Unfortunately, their off-the-field behavior sometimes mimicked their game antics. During a visit to Prime Minister Reijiro Wakatsuki's residence, the ballplayers helped themselves to souvenirs, including Cuban cigars, pens from the prime minister's desk, and even small vases that decorated the shelves in the leader's office.[16]

Despite the American players' behavior, the tour did well financially. Approximately four hundred thousand attended the seventeen games, bringing in 283,191 yen (about $140,000) in gate receipts. The contract called for the Americans to receive 100,000 yen plus all gate receipts above Yomiuri's estimated costs of 15,000 yen. Shoriki, however, had grossly underestimated his costs, as expenditures reached 58,501 yen. The newspaper owner decided to appeal to Hunter, who was handling the American team's finances despite Landis's ruling. Pointing out that the gate receipts had exceeded expectations, Shoriki asked that Yomiuri's expenses be covered before the Americans received their portion. At first Hunter refused, but eventually, perhaps under Fred Lieb's direction, he conceded to give Yomiuri an extra 15,000 yen. Yomiuri lost nearly 29,000 yen (about $15,000) on the tour, but the publicity led to a rise in subscriptions that helped overcome the deficit.[17] By all accounts the tour was a success, especially for Herb Hunter. The baseball commissioner's judgment had been on target—little if any of the gate receipts went to the players, as Hunter managed to pocket most of the profits.[18]

3

Lefty O'Doul left Japan infatuated with its culture. After the injury he spent his time instructing Japanese players and talking with his old acquaintance Sotaro Suzuki. He seemed to love everything about the country—its natural beauty, traditions, food, and especially the people. "I like people who you're not wasting your time trying to help," O'Doul later told baseball historian Lawrence Ritter. "Teaching Americans and teaching Japanese is just like the difference between night and day. The American kid, he knows more than the coach. But not the Japanese kid. They want to learn. They don't think they know everything."[1]

Many think of O'Doul as the greatest American hitter not enshrined in Cooperstown. He won two batting titles (one with a .398 average), and his .349 lifetime average is the fourth best in Major League history, but he played in just seven seasons as a full-time position player. Lefty broke into the Majors as a pitcher for the 1919 Yankees, entering just eleven games over three seasons before being traded to Boston in 1923. The Red Sox gave him a chance to prove himself, but hampered by a sore arm, he posted a 5.43 ERA in twenty-three games before being released. O'Doul returned to his native California and played in the Pacific Coast League, where he abandoned the mound for the outfield. At thirty-one years old he returned to the Majors as an outfielder for the 1928 Giants before being traded to Philadelphia the following season. By 1931 he was back in New York— this time as a Dodger. As a contact hitter O'Doul had few equals, but he was an atrocious fielder, with a poor arm. Bob Stevens, a writer for the *San Francisco Chronicle*, once wrote that O'Doul "could run like a deer. Unfortunately, he threw like one, too."[2]

Within days of returning from Japan, O'Doul wrote Sotaro Suzuki to thank him for the experience and to arrange a future visit. "I sure did have a great time in your country and met some good fellows there. . . . I do want to come to your country again and teach batting to your players."[3] For Suzuki, the request could not have been better timed. After watching the polished Major Leaguers pummel the university teams during the '31 tour, Shoriki concluded that the Japanese would not match the Americans until they had their own professional league. Only then would the Japanese gain enough experience to play the game at its highest level. Shoriki consulted with his baseball advisers and appointed Suzuki to study the idea.

There had been an earlier attempt to create a professional league in Japan. In 1921 former Waseda players formed the Nihon Undo Kyokai (Japan Athletic Association)—the first professional team in Japan. Their goal was to create a team strong enough to compete with American pro teams and thus increase the game's popularity in Japan. Attracting fans, however, proved difficult, as Japanese distrusted professional athletics. From its beginnings at Ichiko, the Japanese had infused baseball with concepts borrowed from Bushido —the supposed code of the samurai warrior that had been reinvented to fit late-nineteenth-century culture. Paramount among these concepts was the idea that sport enhanced not only the body but also the spirit. Intertwined with this was the virtue of frugality—a true samurai should concentrate on developing his spirit and not on acquiring worldly goods. To play for money, rather than for personal enhancement, would sully the spirit. The Great Kanto Earthquake of 1923, which leveled Tokyo and Yokohama, forced the Japan Athletic Association to relocate to Takarazuka, a town near Osaka famous for its female musical theater. Renamed Takarazuka Kyokai, the team played a number of short-lived professional squads and company teams, but its organizers were unable to create a stable professional league. The team finally disbanded in 1929.[4]

Suzuki realized that O'Doul could be the contact needed to establish pro ball in Japan. He seized the opportunity to enlist the American's help and penned a response the day after receiving the letter. "I am planning to organize Professional Baseball in Japan. . . . This is kept in a very secret manner, and nobody, except my three friends, knows about my plan at the present. If things are to be developed smoothly, I must have lots of moral support and help from America, and I am counting you as one of my very reliable friends there in this matter. However, I wish you would kindly keep this matter very secret. Please do not tell anything about this . . . to . . . Mr. Hunter."[5]

O'Doul and Suzuki corresponded throughout the 1932 season, discussing details such as the difference between American and Japanese equipment and helping Hillerich and Bradsby, the makers of Louisville Sluggers, explore the Japanese market. O'Doul returned to Japan in the fall of 1932 along with Herb Hunter, pitcher Ted Lyons, and catcher Moe Berg to coach Tokyo-area university teams. Hunter had organized the expedition without help from *Yomiuri*, as ill feeling remained over the expenses from the 1931 tour. Distribution of the gate receipts had also cost Hunter O'Doul's trust. Outwardly Lefty remained friendly with Hunter, as he needed the baseball ambassador's ties to Japan, but O'Doul continued to work secretly with Suzuki to help *Yomiuri* arrange a future Major League tour without Hunter.

After the start of the '33 Major League season, O'Doul wrote, "Well Suzuki, do you think that a big league baseball club will go to Japan this coming season? If you know about a team going over to Japan this winter, let me know, also let me know if your paper wants to take a team to Japan. . . . I can arrange to bring a first class club over there to your country. I think it would be a wonderful thing for baseball in Japan if we could get Babe Ruth to come to Japan. If you let me know in plenty time I will talk to him and his manager and try to arrange to get him to make the trip." O'Doul closed with an admonishment to keep this plan a secret, especially from Herb Hunter's Japanese friends.[6]

For Suzuki, O'Doul's letter must have seemed like a dream come true. Here, at last, was a chance to actually secure Ruth. "I do not think that a Major League team is coming to Japan this year," he responded. "I am now taking your proposition of bringing [a] Major League Team, in which Babe Ruth [is] included, over to Japan, with Mr. Shoriki. . . . It looks to me that Babe Ruth is getting too old as [a] baseball player, and it may be his last season this year as [a] regular player. If I am right on the above, I think it would be better for Yomiuri to have Babe coming this fall, than to invite him next year.

Can you tell me very confidentially how much does he want for his coming over to Japan and showing the Japanese fans his home run stunts?"[7]

In early July, Suzuki met with Shoriki and outlined O'Doul's idea. Shoriki jumped at the opportunity but established four conditions. First, the team would be organized by O'Doul without Herb Hunter. Second, the tour would have to take place in November 1934, as a full year would be needed to organize and advertise the event. Third, the team must include Ruth and at least five other star players. When selecting the players, O'Doul should "consider their personality and character very carefully." Fourth, with the exception of O'Doul and Lou Gehrig, the players who came in 1931 should be avoided.[8]

Also in early July, before Shoriki's answer would have reached O'Doul, Herb Hunter contacted Philadelphia Athletics manager and part-owner Connie Mack about taking a team to Japan after the '34 season. Hunter told Mack that future trips to Japan would be sponsored by the Tokyo Big Six University League and not *Yomiuri* or any other newspaper. Unbeknownst to Hunter, O'Doul had already approached Mack about the *Yomiuri*-sponsored trip. Like many in baseball, Mack disliked Hunter and told O'Doul of his rival's plans. Still outwardly friendly toward each other, O'Doul and Hunter met in New York to discuss Japan. Hunter confided that he would leave San Francisco on board the *Chichibu Maru* and arrive in Yokohama on September 11 to secure a contract for a 1934 tour. After the meeting O'Doul wrote Suzuki, divulging Hunter's plans and advising Shoriki to reach an agreement with the university teams before Hunter arrived.[9]

Not content to rely on Shoriki and Suzuki, O'Doul thwarted Hunter's plans in the States by enlisting the help of Connie Mack's son Earle. Earle Mack obtained exclusive permission from Commissioner Landis and the club owners to bring a team to Japan in '34. Without Mack's backing Hunter would be unable to bring any Major League players to Japan. Hunter, however, did not give up. Convinced that he alone would get the contract from the Japanese universities, he decided to recruit an all-star team from the Pacific Coast League. O'Doul wrote Suzuki again in August 1933, urging *Yomiuri* to procure a contact with the Big Six University League as soon as possible. In the meantime, O'Doul sounded out ballplayers' interest in traveling to Japan. By August he had lined up A's slugger Jimmie Foxx; Chuck Klein of the Phillies, the 1932 National League Most Valuable Player; and New York Giants ace pitcher Carl Hubbell. Ruth initially declined, but O'Doul remained hopeful that the Bambino would change his mind.[10]

Ruth's response worried Shoriki. Suzuki immediately wrote O'Doul, explaining that Shoriki would not sponsor the team without the Babe. With Ruth's status in doubt, Shoriki was unwilling to sign a contract with the Big Six University League, as O'Doul advised, but he would use his influence to prevent Hunter from attaining one. In 1932 the Ministry of Education had passed an ordinance forbidding students from playing with, or against, professionals. Thus, before the universities could sign a contract to sponsor a Major League team with Hunter, or anybody else, they had to convince the ministry to make an exception to the new rule. Shoriki's friends at the ministry promised that no exception would be made for Hunter.

By the time Hunter arrived in Yokohama, the *Yomiuri* group had their American rival in check. Hunter disembarked on September 11 and, after visiting his allies within Japanese baseball, met with Deputy Minister Yamakawa of the Physical Culture Section of the Department of Education. Yamakawa refused Hunter's request to grant an exemption to the ban against schoolboys playing pros. Hunter next spoke to the minister of foreign affairs, Count Kosai Uchida, to convince him that the university players should be allowed to play for the good of American-Japanese relations, but Uchida was also unmoved. Frustrated, Hunter left Japan on the fourteenth, having spent less than forty-eight hours in the country it took nearly two weeks to reach.[11]

With Hunter gone, Shoriki paid a formal visit to Ichiro Hatoyama, the minister of education, while Tadao Ichioka, head of *Yomiuri*'s sports department, met informally with Yamakawa to discuss allowing the university clubs to play a *Yomiuri*-sponsored Major League team. The initial talks went well, and Suzuki wrote O'Doul, "I am pretty sure that the Ministry of Education will allow the school boys to play games against your team, making some reasons to modify the rules."[12] Shoriki, however, decided not to rely on the ministry or the university teams. Now was the time to bring professional base-ball to Japan. A pro team would not only circumvent the Ministry of Education's ban of schoolboys playing against professionals but also provide a stronger adversary for the Major Leaguers. Shoriki worried that, after watching the Americans pummel their collegiate heroes in 1931, Japanese fans had sated their appetite for Major League Base-ball. He wanted something to rekindle their interest. Ruth would certainly help, but a professional Japanese team would make the games more exciting and probably bring fans to the parks. In Sep-tember 1933 Shoriki and his *Yomiuri* advisers began organizing two professional clubs—one in Tokyo and another in Osaka. The Tokyo club was created first and would be given the honor of playing the opening game against the visiting Major Leaguers the following fall.[13]

O'Doul promised to come to Japan to complete the plans after the World Series. The outfielder had been traded by Brooklyn to the Giants in June, and after coasting to the pennant, New York faced the Washington Senators in the 1933 World Series. O'Doul rode the bench throughout the series, having just one at bat—a two-run pinch-hit single that helped the Giants win the second game and capture the championship. At the close of the series he left for Tokyo.

Lefty met with Shoriki and Suzuki at *Yomiuri*'s headquarters to draw up the tour's contract on December 23. The terms were simi-lar to the 1931 agreement. Yomiuri would organize the tour and pay the Americans' expenses plus a guaranteed sum of 150,000 yen (with the declining yen equivalent to about $40,000). If the gate receipts totaled more than 150,000 yen, then *Yomiuri* would first recover its expenses up to 35,000 yen before turning the remainder over to the American players. To celebrate the deal, Shoriki ordered coffee from the cafeteria. Suzuki cringed. O'Doul raised the cheap paper cup to his lips and sipped.

As surprise fluttered across O'Doul's face, Shoriki beamed with pleasure. "What do you think, Mr. O'Doul?" Shoriki asked. "Isn't the taste of Japanese coffee exceptional?"

"Great, great, Mr. Shoriki," O'Doul stammered while maintaining a straight face. "There's no coffee like this in America."

"Well, have another cup, then!"

"Oh, no thank you," O'Doul said diplomatically.[14]

At O'Doul's and Connie Mack's direction, John D. Shibe, vice president of the Philadelphia Athletics, announced in the December 28, 1933, issue of the *Sporting News* that in 1934, an all-star American League tour would start in Canada and include "one game in Honolulu, two weeks stay in Japan, a visit to Shanghai, a short stop in the Philippines, followed by a trip to Australia." Shibe added, "India, Egypt and some of the European countries may be visited before the All Stars return."[15] O'Doul returned to San Francisco in January, forwarded the contract to Earle Mack and baseball commissioner Landis for their approval, and readied himself for spring training. In the meantime, Shoriki continued to organize his professional team.

As O'Doul trained with the New York Giants, a strange report came across the United Press wires. New York City police had arrested Herb Hunter for stealing jewels worth twenty thousand dollars from Mrs. Clifford Roberts of Queens, New York. The news blurb provided no details and the police dismissed the charges a few days later, but the arrest ruined Hunter's reputation. Suzuki almost gleefully wrote O'Doul that an American friend told him, "Should Mr. Hunter come to Japan, no foreigner in Japan would speak to him. . . . I do not know what attitude the Japanese baseball fellows will take . . . but I should say that he is through in Japan as far as baseball is concerned."[16] He was not. Although Hunter would never bring another professional team to Japan, he would lead the Harvard nine on an eleven-game tour against the Big Six universities in August 1934.

Throughout the '34 Major League season, O'Doul recruited players for the tour. Many turned him down, while others needed hours of persuading. Visiting Japan in 1934 was difficult. It was a long journey—almost two weeks by ship from the West Coast. Before modern world markets and media made Japan familiar to Americans, the radically different culture often baffled visitors. Diplomatically the United States and Japan were at odds, with each vying for naval domination of the Pacific and control of trade in China. Furthermore, racial prejudice against Japanese, and Asians in general, was high. Most Americans knew little about Asians beyond stereotypes, and the stereotypes of the times were not pretty. Cartoons depicted Asians as small yellow men with buckteeth, disproportionate snoutlike jaws, and slanted eyes often protruding from round, thick glasses. They were depicted as utterly alien, even subhuman. They were caricatured as innately dishonest, cruel, full of avarice, and irrational to the point of stupidity but at the same time devious. The archetype was Sax Rohmer's fictional Dr. Fu Manchu—the diabolical genius intent on enslaving the Western world. Rohmer's books, subsequent radio shows, and movies, as well as other so-called Yellow Peril literature (which depicted Asians as a threat to both American and international stability), were immensely popular in the interwar years and would have been familiar to nearly every ballplayer.

Although the trip was a hard sell to the best players, O'Doul was a talented salesman. Ruth, of course, was O'Doul's primary target. "Why would I want to go there?" was the Babe's first response. O'Doul explained that the Japanese were crazy about baseball and all his expenses would be paid, but Ruth remained reluctant. Lefty decided to resort to more devious tactics. His wife, Abigail, who had accompanied him on the '31 tour, began to work on Claire Ruth, describing the wonders of Japan and how much the Japanese adored the Babe. The ploy worked, and soon Claire's daughter, Julia, was also trying to convince her stepfather to make the trip. By mid-July the women had won. Ruth agreed to go.[17]

On July 18 *Yomiuri* announced that Ruth would come to Japan. Two days later the several hundred thousand readers who turned to page 5 saw a photograph of Ruth dominating the upper-left corner of the newspaper page. The accompanying article, written by Suzuki, proclaimed that Ruth was strong enough to hit a ball out of Meiji Jingu Stadium, a feat accomplished by just a few, including Negro League legend Biz Mackey, who hit three out during the Philadelphia Royal Giants' visit in 1927. Suzuki's piece outlined Ruth's achievements in the Majors and speculated about what he would accomplish in Japan.[18]

Having secured Ruth and Jimmie Foxx, the 1933 American League home run king, Shoriki now wanted Chuck Klein, the National League 1933 home run champ. Klein had originally agreed to accompany O'Doul, but after winning the 1933 Triple Crown, the incompetent and cash-starved Phillies traded him to the Chicago Cubs for sixty-five thousand dollars and three players of little consequence. Perhaps under pressure from his new team, Klein no longer wished to travel to Japan. O'Doul tried to change his mind but to no avail.

Nevertheless, by late August, O'Doul had assembled one of the strongest baseball teams in history. Nine future members of the Hall of Fame in Cooperstown agreed to go. The infield would be Lou Gehrig of the Yankees at first, Charlie Gehringer of Detroit at second, Jimmie Foxx from the Athletics at third, and Joe Cronin of the Senators at short. The great Rodgers Hornsby, now thirty-eight years old and managing the St. Louis Browns, would fill in as needed. The outfield consisted of Ruth, Indians slugger Earl Averill, and Senators star Henry "Heinie" Manush. The only position not filled by a future Hall of Famer was catcher. Here, Charlie Berry, a promising youngster on the Athletics, would gain needed experience. Pitching would be provided by Yankees ace Lefty Gomez, the Senators' twenty-game winner Earl Whitehill, and Clint Brown of the Indians. Rounding out the team would be Pinky Higgins from the A's, Ben Chapman of the Yankees, and O'Doul. There were also rumors that pitchers Carl Hubbell and Lefty Grove would join the squad. A slew of baseball dignitaries would accompany the team to Japan, including Connie Mack, the Philadelphia Athletics' venerable manager and part-owner; his son, and A's executive, Earle Mack; the Washington Senators' owner, Clark Griffith; Cleveland general manager William Evans; American League president William Harridge; and perhaps even Commissioner Landis.[19]

The group would barnstorm in Northwest Canada before leaving Vancouver on board the *Empress of Japan* on October 20. Ruth, the *Sporting News* noted, had already picked out his suite on the luxury ocean liner. After a stop in Honolulu, the squad planned to stay in Japan for a month before playing a game in Shanghai and three in Manila. Plans to continue the tour around the world had been abandoned, but several players including Ruth and Gomez would encircle the globe on their own.

4

Sotaro Suzuki stared up at the ship's three smokestacks towering above him. At 16,810 tons the *Empress of Russia* was nearly 10,000 tons smaller than the *Empress of Japan*, but moored in Yokohama Harbor the 590-foot vessel seemed tremendous. After nearly two years of hard work and only six weeks left before the tour would begin in November, the preparations were nearly complete. The contracts were signed, the roster set, the travel arrangements made. Only minor details remained, such as getting balls and bats autographed by Ruth, Gehrig, and Foxx for raffle prizes.

This excursion to the States should be fun, Suzuki thought to himself. He would disembark in Vancouver and take a train across Canada—a good chance to enjoy the Rockies and the magnificent countryside—to Montreal and then down to New York to meet with Lefty O'Doul and Earle Mack. He would then accompany O'Doul to the World Series before spending a week meeting with Pacific Coast League owners to discuss bringing *Yomiuri*'s professional team to California in the spring of 1935. Finally, Suzuki would meet the All American players in Seattle and accompany them to Japan.[1]

The first day of the voyage was pleasant enough. Suzuki strode about the deck savoring the fair weather and salt air, spent the afternoon in his cabin writing an article, presumably on baseball, and in the evening enjoyed the "talkie" *So This Is Africa* (a Bert Wheeler and Robert Woolsey slapstick comedy) in the ship's theater. Before retiring, he recorded the events in his journal—a habit he had continued since living in New York. The next morning the ship crossed the meridian, forcing the passengers to relive September 19. It was on this second September 19 that things began to go wrong.

Rain pelted the ship, preventing Suzuki from exercising on deck.

The wind increased, and high waves began rocking the ocean liner back and forth. Although a seasoned traveler, Suzuki felt seasick and skipped dinner. During the night the storm increased. Suzuki awoke at a quarter to eight, bathed, but immediately returned to bed. In the evening he ventured out of his cabin to the dining hall. Most of the passengers remained in their cabins, but Suzuki managed to get down a rice ball, some Chinese food, and a melon before returning to bed to write in his journal.

When Suzuki awoke the next morning, fog engulfed the ship, but the sea was calm. The storm had sped west, smashing into Japan on Friday, September 21. Winds of 135 miles per hour, at that point the highest ever recorded in Asia, accompanied by driving rain hit the Osaka-Kobe area around eight o'clock. Telephone, telegraph, and electric lines crumpled. High waves pounded the shoreline, raising the sea level ten feet and flooding tens of thousands of homes. The strongest gusts came just as schoolchildren met for opening assemblies. Unable to withstand the high winds, 146 schools collapsed. More than 500 children were crushed to death, and another 1,700 were injured. The storm overturned trains, including the Number Seven Express bound for Shimonseki, which derailed on the bridge crossing the Setagawa River, killing 8 and injuring 154. In Osaka the famous five-story Shitennoji Pagoda swung to and fro before collapsing in a heap, burying 20 people who had taken shelter on the ground floor. Now known as the Muroto Typhoon, the storm killed more than 3,000, injured another 15,361, and destroyed 92,323 homes.[2]

On September 22 news of the devastation reached the *Empress of Russia* by telegraph. The captain informed Suzuki about the tragedy personally, and other non-Japanese passengers sought him out to express their sympathy. Their actions touched him, and he noted in his journal "very impressed" next to the entry.

A telegram awaited Suzuki when he arrived in Vancouver two days later. "Welcome to America. Wire me care of Giants the time you arrive [in] New York so I can meet your train. Will be very happy to see you. O'Doul." There were no hints of problems, so, according to the diary, Suzuki boarded the Canadian Pacific Railway to Montreal relaxed. The train sped across Canada through the Rockies and across the Alberta and Saskatchewan plains. Suzuki watched the towering peaks, the glaciers, Lake Louise, which he found "more beautiful than in the photographs," and the snow-covered plains dotted with buffalo, deer, sheep, and cattle rush by. He wrote in his diary, "If the living place influences the heart of humanity greatly, it is no wonder that Japanese are ragged and Canadians and Americans are composed." At Montreal Suzuki changed trains for the 331-mile trip to New York's Grand Central Station. He sat back, enjoying the orange maples, yellow birches, and glistening water of Lake Champlain, unaware that the tour's success was in jeopardy.

Since O'Doul had last written, players had begun to back out of the trip. In early September, prior to Suzuki's departure but before a letter could reach him, the National League owners, fearing injuries to their stars, forbade their players from participating in the tour. This cut Rodgers Hornsby, Carl Hubbell, and even O'Doul from the roster. Lefty would make the trip as a coach, not a player. About the same time Clark Griffith, the miserly owner of the Washington Senators, decided not to accompany the squad to Japan or allow his players to make the trip. This forced outfielder Heinie Manush and pitcher Earl Whitehill off the roster and would have removed shortstop Joe Cronin if he had not already broken his wrist. Red Sox owner Tom Yawkey followed suit, ensuring that Lefty Grove, the star of the 1931 Japan tour, would not return in '34.

It was too late to convince other stars to make the trip, so O'Doul and Earle Mack settled on Philadelphia Athletics to fill the holes. Bing Miller, a career .300 hitter, but now close to retirement, would replace Manush. Eric McNair, whom Connie Mack once called "the best defensive infielder in the American League," replaced Cronin at shortstop. Griffith relented and gave Whitehill permission to join the squad.

O'Doul probably explained the changes to Suzuki after meeting him at Grand Central. The two drove to the hotel and chatted until one in the morning. By the time he had finished his journal and turned in, it was two o'clock. Nonetheless, O'Doul woke Suzuki early the next morning, and together they rushed to Grand Central. Earle Mack had come up from Philadelphia to meet with Suzuki and deliver the news in person. Babe Ruth had changed his mind. He now refused to go to Japan.

5

All Suzuki could do was wait. And wait. Ruth was in Washington DC. playing out the last two games of the 1934 season. He would return to New York in two or three days. Suzuki spent the time visiting his haunts from his days at Columbia, watching a Giants game at the Polo Grounds, and meeting with Ruth's agent, Christy Walsh, and Lefty O'Doul to determine how to convince the Babe to honor his commitment. The nights were bad. On the twenty-ninth, Suzuki turned in at one but tossed and turned until three. He awoke just an hour later, dressed, and began another fret-filled day. The next night was even worse. Exhausted, he went to bed early but stared at the ceiling until sleep finally came at four.

At ten o'clock, October 1, an associate of Christy Walsh arrived at the hotel to take Suzuki to see Ruth. Sotaro grabbed a bag before they drove to a barbershop on West Eighty-Eighth Street. Ruth sat in the barber's chair, his back to the door. Butterflies filled Sotaro's stomach. The next few moments would determine the success of the tour, perhaps the future of Japanese professional baseball, and probably his job. Swallowing hard, he entered. Seeing Suzuki's reflection in the barbershop mirror, Ruth smiled his big ear-to-ear grin and said hello. Taking his large paw from beneath the white cloth, he grasped Suzuki's hand. A few moments later the barber finished, and Ruth heaved himself from the chair with a scowl.

"I'm not going to Japan," the Babe growled.

Although Suzuki had expected the message, the forcefulness of Ruth's announcement surprised him.

Ruth was in a foul mood. Unbeknownst to Suzuki, Ruth's dream of managing the Yankees had just been shattered, and his future in Major League Baseball was now uncertain.

In the summer of 1929 Yankees manger Miller Huggins contracted erysipelas, a bacterial infection of the skin, now treatable with antibiotics, but not then. Complaining of fatigue, headaches, and a painful carbuncle near his eye, Huggins entered St. Vincent's Hospital in Manhattan on September 20. He died five days later. Huggins's sudden death shook Ruth and left a hole at the Yankees helm. Head coach Art Fletcher filled the void for the remaining eleven games, but refused to manage the following season. As the newspapers speculated who would get the job, Ruth wondered, "Hey, what's the matter with me?" Many stars went straight from the diamond to the helm without apprenticing as a coach or Minor League manager. Some, like Rogers Hornsby and Joe Cronin, became player-managers, gradually reducing their playing time as their skills decreased. As a former star pitcher and the premier hitter in baseball history, Ruth believed that he understood the game better than most managers.[1]

In typical Ruth fashion, the impetuous Babe hurried across Central Park to Yankees owner Col. Jacob Ruppert Jr.'s office at the Yorkville brewery and presented his case. Ruppert listened impassively and, when Ruth finished, shook his head sadly. "You can't manage yourself, Ruth. How do you expect to manage others?"

"Listen, Colonel, I've been through the mill. I know every temptation that can come to any kid, and I know how to spot it in advance. And if I didn't know how to handle myself, I wouldn't be in baseball today."

"I know you're sincere about this, Ruth. Let me think it over for a day or two. Then I'll be in touch with you."

Ever the optimist, the slugger didn't realize that he had just been turned down and went home to wait for Ruppert's response. A few days later as he was contemplating calling the owner, the Bambino read in the paper that the Yankees had offered the job to pitching coach Bob Shawkey.

Shawkey's tenure as manager lasted just one season, as the Yanks finished third, sixteen games out of first place. In the fall of 1930 Ruppert and Yankees general manager Ed Barrow quietly signed former Chicago Cubs manager Joe McCarthy to lead the team. Shawkey discovered that he was being replaced when he stumbled upon Ruppert, Barrow, and McCarthy meeting with reporters at the Yankees' offices.[2] Ruth seethed when he heard of the appointment, feeling that the job was rightfully his. He complained to Ruppert, who patiently told his star that he wanted Ruth to concentrate on hitting and not be distracted by the rigors of management. Not placated, Ruth left.

McCarthy was a rigid disciplinarian and rule maker. He banned shaving and card playing in the clubhouse, claiming that both were unprofessional, and required the players to wear jackets and ties when traveling. Fuming at both McCarthy's presence and his rules, Ruth despised his new manager, deriding him to anyone who would listen. For three years they coexisted, rarely speaking to each other.

Starting in 1932 other teams considered hiring Ruth to manage. The Red Sox approached him during the '32 season, but the Babe was not interested, as he was leading the Yankees to a championship season with a .341 average and forty-one home runs. Based on those stats, the Yanks signed Ruth for '33 at fifty-two thousand dollars, but the Babe's long-abused body aged rapidly, and soon his salary outstripped his contributions on the field. Stuck with the overpaid superstar, Ruppert and Barrow encouraged the Babe to consider retiring and manage elsewhere.

The Babe's best chance came in October 1933. After the World Series, Frank Navin, the owner of fifth-place Detroit, asked if the Yankees would be willing to let Ruth manage the Tigers. Ruppert and Barrow jumped at the chance to move Ruth and urged the Babe to pursue the job. Navin asked the Babe to come to Detroit to work out the details, but Ruth declined, saying that there was not time before his trip to Hawaii on October 15. Barrow advised Ruth to reconsider, but the Bambino responded, "There's plenty of time. The season doesn't begin for six months. I've got things all set in Hawaii. I'll call him when I get back."

En route to the Honolulu-bound SS *Lurline* in San Francisco, the Ruths stopped in Chicago to view the World's Fair. They visited the exhibits, sampled exotic foods, and even watched a puppet show featuring none other than the Bambino himself. Detroit was a mere 237 miles to the east. Ruth could have met with Navin for a day and still have had time to witness his puppet self. But he did not. Arriving in San Francisco, Ruth realized his mistake and late one night telephoned Navin at home. Unfortunately, Ruth forgot about the time difference. The phone rang at three in the morning, Detroit time. A sleepy and grumpy Navin, who was generally cranky even in daylight, heard Ruth demanding if he would be the Tigers' next manager. He needed a yes or no that moment. "No," said Navin and hung up.

While Ruth relaxed in Hawaii, Navin traded for star catcher Mickey Cochrane and installed him as a player-manager. Under Cochrane the Tigers walked away with the pennant in '34, finishing seven games in front of the second-place Yankees.[3]

Ruth spent the 1934 season under McCarthy's thumb in right field, but he was no longer the Sultan of Swat. He had put on weight, and his weak legs made him a defensive liability and reduced his power at the plate. His .288 batting average was his lowest since 1916 when he was a still a full-time pitcher, and his twenty-two home runs were the lowest since he became an everyday player in 1919. In August he announced that 1934 would be his last as an active player. When asked what he would do next, Ruth told reporters that he would like to manage, with some pinch hitting now and then. He still openly coveted McCarthy's job.

The day before Suzuki cornered him at the barbershop, the Babe had marched into the brewery and confronted Ruppert and Barrow. The Yankees had finished in second place for the second year in a row. "Are you satisfied with McCarthy as your manager?" Ruth demanded.

"Why yes. Of course, I am. Aren't you?" responded Ruppert.

"No, I'm not," growled Ruth. "I know I can do a better job than he can!"

"Really? Well, that's too bad, Ruth. I'm sorry, but McCarthy is the manager, and he will continue as manager."

"That suits me! That's all I wanted to know!" Ruth stormed out, knowing that his career as a Yankee was over.[4]

Now, the Babe stood beside the barber's chair scowling. Suzuki cajoled. "The Japanese fans are waiting to see you . . ." "The tour will fail without you . . ." "You signed a contract . . ." Nothing worked. Ruth remained adamant. He would not go to Japan.

The door behind Suzuki opened, and O'Doul and Walsh entered. The argument continued—more forcefully now that the two Americans were aiding Suzuki. They were getting nowhere when Suzuki had an inspiration. Reaching into his bag, he withdrew a *happi* coat, a thin cotton jacket usually worn at festivals, with Ruth's image on the front. Ruth stopped and looked. This jacket, Suzuki explained, would be worn by men delivering the *Yomiuri* newspaper. Sotaro reached in a second time and pulled out a large folded paper. Suzuki unfurled a three-by-four-foot advertising poster for the tour. Massive red kanji down the right side and bottom and blue kanji across the top proclaimed that *Yomiuri* was sponsoring a Japanese-American baseball series on November 4 and 5 at Meiji Jingu Stadium. Dominating the poster was a pen-and-ink portrait of the Babe. Drawn with exquisite detail, showing the lines in his face and the famous large nose, the portrait captured Ruth as he was in 1934, aging and a bit melancholy. The artist made a significant change in Ruth's face. His eyes were almond shaped with the distinctive downward slant of an Asian and not the rounder eyes of a Westerner. Below the portrait a caption read "Baseball King Babe Ruth."

Once again Sotaro explained how much the Japanese were looking forward to his visit. But this time, the Bambino did not argue. He boomed a mighty laugh—perhaps his first in days—and agreed to play.

That night, Suzuki slept well.

6

As Sotaro Suzuki slept, Jimmy Horio steamed toward Japan, hoping to become the first Asian in the Major Leagues.

In 1890 his father, Shimataro Horio, and his family joined the tens of thousands who fled Hiroshima for Hawaii as an economic downturn hit the southern province especially hard. Food became scarce, forcing some unfortunates to subsist on bark and roots. Labor recruiters traversed the prefecture, explaining the need for workers on a tropical island paradise known as Hawaii. There an entire family could find work and save enough money to return to Japan in style or make a new comfortable home in the islands. With little economic future in Hiroshima, Shimataro signed a labor contract and with his wife, Shimo, and their two young daughters boarded a Hawaiian-bound steamship.[1]

The passage was brutal. For three weeks the Horios would have been packed belowdecks with hundreds of other passengers. Families rigged up cloth screens for privacy, but they did not keep out the smell. Passengers relieved themselves in buckets that during rough seas would remain full for days in the enclosed space. Diseases spread quickly. This was just the first indication that the recruiters may have deceived them.

The family settled at Pa'ia Plantation on the island of Maui. The Horios were accustomed to hard work, but life on the plantation was harsh. Laborers worked from dawn to dusk with few breaks from the tropical heat. To protect themselves from the razor-sharp cane leaves, workers wore heavy clothing, which led to heat exhaustion. On the most brutal plantations, mounted overseers armed with whips rode behind the laborers to ensure that they kept pace. Despite the hard conditions, the family grew, and Shimo bore six more children, including James Fumito Horio, the seventh of the eight children and youngest son, in 1907. By 1913 Shimataro Horio had enough of Hawaii and moved his family back to Hiroshima. The Horios spent the next six years in Hiroshima before packing up and returning to Maui.

Jimmy most likely learned to play ball as a youngster in Maui by tagging along with his older brothers. He refined his skills while attending elementary school in Japan and, after returning to Hawaii, played in Maui's plantation league. Horio stood nearly five foot eleven and towered over the island's issei and nisei (first- and second-generation Japanese immigrants). Few boys from the plantations followed professional baseball. Games from the mainland were rarely broadcast on the island, and even when they were, radios were scarce. The local papers carried Major League news but rarely featured it—local sports action was more important to most Hawaiians. Horio, however, was one of the few kids who followed the sport and from a young age dreamed of playing in the Major Leagues.

In 1928 Shimataro Horio once again returned to Hiroshima. He acquired property, either through inheritance or with his carefully saved plantation wages, and this time settled in the city permanently. Instead of relocating with his parents, Jimmy, now twenty-one, decided to move to Los Angeles and pursue his dream of playing professional baseball.

Jimmy played for the amateur Grand Central Market team before joining the Los Angeles Nippons, the area's top nisei semipro squad, in 1930. The following spring the LA Nippons traveled to Japan. For most of Horio's teammates it was the first visit to their parents' homeland. Many were overcome with emotion as they visited the country's national monuments and were welcomed by thousands of fans.

It was not easy being Japanese in the United States, even in the so-called Japan towns of the West Coast. Prejudice ruled the day. Laws precluded many Japanese Americans from owning land, Japanese American laborers were excluded from certain industries, and signs proclaiming "No Japs Allowed!" hung outside many white-owned businesses. In Japan the nisei players could visit any restaurant, enter any store. They were treated as equals by the majority of the population, perhaps for the first time in their lives.

The LA Nippons nisei, with their American diets, were physically larger than the native Japanese and played a more aggressive brand of baseball. They dominated their Japanese collegiate and club opponents, winning twenty of their twenty-five games. Horio impressed the Japanese with his power as well as his defense and strong arm. As he was bilingual, Jimmy befriended several of the Japanese players, a minor act at the time but one that would change his life.

After returning from Japan, Horio spent three more years with the LA Nippons, but he was no closer to making the Majors. No Major League scout had made him an offer, and he would turn twenty-seven on March 15, 1934. Knowing that he would soon be too old to interest a Major League team, he realized that it was time to leave Los Angeles. He joined the Sioux Falls Canaries of the Class D Nebraska State League for the '34 season. Speedy Horio hustled on the base paths, scoring sixty runs in the short season, and developed a reputation as an outstanding defensive outfielder. He was soon dubbed "the Yellow Peril"—a phrase popularized by turn-of-the-century racists to describe the perceived threat of Asia's growing population. Whether he embraced the condescending name with irony or hated it is unknown, but Horio rarely let racial slights go unchallenged. He was the only Japanese in the Nebraska State League and bore the taunts of opponents and fans alike. He retaliated by sliding hard on the base paths and even entering the opposing dugouts to confront hecklers. Once, when a fan repeatedly yelled "Chink," Jimmy challenged the heckler to come onto the field to settle the matter.

But racism would not be the primary barrier preventing Horio from making the Majors. He was, in truth, not a strong hitter. In his 413 at bats in Class D ball, Horio hit just .264, with 5 home runs and a .383 slugging percentage. His spirit, hustle, and defense could not overcome his weak hitting. Late in the season, Charlie Bartlett, a scout for the St. Louis Cardinals, watched Jimmy carefully but made no offer. Jimmy must have known that his dream was slipping away.

Then in early autumn, Horio heard about the All American barnstorming tour to Japan and, more important, of *Yomiuri*'s plan to create the All Nippon team. He had excelled against the Japanese in '31 and felt that he was a better player than many of their stars. A crazy idea came to him—an incredible gamble. He would play for the Japanese and prove to the Major Leaguers that he was their equal. Then he would finally gain the coveted Major League contract.

The tour would start in a month. Jimmy did not have time to write to the *Yomiuri* organizers or have friends make introductions for him. With his wife, Yoshiko, he boarded the next ship to Yokohama.

7

Moe Berg opened his trunk and began to pack. In went a number of dark-gray suits, high quality and identical. In went matching white dress shirts and several identical black ties. Black shoes followed. Dressing was easy for Berg, as he wore the same outfit every day, a ritual he would follow for more than fifty years. Once his teammates, convinced that Berg never changed his clothes, sneaked into his hotel room and peeked into his closet, only to find eight identical suits.[1]

Unlike most of his All American teammates who were taking their first overseas trip, Berg was a seasoned traveler. He had already visited more than a dozen countries on four continents and could speak or read at least twelve languages with varying degrees of competency. He spoke a few fluently, such as French, but understood just a smattering of Japanese, Sanskrit, Greek, and others. Although Berg had an extraordinary faculty with languages, sportswriters exaggerated his abilities, often claiming that he spoke a dozen fluently. Berg did little to correct the misconception and often paraded non-English newspapers in the clubhouse. His linguistic ability and low batting average caused a teammate to quip that Berg could speak a dozen languages but could not hit in any of them.

Berg was an odd Major Leaguer. Moe, short for Morris, was the third child of Bernard and Rose Berg, Ukrainian Jews who immigrated to New York in the 1890s. Like most immigrants, Bernard started near the bottom, slaving over an ironing board in a Lower East Side laundry. Within two years, he was running his own laundry and taking classes at the New York College of Pharmacy. In 1902 Moe was born in Harlem, where his father now worked as a pharmacist. Four years later, Bernard bought a pharmacy in Newark, and the family moved to New Jersey. Although born in a Ukrainian shtetl,

Bernard abandoned Judaism and forbade Yiddish from being spoken in his house.

Moe became a star athlete and student at Barringer High School and at sixteen years old enrolled at New York University for the 1918 academic year. The following year, Princeton University accepted him as a freshman. Despite his secular upbringing, the prevalent anti-Semitism at Princeton caused Berg to accept his Jewish ethnicity. He presided over Friday-night services when some of his few Jewish classmates organized the events (although the services may have been an excuse to get out of the mandatory Sunday chapel for Gentiles).

At Princeton Berg combined athleticism with scholarship. He excelled at foreign languages, studying Latin, Greek, French, Spanish, Italian, German, and Sanskrit before graduating magna cum laude in 1923. He starred at basketball and baseball. He played three varsity seasons in those sports, becoming the baseball team's star shortstop and leading the Tigers to a 21-4 record his senior year. Within hours of playing his last game for Princeton, Berg signed a professional contract with the Brooklyn Dodgers for five thousand dollars. The following afternoon he played three innings against the Phillies, gaining a single in his first at bat.

That first at bat, however, was not a portent of a great baseball career. Berg played in forty-nine games during the summer of '23, hit an embarrassing .186, and committed twenty-two errors at shortstop. His signing bonus, however, went to good use—funding a semester at the Sorbonne. Berg spent the off-season in Paris, enrolling in twenty-two classes, including courses in romantic languages, history, literature, and medieval Latin. After touring Italy and Switzerland, he headed home for spring training.

Berg failed to make the Dodgers in '24 and spent the season in the Minors. He returned to school in the fall, studying French and Spanish at Columbia University's Graduate School of Arts and Sciences, and squeezed in a season with Reading of the International League before enrolling at Columbia Law School in September 1925. During the off season, the Chicago White Sox purchased his contract from Reading. His chance to return to the big leagues would begin at spring training in March 1926. Berg, however, informed his new club that he would skip spring training to finish his first year at law school. Shocked, the team sent officials and players to dissuade him but to no avail. Berg joined the Sox on May 28 and spent the season on the bench, seeing action in just forty-one games as a utility infielder. He returned to Columbia in September, once again missed spring training, and rode the bench in 1927. The following year Berg decided to focus on baseball. He secured a leave of absence from Columbia in February 1928 and reported to spring training on time.

A plodding runner, Berg was too slow to play shortstop at the Major League level, but luck would prolong his professional career. The 1927 White Sox carried two catchers on their roster as well as player-manager Ray Schalk, Chicago's starting catcher from 1913 to 1926. Between July 21 and August 5, all three catchers fell to injuries. As the exasperated Schalk pondered his dilemma, Berg supposedly told him, "You've got a big league catcher sitting right here." Berg had meant backup first baseman Earl Sheely, who had caught in the Minors, but Schalk misunderstood. "All right, Berg, get in there." Without correcting his manager, Berg put on the equipment and announced to the dugout, "If the worst happens, kindly deliver the body to Newark." He survived, playing ten games behind the plate until the regulars returned.

Entering the 1928 season, Berg had decided to catch full-time. Although slow for a shortstop, he was spry for a catcher and easily mastered pitching strategies. He learned the finer points of his new position and became the team's top catcher in '28 and '29. His batting average even rose to a respectable .287 in 1929. With his rise in baseball, law school suffered. Berg failed Evidence that fall and would need to retake the course in 1930 to graduate, but he had fulfilled his dream of becoming a starting Major Leaguer. Then, on April 6, days before the start of the 1930 season, Berg injured his knee. He would never get more than 150 at bats in a season again.

Berg was an odd duck, never fitting in socially with his fellow ballplayers. He left the ballparks directly after games, rarely joining his teammates for dinner or outings. Even on the road, where players are forced together, Berg would leave the hotel alone—his destinations known only to himself. He would occasionally attend lectures, visit museums, and, after joining the Senators in 1932, attend embassy and government parties, where he would make connections that would eventually lead to a more shadowy career. Then there were the newspapers. Berg usually carried a stack with him: the *New York Times*, *Washington Post*, *Boston Globe*, local papers, and often specially ordered British and French papers. He forbade others from touching them until he had finished reading. They were alive, he would claim, until read. Once finished, he would pronounce the paper "dead" and often discard it on the floor.[2]

Despite Berg's eccentricities, his teammates liked him. Most found him to be kind and funny, even charming. He was even more popular among the reporters. Berg was always ready with a good quote. Strangely, as his skills faded and he became less important on the field, he became more of a celebrity. *New York Times* columnist John Kieran made Professor Berg's antics a regular topic in his "Sports of the Times," which eventually led to Berg's appearance on the popular radio quiz show *Information, Please!*

After the 1932 season, Berg joined Herb Hunter, Lefty O'Doul, and Ted Lyons on the trip to Japan to instruct the Tokyo Big Six University teams. As a backup catcher, Berg seems an odd choice, but he was a friend of Lyons, had a lust for travel and a gift for languages, and was a good teacher. During the two-week trip to Japan, Berg studied the language. He memorized katakana, a phonetic alphabet used to write foreign words in Japanese, but seems to have ignored hiragana, the phonetic system for Japanese words, as well as the more challenging kanji characters.

Following a thin book on Japanese grammar, Berg wrote out sample sentences in English followed by their Japanese equivalent in the roman alphabet and then in katakana. His choice of sentences bordered on the bizarre. "Is there a man here who makes toys?" "How many soldiers in one regiment?" "Is there only one kind of Japanese dog?" And just in case you encountered said Japanese dogs, "Are there two or three dogs in the garden?" By the time his ship docked in Yokohama, Berg understood the basics of the language and could communicate simple ideas, although he would often need to write them in katakana and pass the note to a native speaker.[3]

Berg was infatuated with Japan from the first day. He wrote his family, "I have never enjoyed a visit or anything any more in my life than this one. . . . So this is the Orient—saw rikshaws and jinrikshaw-men . . . , smelled some of the distinctive odors of Japan—the ride [from the dock to the hotel] was a page out of a dream—streets, narrow, lined with shops, thousands of people going home from work on bicycles, street cars packed with people, everybody moving."[4]

The Americans spent their days instructing college teams on the finer points of the game. They ran drills, such as trying to steal second base on Lyons and Berg (Berg threw out most of the runners), and worked on hitting. They also supervised intrasquad games—occasionally halting play to point out a strategic error or correct a fault. Berg noted that "the boys are usually small—none as tall as I—but wonderful imitators and on the whole good students—they learn quickly—they are not good hitters and play what we call in the U.S. a passive game."[5]

When not instructing the players, Berg wandered the streets, filming life in Tokyo—young women in bright kimonos, old men pulling wagons loaded with crates, bargemen punting through the city's canals, young boys with shaved heads mugging for the camera. In the evenings he and the other Americans sampled traditional Japanese entertainment. They watched a sumo match, attended a play, went drinking, and spent at least one night with the infamous female denizens of Yoshiwara—often mistaken for geisha by foreigners.

Berg also spent hours at Meiji University with Takizo "Frank" Matsumoto. Frank was born in Tokyo in 1901 and given the Japanese name Takizo. Soon after his birth, the Matsumoto family moved to Fresno, California. They had barely settled when Takizo's father died. His mother, Kiyo, now a young widow, quickly married restaurant owner Hichiza Narushima, and Takizo soon became known as Frank Narushima. Like many American boys, Frank excelled at sports. He played football at Fresno High School, ran track, and fell in love with baseball. After graduating in 1919, he helped start a Japanese American baseball team at the Fresno Athletic Club. The following year Kenichi Zenimura, the most pivotal figure in Japanese American baseball, joined the club. Frank did not remain with the Fresno team long, as he moved to Pasadena to attend the California Institute of Technology for two years. In 1922 he returned to Japan, enrolled at Meiji University, and reassumed his Japanese name.

At twenty-three Matsumoto may have been too old to play on Meiji's baseball squad, as he instead became the team's manager—a position closer to traveling secretary than field manager. With Matsumoto's help his old friend Kenichi Zenimura brought the Fresno Athletic Club to Japan in 1924. Ties between Meiji and Fresno were strengthened two years later when Kenichi's cousin Tatsumi Zenimura enrolled at Meiji and joined the ball club. In 1927 Kenichi brought Fresno to Japan for a second time, and the two friends helped promoter Lon Goodwin bring the Negro League Philadelphia Royal Giants to Japan. In turn Zenimura hosted the Meiji ball club in California in 1929. By the time Matsumoto graduated and was hired by the university to teach English and economics, the pair of old friends had extensive experience in organizing international baseball tours. They probably helped organize the Royal Giants' second tour of Japan in 1930 and may have played a small role in the *Yomiuri*-sponsored 1931 Major League tour.[6]

Matsumoto and Berg quickly became fast friends. Matsumoto tutored Berg in Japanese, and Berg returned the favor with French lessons. Berg also became a guest lecturer in Matsumoto's English courses at Meiji University. Once his coaching duties were over, Berg and Matsumoto toured southern Japan. They visited Kyoto, Nara, Osaka, and Kobe before taking a boat to Beppu to enjoy the hot springs. Berg left Japan through the southern port of Shimonoseki, embarking on a whirlwind tour of Asia. He stopped in Korea, Manchuria, Shanghai, Peking, Saigon, Cambodia, Bangkok, India, Egypt, Palestine, and finally Germany before heading home and to spring training.[7]

During the 1933 and '34 seasons, Berg spun tales about Japan during the tedious hours watching the games from the bullpen, probably wondering if he would ever get a chance to return. In August 1934 the opportunity came. All-star catcher Rick Ferrell decided not to join the American team, leaving the squad without a backstop. Earle Mack asked Berg to fill the void. On August 30 Mack sent Berg an urgent telegram, "Kindly advise if there is a possibility you will make the trip. Must send over final lineup by September 1 as want to get started on programs and scorecards. Also must get uniforms made." Berg, thrilled to be returning to Japan, agreed.

As he finished packing, Moe Berg focused on a small but heavy rectangular brown box. A brass lock sealed the opening of the cardboard case covered with cheap leather. It contained his 16-mm Bell and Howell movie camera. A rugged piece of machinery, constructed of steel and magnesium, the B&H 70a weighed six pounds without the lens. It cost just under two hundred dollars, a sizable sum at the time but affordable to a ballplayer like Berg. He had lugged it around the world in 1932, taking films of Japanese temples, the Great Wall of China, and the Egyptian pyramids. This time he had a contract with Movietone News to record highlights of the trip to Japan for their newsreels.[8]

He also packed a letter from Cordell Hull, the secretary of state of the United States of America. It read:

To the American Diplomatic and Consular Officers:

At the instance of the Honorable Chester C. Bolton, representative in the Congress of the United States from the State of Ohio, I take pleasure in introducing to you Mr. Morris Berg of Newark, New Jersey, who is about to proceed abroad.

I cordially bespeak for Mr. Berg such courtesies and assistance as you may be able to render consistent with your official duties.

Cordell Hull
Secretary of State[9]

It was a strange letter for a ballplayer to carry, but Berg's behavior in Japan would be even stranger. During World War II Moe Berg would become an operative for the OSS. Several baseball writers would later argue that the letter was intended to help Berg in a secret mission for the State Department. Berg, they would say, was already a spy in 1934. His mission was to gather information on the Japanese and photograph significant military and industrial sites while he toured the country as an honored guest. After all, nobody would suspect a ballplayer of espionage.

Berg boarded a United Airlines flight from New York and arrived in Chicago to rendezvous with members of the All Americans. Together, they would take a train to Seattle to unite with the rest of the team. In Chicago Berg met Babe Ruth, who arrived with his wife, Claire; eighteen-year-old stepdaughter, Julia; and nearly twenty pieces of luggage. An amazed Berg wrote his parents that one of the Bambino's bags contained nothing but chewing tobacco. They left the Windy City on October 15. As the train passed through the Illinois countryside, throngs of fans lined the depots to catch a glance of the mighty Babe. He usually made a brief appearance at a window, waving a great paw and shouting hellos. Ruth surprised Berg. Perhaps expecting him to be a coarse but lovable clown, Berg found the Babe to be "a born actor, good natured and not dumb at all," but noted that "he can drink and eat more than any two men."[10]

Joining Berg and Ruth were manager Connie Mack and an old friend of Moe's—Charlie Berry. Berry also hailed from New Jersey, and Berg had tried, unsuccessfully, to get him into Princeton in 1921. Instead, Berry attended Lafayette College, becoming an All American football player. He later played in the fledgling NFL and led the league in scoring in 1925. That same year he joined the Philadelphia Athletics as a backup catcher. For the next few years Berry spent his summers in the Minors and falls on the gridiron until leaving football and returning to the Majors in 1928. No animosity remained between Ruth and Berry from their 1931 home-plate collision that left Ruth unconscious and sidelined for two weeks, and the four men spent their days in the Pullman coaches "telling stories and lies."[11]

During a two-hour stopover at St. Paul, Minnesota, a friend of Berry's met the train and invited Berry and Berg for a drive. As they entered the car, Berry collapsed against the door. Moe rushed over to help. Clutching his stomach, Berry explained that he felt sharp pains and had not gone to the toilet all day. It was nothing that an enema wouldn't fix. Moe disagreed. He had picked up basic medical knowledge from his brother Sam—the doctor. Berg insisted that they forgo the pleasure drive and rush to a doctor. He was right. A blood test revealed that Berry's white corpuscles were over two thousand—a sign of appendicitis. The doctor, however, insisted that Berry was in no immediate danger and should continue to Seattle. Back on board the train, Berg brought Berry an ice pack, and the pain subsided. By five in the morning it became obvious that the doctor had been wrong. The pain was unbearable. Making an emergency stop in Valley City, North Dakota, Berry was rushed to the hospital to have his appendix removed. On a tight schedule, the All Americans could not wait and left their teammate as the train continued to the West Coast.[12]

Berry's departure left Berg as the squad's lone catcher. Mack wired Philadelphia and ordered Frank Hayes, a twenty-year-old Athletics prospect, to take Berry's place. Hayes would have to leave immediately and take a rare cross-continental flight to Vancouver. If the weather cooperated, he would make it just in time for the team's October 20 departure by ship to Japan.

More bad news awaited Connie Mack in Seattle. Earle Mack had led about half of the All American squad on a barnstorming tour from the East Coast to Seattle. They played local nines and semipro squads and lost to a Negro League all-star team (featuring Chet Brewer) as they traveled across the country. On October 8 they stopped in Winnipeg to challenge a mixed-race team of Minor and Negro leaguers called the North Dakota All Stars. On the mound for the first game of a proposed doubleheader was eventual Negro League all-star Barney Brown, who would play professionally for the next twenty-two years. But that October "Lefty" Brown was only a few years into his career. Later he would be known for a devastating screwball, pinpoint control, and a fiery competitive spirit. That afternoon, however, a pitch got away, drilling Athletics slugger Jimmie Foxx in the head. Foxx toppled over, unconscious. Locals rushed him to a hospital. He would live, initial reports concluded, but might never be able to play ball again. After further observation and X-rays, doctors decided that Foxx's skull was not fractured and there would be no brain damage. He had suffered a serious concussion and would recover. Foxx remained hospitalized for four days and then headed west to rejoin the team.[13]

The All Americans on the Japan tour finally united in Seattle on October 18. That evening they played against a group of barnstorming American Leaguers including pitcher Ted Lyons, who had traveled with Berg to Japan two years earlier. During the game Jimmie Foxx, his head bandaged and still in a stupor, approached Sotaro

Suzuki to promise him that he would make the trip to Japan. American League president William Harridge, however, would not make it. Suzuki had just received a telegram informing him that Harridge's wife had injured her leg, making travel impossible.

Following the game both teams took a train to Vancouver and settled in at the Vancouver Hotel. A mob of young boys filled the hotel lobby. To the surprise of the ballplayers, many of the boys already had papers full of signatures and were clamoring after a group of young men on the other side of the lobby. The *Winnipeg Free Press* called the evening one of "the best opportunities on local record for autograph hunters," as Canadian lacrosse champion Orillia Terriers and former world champion Gene Tunney were also hotel guests.[14]

Rain began soon after dawn and continued throughout the day. The game against Ted Lyons's barnstormers should have been canceled, but the All Americans needed practice and fans had begun to line up outside of Athletic Park. With all of the Major League teams located east of the Mississippi (except St. Louis), West Coast fans had few opportunities to see big league ball, and the All Americans were not just any big leaguers but probably the most talented squad ever to play in Vancouver. Some fans had traveled for hours to see the team, and especially the Babe, in person. Eighteen-year-old Rud Haar came by steamship from the small mill town of Woodfibre. After the three- to four-hour trip, Haar waited in the rain for a seat in the tiny ballpark, but he felt it was a small price to see Ruth and the All Americans. The downpour evidently did not spoil his love for the game, as Haar would later become the head groundskeeper at Vancouver's Nat Bailey Stadium in the 1980s.[15]

Puddles dotted the field and spray flew into the air each time a ball skidded across the outfield grass, but the two teams did their best to please the Vancouver fans. Ruth did not play well, trying too hard to hit one out, but two drives in foul territory left the ballpark, landing on Sixth Avenue. The *Vancouver Sun* claimed that the fouls "traveled farther than any two balls ever hit before at Athletic Park." The rain intensified in the sixth inning and the umpires finally decided to end the contest, but Ruth supposedly jogged in from the outfield announcing, "If these people can sit here and watch us, we can stay out here and play." The game continued a full nine innings when it ended as a 2–2 tie.[16]

The soaked players trudged back to the Vancouver Hotel, changed, dined, and met in Connie Mack's room. At seventy-one years old, Mack was by far the oldest manager in the Majors. He had been at the Athletics helm since 1901, always dressed in a suit, never a uniform. Known as the ultimate gentleman, Mack did not curse, smoke, or drink, but the players respected him just the same for his fairness and knowledge. He addressed the All Americans in a quiet, serious voice, and the players settled down to listen.

In the morning, Mack explained, they would board their ship and leave the United States. During this trip they would be more than baseball players; they would be ambassadors, he said. Their behavior, both on and off the field, would reflect not only on themselves but also on Major League Baseball and their country. Every player must promise to always try his best, be friendly and sincere toward his hosts, teach the Japanese players, be nice to the fans, and always be respectful. "If you cannot keep this promise," Mack continued, "please leave this room and you can go wherever you want." Nobody stirred.

Ruth, sitting in the front row, raised his right hand and swore that he would follow the rules. Each of the other players followed in turn, swearing to follow Mack's tenets. Mack then made some brief announcements and dismissed the team. As Suzuki left Mack pulled him aside and promised to help him create a professional league. The two grasped hands tightly, sealing the friendship.[17]

The next morning, October 20, the All Americans left the hotel and paraded through the streets of Vancouver to the docks, to board the jewel of the Canadian Pacific fleet, the *Empress of Japan*. A throng of well-wishers packed the pier, forcing the players to push their way through the crowd. As the other players checked into their cabins, the new catcher, Frank Hayes, met with diplomatic officials from the United States, Canada, Japan, and China. Hayes had arrived by airplane the night before as planned, but having come on such short notice, he had not had time to apply for a passport. The officials issued Hayes the passport and appropriate visas as the crew readied for departure.[18]

The ship's orchestra struck up a tune on the main deck as the passengers lined the gunwale to wave their good-byes. Ship employees ran down the decks, distributing serpentine confetti as cameramen for various newsreels took their last onboard footage. At last, the *Empress of Japan* pulled away from the pier as the band played "Aloha," and passengers tossed confetti on the dock below. Amid the cheering, music, and blasting horns, tears slid down the Babe's broad cheeks.

The adventure to Asia had begun.

8

Capt. Koji Muranaka bowed before the main altar at the Jikishin Dojo (Direct Mind Training Center) in the Koishikawa section of Tokyo. Before him stood a large tablet dedicated to Amaterasu Omikami, the Sun Goddess and progenitor of the imperial family. The wall to the left of the altar contained three rows of photographs depicting the nation's leading patriots. To its right stood an alcove containing a flower arrangement, a pair of samurai swords, and a scroll bearing the command "Enemy Countries Surrender!"[1] The early-morning sun shone through the many windows on Muranaka's left, casting light on the large room's tatami floor.

Now thirty-one years old, Muranaka had a nondescript yet pleasant face—high cheekbones, a firm jaw, a small nose, and a slightly receding hairline. Without his uniform, he would have blended in with Tokyo's thousands of salarymen. His father, after all, was a successful businessman in Hokkaido. But Koji had chosen a different, more violent, path.

Muranaka was a rising officer in the Imperial Army. He had attended a military school in Sendai before being accepted to the Thirty-Seventh Class of the Imperial Japanese Army Academy in the Ichigaya section of Tokyo. Exceptionally bright, articulate, and fluent in German, he graduated in 1925 and became a full lieutenant in 1928 with the Twenty-Sixth Infantry and a captain in 1934. In 1932 Muranaka was admitted to the elite Army War College, the springboard to higher command. But his destiny would change when he met Mitsugi Nishida.[2]

Although the son of a sculptor of Buddhist images, Nishida had been pushed toward the military as a child. Born in 1901 he attended the Hiroshima Regional Army Cadet School and the Central Army

Cadet School before entering the Imperial Japanese Army Academy in 1920. While at the academy, he met activist Ikki Kita. Kita, a former Waseda University student, member of the Black Dragon Society, and spy for the Japanese in China, was the leading theorist for National Reconstruction. Kita believed that Japan faced both an international and a domestic crisis. Despite Japan's defeating China in the Sino-Japanese War in 1894 and Russia in the Japanese-Russian War in 1905 and joining the Allies in World War I, the Western nations did not recognize Japan's right to establish a controlling interest in China or expand its territories. As a result Japan stood alone, confronted by hostile Western nations. But before Japan could successfully expand its interests in China, it needed to be strong internally. Kita argued that Japan's rapid Westernization in the late nineteenth century had benefited only elites and left it socially and economically fractured. Indeed, following World War I, the Japanese economy had slumped, causing widespread unemployment and inflation that led to labor strikes and rioting. In his book *An Outline of Measures for the Reorganization of Japan*, Kita called for a complete social and economic reorganization of the country.[3] Rejecting the Western ideologies of democracy and communism as unsuitable for Japan, he advocated that power be turned over to the divine emperor as the "representative of the people and as pillar of the nation."[4]

Japanese tradition held that the first emperor, Jimmu (AD 509–71) was the direct descendant of the Sun Goddess, Amaterasu Omikami. As the imperial line had remained intact since Jimmu's reign, it followed that subsequent emperors were themselves divine, embodying the true spirit of Japan and the wisdom of the gods. The emperors, however, had rarely concerned themselves with the daily mechanisms of government. Instead, they allowed advisers and military rulers, known as shogun, to run the country as they focused on their role as head of the Shinto religion. From time to time disenfranchised groups would seize power under the guise of returning control to the emperor, dispatch his advisers, and set themselves up as his new advisers. The most famous "restoration" was the Meiji Restoration of 1867 when the abrupt arrival of Commodore Matthew Perry and his black ships in Yokohama Bay in 1853 sparked a series of events that toppled the 350-year reign of the Tokugawa shogunate and transferred power to rival lords, who modernized the country in the name of the young Meiji emperor.

Kita, like many nationalists, believed that the Meiji Restoration remained unfulfilled. Instead of allowing the emperor to control the government, he thought, a group of corrupt advisers, bent on a plan of Westernization, dictated Japanese policy. These advisers, known as the genro, remained in power after Meiji's death in 1912 and continued to direct the policies of the current emperor, Hirohito, known formally as Showa. Kita, therefore, called for a Showa Restoration that would free Emperor Hirohito from the genro and allow him unlimited power to run the nation.

To accomplish the restoration, members of the military motivated by pure patriotism would need to seize the government in a coup d'état. These troops would then declare martial law, dissolve the cabinet and diet, suspend the constitution, and purge the Imperial Court and the emperor's advisers before "restoring" the emperor to power. Unlike Emperor Meiji, the Showa emperor would use his divine abilities to set policy, although an appointed cabinet and a nationally elected diet would help implement these policies. In the words of the Jikishin Dojo's founder, Roshi Omori, "We believed that the benevolence of the August Mind of his Majesty would pour down on all the people just as the rays of the sun in spring flood the earth with warmth."[5]

To end Japan's social and economic divisions, the restored emperor would then disband the peerage system, turn all imperial property over to the nation, place a cap of one million yen on a family's personal property and nationalize the excess, nationalize all property within city boundaries, nationalize large forests and large-scale agricultural enterprises, end large business by limiting private industry to capitalizations of one hundred million yen, institute profit sharing between workers and employers, create an eight-hour workday, and ban child labor.

Once Japan's domestic inequalities had been abolished and its reconstructed society was running smoothly, it was the military's duty to expand Japan's influence and bring their enlightened society to other lands, the movement contended. A leading nationalist magazine proclaimed, "We the Japanese should lead the war of emancipation of the human race. . . . It is not sufficient to aim at the reform or revolution of Japan herself . . . because it is Japan's mission to liberate the whole world."[6]

After becoming Kita's disciple and graduating from the academy in 1922, Nishida served with the Twenty-Seventh Cavalry in Korea and the Fifth Cavalry in Hiroshima before retiring in 1925 due to poor health. During his active military duty and his retirement, Nishida spread Kita's ideas among the younger army officers and academy cadets. In the mid-1920s he formed the Heavenly Swords Society (Tenken-to) "to be the fundamental power for enforcing the logical reconstruction." The group readied itself for the assault needed to spearhead Kita's restoration, promising to "fight constantly with mob-uprising, commotion, assassination, sabotage, destruction, occupation, denunciation and propaganda."[7] As a second Lieutenant, Koji Muranaka not only had joined Nishida's Heavenly Swords but was also listed in the 1927 newsletter as a local organizer.[8] The Heavenly Swords Society, however, never fulfilled its mission. Military police learned of its existence and forced Nishida to disband the group in the late 1920s.

Starting in the early 1930s other ultranationalist groups attempted to initiate the Showa Restoration. Most were poorly organized and ill-conceived plans by small civilian groups that went nowhere, but there were six serious attempts, three involving military personnel, between 1931 and December 1933.

The first came in March 1931, when a group of senior military officers, with no ties to Nishida, formed the Cherry Society and planned a coup d'état to replace the ruling cabinet with a reformist cabinet headed by the minister of war, Gen. Kazushige Ugaki. Just before the planned coup Ugaki backed out, forcing the group to abandon, or at least postpone, their plans. In October of the same year, several members of the Cherry Society were ready to try again. This time they planned to massacre the cabinet, seize strategic areas of Tokyo, and create a reform cabinet headed by Gen. Sadao Araki. The plotters contacted Nishida, who readily committed his young followers to the cause. As a former member of the Heavenly Swords, Muranaka was probably among Nishida's men. This attempt also failed, as the war minister discovered the plan, confined the plotters to their barracks, and later transferred the ringleaders from the capital. Nishida and his followers remained unscathed from the incident, but the young officers lost confidence in the Cherry Society and began to question the senior officers' commitment to true reform. From that point on Nishida and his group would take matters into their own hands.

The next major plot came only five months later, when a group of naval officers and civilians, led by the Buddhist priest Nissho Inoue and known as the League of Blood, banded together to assassinate twenty leading businessmen and liberal politicians. Inoue assigned a target to each of twenty followers and ordered his men to kill their targets whenever an opportunity presented itself. The conspirators hoped that the ensuing chaos after the assassinations would enable the military to seize power, declare martial law, and enact the restoration. Inoue had initially asked Nishida to join the uprising, but Nishida declined, stating that the timing was not right. The League of Blood killed former finance minister Junnosuke Inoue (no relation to Nissho Inoue) and the head of the Mitsui trading company Takuma Dan, before police broke the conspiracy and arrested Inoue and his followers on March 11, 1932. The involved naval officers, however, remained undiscovered and decided to continue the plot.

The naval conspirators once again asked Nishida to join, but again he declined. On March 20 the naval officers met with Muranaka, several other young army officers, and a group of cadets from the Imperial Japanese Army Academy, where Muranaka was now an instructor, at the barracks of the Third Infantry Regiment in Tokyo. Muranaka and his fellow officers followed Nishida's lead and refused to join but did not forbid ten cadets from participating.[9]

At dusk on May 15 they struck. Dividing themselves into four groups, they killed Prime Minister Tsuyoshi Inukai at his home and tossed grenades into Mitsubishi Bank, the Seiyukai Party headquarters, the Bank of Japan, and the residence of Count Nobuaki Makino, a close adviser to the emperor and the keeper of the Privy Seal. The grenades, however, caused little damage. The group had toyed with but eventually abandoned the idea of murdering Charlie Chaplin, who was visiting Tokyo. The conspirators then drove to the military police headquarters and surrendered. Meanwhile, a group of associated civilians attacked several electric power stations in an effort to plunge Tokyo into darkness, while another civilian attempted to assassinate Mitsugi Nishida in retribution for not participating and to settle a personal score. The attempt on the power stations failed miserably, but the attack on Nishida left him critically wounded with eight gunshot wounds (he would recover). Despite killing the prime minister, the insurrection was a failure. The army stayed in its barracks, martial law was not declared, and the structure of Japanese government remained intact.

In the summer and early fall of 1933 Lt. Yasuhide Kurihara, an ardent follower of Nishida, began organizing fellow officers, cadets, and civilians for another coup d'état attempt. Some accounts place Muranaka among the initial plotters. Concluding that the coup of March 1932 failed because of poor execution, Kurihara trained his followers in the tactics of insurrection, including mock assaults on the residence of the emperor's trusted adviser, Count Makino. Nishida, however, convinced Kurihara that the timing was not right for a coup attempt, and Kurihara canceled his plans. But a group of Kurihara's civil followers plunged ahead. Calling themselves the Volunteer Squad of Saitama Young Men for the Rescue of the Country (a name that sounds more impressive in Japanese than English), they planned to assassinate the head of the Seiyukai political party and other leading politicians. Police uncovered the plot the day before the planned attack in November and arrested the conspirators.

A few months earlier civilians calling themselves the Shimpeitai (Sacred Soldiers) planned to rescue Nissho Inoue from jail and overthrow the government by assassinating the cabinet. The plot involved no military personnel, excepting Inoue's brother, who was a navy pilot, but among the ninety-plus conspirators was Roshi Omori, the founder of Jikishin Dojo.

Later in his life Omori, using the first name Sogen, would become a Buddhist priest and be called "the greatest Zen master of modern times," but in the 1920s and '30s he was an ardent supporter of the Restoration. Born in 1904, Omori took up kendo at the age of fourteen, progressed rapidly, and trained under some of Japan's master swordsmen. At nineteen he began to study Zen to improve his swordsmanship. About the same time Omori met and became friendly with Mitsuru Toyama, the unofficial leader of Japan's ultranationalist movement and recognized head of the Japanese mob, and his son Ryusuke Toyama. Impressed with the men and their convictions, the twenty-three-year-old Omori joined the Imperial Flag Society, an organization founded to create an emperor-centered society. Five years later, in 1932, Omori founded the League for Loyalty to the Emperor and the Restoration, which, as its name implies, advocated for the Showa Restoration.

In 1933 Omori had his first Zen "enlightenment experience" while urinating. "I heard the sound of the urine hitting the back of the urinal. It splashed and sounded very loud to me. At that time I thought 'Aha!' and I understood. I had a deep realization."[10] Believing himself enlightened, Omori joined the Shimpeitai and plotted to bring about the Showa Restoration by assassinating the entire Japanese cabinet, the presidents of the two largest political parties, the head of the Tokyo Metropolitan Police, and various other political and economic leaders. Police foiled the coup hours before its start and arrested ninety-five participants. Omori, however, had decided not to participate at the last moment and, having fled to Nagoya, escaped arrest.

On January 1, 1934, Omori founded the Jikishin Dojo to instruct like-minded patriots in the arts of sword fighting, judo, calligraphy, and Zen. With Mitsuru Toyama's blessing, Ryusuke Toyama became the dojo's adviser. Its founding statement read:

Based on our respect for the Founder of the Empire [Emperor Jimmu], we reverently seek to promote the prosperity of our glorious Imperial Throne by respectfully revealing the fundaments of statesmanship and investigating through our own persons the essentials of governance. The spread of the emperor's work is the national policy of Japan while the mission of the people is to assist in this endeavor. It is for this reason that we have taken it upon ourselves, first of all, to aid each other in cultivating divine justice. Therefore, we have established the Jikishin Dojo in order to resolutely promote the true practice of the way of the warrior.

We pray that by hiding nothing, we will encounter excellence; by exerting ourselves to the utmost, we will foster our

talents; and by pointing directly at the source of the mind received from our ancestors, we will encounter our divine, im-
mortal native spirit. Furthermore, we have made the reverent
accomplishment of the [Showa] Restoration a pledge of steel in
which mundane, personal interests have no place.[11]

The dojo stood in a quiet neighborhood, surrounded by three
Buddhist temples and a Shinto shrine. More important, as it was not
far from the military academy, the new dojo attracted Mitsugi Nishida's followers, including Koji Muranaka. After becoming disillusioned
with the more senior members of the Cherry Society, Nishida's young
disciples had coalesced into a group known as the Young Officers.

The dojo's thirty live-in students awoke at six, cleaned the prem-
ises, and meditated for forty-five minutes before starting their
morning Shinto prayers before the tablet of the Sun Goddess. Each
afternoon they practiced kendo and judo at four o'clock and afterward on Mondays, Wednesdays, and Fridays read and discussed
patriotic literature. Each month at dawn, they went as a group to
worship at the Meiji Shrine.[12]

Muranaka looked around the room at his comrades. The men had
come for their monthly five-day period of intensive *sesshin* (Zen med-
itation). The sessions started at four in the morning and lasted until
ten at night. Their purpose was "the realization of our great pledge
[to achieve the Showa Restoration] by acquiring an indestructible
and adamantine body of indomitable resolve through introspec-
tion and Zen practice."[13] Alongside the regular students sat Mitsugi
Nishida and the core of his followers, including Lt. Asaichi Isobe,
with his flat face and round Coke-bottle glasses—a face that only a
mother could love.

Isobe had been in the class behind Muranaka at the military academy. After a brief stint as a lieutenant with the Eightieth Infantry,
he enrolled in the Army Finance School in 1932 and now served in
the First Artillery Division. He was fanatically committed to the restoration, believing he was divinely inspired to save Japan. Historian
Herbert Bix, in his Pulitzer Prize–winning biography, *Hirohito and the
Making of Modern Japan*, would call Isobe "the most deranged of the

ringleaders" for the Showa Restoration.[14] Two years later, as Isobe sat in prison, he would write:

> The Japan of today is not for us. This rotting nation that is without virtue or faith will receive retribution from our True Nation of Divine Japan. . . . The only path for Japan is the reform movement. . . . Killing traitors is not a crime, but the duty of the patriot. . . . Punish all the criminals in Japan and burn them away. Do not quit until there are no criminals . . . even if you have to turn all of Japan into a sea of flames. Burn! Burn! Become a soul of fire and burn everything. . . . I will go not to heaven, but definitely to hell. This gives me great joy. I am confident I can be a great demon, a great demon of hell. I must start building my character now, so that I may be a cruel and ruthless demon. I shall be a demon without a single drop of tears or blood. . . . My soul will not submit; forever resisting and battling; never retreating even an inch, even if suppressed by the power of country and the force of the military, one indomitable soul will scream for justice, ceaselessly persecuting evil.[15]

After the failed plots and coups of the past few years, Nishida counseled patience. The time is not yet ripe, he would tell his followers. We must first prepare the populace. To that end the Jikishin Dojo published its first issue of a magazine titled *Kakushin* (Essence) on September 18, 1934. The lead article, "Destroy the False and Establish the True—Risk Your Life in Spreading the Dharma—the Great Essence of the Showa Restoration," was a call for patriots to unify, take up arms, and create a new society.

> The Restoration is a holy war to destroy the false and establish the true. . . . [W]e must support and promote the Imperial Army and Navy as the main force backing the Restoration while reverently seeking the promulgation of an Imperial Order that will promptly disperse the black clouds engulfing us. This is the proper duty of all citizens, who cooperate with, and support, imperial policy. Duty is heavier than mountains while death is lighter than feathers. Given this, how is it possible that the

epoch-making, great undertaking [of the Showa Restoration] can be accomplished without the valiant, dedicated spread of the Dharma at the risk of your life?[16]

Two days after its publication, police impounded all copies of *Kakushin*. Just writing about the restoration was fruitless, thought Muranaka. It was time for action.

9

The *Empress of Japan* left port just in time. The downpour that had ruined the game on October 19 intensified into a gale. It came from the southwest, battering Seattle, Portland, and Vancouver with driving rain and winds up to eighty-three miles per hour. A cyclone smashed into downtown Vancouver, tearing signs, streetlights, and awnings from their ties, hurling them through plate-glass windows. In Washington State, the storm killed twenty-one and injured more than one hundred. Although the *Empress of Japan* had escaped, the transpacific ocean liner SS *President Madison* was less fortunate. Docked at Pier 41 in Seattle, the winds severed the ship's moorings before driving the 535-foot liner into the sternwheeler *Harvester*. The collision failed to slow the 14,124-ton *President Madison*, which next slammed into the freighter *North Haven* and several smaller vessels as the *Harvester* sank.[1]

Out at sea huge waves pounded the *Empress*, rocking it wildly. At 26,033 tons, the massive ocean liner was in little danger, but many passengers felt that death was imminent. The roars of the wind woke Stuart Bell in his deck cabin at five thirty in the morning. The sports editor of the *Cleveland Press* opened his porthole and stuck out his head to investigate. Squinting through rain and spray, Bell watched seamen rush to secure the lifeboats as waves crashed over the side of the seven-deck ship. The *Empress* rolled to port, sending Bell's trunk scurrying across the small cabin. The writer closed the porthole and captured the sliding trunk. As he bent to close the top, his typewriter plummeted off the table, just missing his head. With both sleep and the ability to write nearly impossible, Bell dressed and stumbled through the pitching corridors to the opulent first-class dining room for an early breakfast. The cavernous room stretched the entire 83-foot width of the ship and was 120 feet long. More than fifty-five tables, covered in the finest linen, spread across the wood and marble floor. Ornate brass work decorated the paneled walls and ceiling and framed the orchestra balcony over the buffet.[2] According to a 1936 travel guide, a typical Canadian Pacific first-class breakfast began with exotic fruits—Hawaiian pineapple, persimmon, pomegranate, pomelo, and mango—and continued with "more cereal and egg variations than you knew had ever been invented, then a symphony of pig, until at last you arrive at waffles and maple syrup."[3]

Bell dined alone. The waiter commented that they expected few diners due to the rough seas. Then the Babe entered, hungry as usual. Unaffected by the violent lurching, Ruth ordered his usual breakfast of two steaks. Soon Moe Berg arrived, movie camera in hand. After breakfast he would visit the bridge to film the *Empress* from above as its bow plowed through dark, mountainous waves, sending "giant clouds of spray over the bridge."[4]

The Gehrigs entered next. Lou and Eleanor had been married the previous September and were using the tour to Asia and a subsequent trip around the world as their belated honeymoon. The couple ignored Ruth and sat by themselves. Although the two sluggers had been friendly for years, they had a falling out in 1933 and no longer spoke. The feud began when Ruth's natural daughter, Dorothy, visited Lou's parents wearing hand-me-downs. Christina Gehrig, Lou's controlling mother who adored Dorothy, questioned why Claire's stepdaughter was always dressed so shabbily when her natural daughter, Julia, sported the latest fashions. Claire heard about the comment and overreacted. Furious at the slight, she forbade Dorothy from visiting the Gehrigs and vented about the Gehrigs to the Babe. The following day Ruth spoke to Gehrig in the locker room, and the conversation became heated. By game time both had vowed not to speak to each other again.[5]

After breakfast Bell bumped into a ghostly pale Clint Brown and a staggering Earl Averill. Brown meekly suggested getting a sandwich, but Averill's less than enthusiastic reply ended the issue and the two Cleveland Indians wandered off. Most of the party was nowhere to be seen—languishing in bed clutching their stomachs with seasickness when they were not sprinting to the bathrooms to throw up. Besides Bell the All American party contained forty people— fifteen team members; thirteen players' wives; Julia Ruth; umpire John Quinn; Philadelphia Athletics trainer Edward "Doc" Ebling; J. A. Hillerich, manufacturer of the famed Louisville Slugger, and his wife; the Athletics' business manager, Robert Schroeder, and his wife; Elfreda Macfarland and Mary A. Reach, daughters of Athletics co-owner Ben Shibe; Connie Mack's good friend Walter M. Warren; Sotaro Suzuki; and Mack himself.

The storm cleared the next morning, and work began. Connie Mack, Ruth, and O'Doul met in Mack's estate room to discuss the team and plan practices. Fitting his personality, Mack had rented a modest room, quite unlike Ruth's opulent three-room suite that cost three thousand dollars for the twelve-day journey. The venerable manager was only a figurehead on this trip—an envoy of Major League Baseball commissioner Landis. Ruth would manage the team. The Babe would finally get to prove that he could lead.

Earlier that year Mack had hinted that he might retire. He had been in professional baseball for forty-five years, first as a catcher for Washington, Pittsburgh, and Buffalo from 1886 to 1893; then as a player-manager for the Pirates from 1894 to 1896; and finally as a skipper, general manager, and part-owner of Philadelphia since 1901. He now dabbled with the idea of abandoning the dugout for the front office. Hiring Ruth as his replacement intrigued Mack. After winning the World Series in 1929 and '30 and an American League pennant in '31, the Athletics, strapped for cash, had sold their star catcher, Mickey Cochrane, to Detroit in October 1933 and plummeted to fifth place in '34. Attendance, already suffering during the Depression, fell. Only 305,847 fans attended Athletics home games in '34, down from 627,464 in 1931. Ruth's Yankees, on the other hand, drew 854,682 during the past season. If the Bambino took the Athletics' helm, his personality would bring fans back to the ballpark, Mack believed. For the next six weeks Ruth would be on an extended job interview. Unbeknownst to the Babe, Mack would scrutinize his behavior and on-the-field tactics to assess his ability to take over the Athletics.

While the squad steamed to Japan, reporters on the East Coast learned of Mack's intentions. On October 26 the *New York Times* reported that "Mack invited Ruth to make the trip with him for the purpose of training him in the Mackian system of handling baseball teams and that when they return the announcement will be made of the retirement of Mack and the engagement of Ruth." Yankee owner Col. Jacob Ruppert commented that he would allow Ruth to leave New York, providing that the Babe was offered a Major League managerial position. General manager Ed Barrow, however, added that "he did not believe that [the rumor] had any foundation in fact."[6] To many, Barrow's denial verified the story.

As Mack, Ruth, and O'Doul worked, the other travelers enjoyed the ship's amenities in the pleasant weather and now calm waters. Besides the elegant first-class dining room, the *Empress* sported a first-class cocktail lounge, dining rooms and lounges for the other classes of travelers, below-deck and on-deck swimming pools, a movie theater, a gymnasium, a beauty parlor, electric and Turkish baths, a tanning salon, and a variety of shops. The ship could carry 1,159 passengers (399 in first class) and needed 579 crew members to sail and attend to the passengers' whims.

Most of the players congregated on the first-class promenade to lounge, stroll, or play deck games. Earl Averill tried shuffleboard for the first time and became addicted. Soon he was organizing his teammates for the ship's shuffleboard tournaments. Teaming with Clint Brown, the rookie shuffleboarders took on all challengers, including a formidable team of the Babe and Sotaro Suzuki. Lefty Gomez preferred Ping-Pong. Holding the paddle by the blade instead of the handle, he battled birthday boy Jimmie Foxx. As the ballplayers pounded the plastic ball back and forth, a young girl watched, probably lacking the courage to ask for a game. Ruth strode on deck and, understanding the girl's longing eyes, challenged her to a game. Stuart Bell likened the opponents to an elephant and a lamb, but noticed that Ruth always returned the ball within the girl's reach, probably with a twinkle in his eye.[7]

Moe Berg spent most days in a lounge chair with language books and note cards, working on his Japanese. Despite claims that he spoke the language fluently, he had just a rudimentary understanding. At the beginning of the voyage Ruth had asked him if he spoke the language, and Berg, straight-faced, answered, "No, I never had occasion to learn it." Later, when Berg greeted somebody in Japanese, Ruth looked up in surprise. "Wait a minute, you told me that you didn't speak Japanese!" "That was two weeks ago," Berg replied.[8]

The second day at sea ended with the team, dressed in formal attire, meeting in the dining hall to celebrate Foxx's twenty-seventh birthday. Berg surprised the company by having a large birthday cake baked for the occasion and then danced the night away with Julia Ruth and Peggy Bolton, the niece of the Canadian ambassador to Japan.

The next morning, manager Ruth called the squad together for their first floating practice. The team met on the top deck, known as the sports deck, for light exercise and catching. Nets surrounded the area to contain errant throws, but there was no room for batting practice. The players dressed casually in polo shirts and flannel trousers. Ruth alone wore shorts—his spindly, long white legs sticking out from under his massive round trunk.

The Babe supervised, a large cigar between his teeth, as Lefty Gomez pitched to Moe Berg and Clint Brown threw to Lefty O'Doul. The sound of Gomez's pitches smacking into Berg's mitt soon drew Ruth's and Mack's attention. They watched in amazement as his fastballs blazed along the deck and his curves bit sharply. Gomez was among the top pitchers in the league, but this display was superhuman. Neither Ruth nor Mack had seen him pitch like this before. Slowly, it dawned on them. The jokester had set up with his back to the ship's bow. The stiff ocean breeze and the rush of the ship traveling at twenty-two knots propelled the ball down the deck toward Berg, enhancing the speed of each pitch.[9]

Ruth's protruding belly, so visible above his shorts, worried Sotaro Suzuki. The Babe had arrived in Vancouver in terrible shape, no longer resembling a professional athlete. The Japanese were expecting a baseball god. Would his physical appearance disappoint the fans? Would he be able to perform as expected? What if, after finally procuring the great Bambino and staking *Yomiuri*'s reputation and financial security on him, the Babe could no longer play and became a laughingstock? Somehow, Ruth recognized Suzuki's concerns. The Bambino explained that he understood the importance of the trip and would not let down the Japanese fans. As the other players lounged on deck, Ruth spent hours in the ship's gymnasium working out with the latest exercise equipment—electric horses, stationary bicycles, weights, and rowing machines. Slowly, Ruth began to firm up, and Suzuki's anxiety decreased.[10]

The Babe woke Julia at dawn on Wednesday, October 24, and the two hurried on deck. Stuart Bell and Connie Mack were already leaning over the railings pointing toward the water, occasionally crying out in delight. The Ruths hurried over. Julia followed their gaze but saw nothing save the gently rolling ocean. "You'll see them soon," the Babe probably explained. But nothing happened. Minutes past and Julia became suspicious. Finally, she decided that she had been tricked. They could not be real. Fish do not fly. And then, without warning, they came—leaping out of the water, skimming a foot above the ocean for fifty feet with small, thin wings before diving back into the depths. Eventually, most of the passengers lined the railings to watch the fish perform their acrobatics.[11]

Later, the passengers reassembled on the sports deck to watch the ballplayers practice. Jimmie Foxx grabbed a catcher's mitt to warm up Earl Whitehill. Although Foxx had caught thirty-seven Major League games from 1925 to '28, he spent most of his career at first or third base. After trading Cochrane the year before, Mack needed a hard-hitting catcher. Mack reasoned that Foxx's vast baseball knowledge would be an asset behind the plate and that having Foxx's bat in a spot often filled by weak hitters would help the Athletics score more runs. With Ruth's consent Mack planned to test Foxx at catcher against the Japanese.

Just before eight on the morning of October 25, the *Empress of Japan* steamed past Diamond Head, the extinct volcano that dominates Honolulu. One hundred and fifty thousand years ago Diamond Head's last eruption ripped off the top of the cone, leaving the rugged, nearly symmetrical base that still rises 760 feet above sea level. Although it was Hawaii's most famous landmark, few knew that the majestic Diamond Head contained a series of secret tunnels, radio rooms, and batteries of guns capable of hurling twelve-inch shells miles offshore. "Well, boys, there she is," exclaimed Ruth to the group of ballplayers and wives crowded on deck.[12]

A motorboat began to circle the white ocean liner, the driver waving to the crowd. Ruth, who seemed to know everybody, everywhere, yelled, "Hey Frank!" as he recognized golfer Francis Brown. The two had become good buddies during the Babe's trip to Hawaii the previous winter—the excursion that had cost him the managerial job with Detroit.

When the *Empress* weighed anchor at the quarantine station at Honolulu Harbor, small boats crowded with young Hawaiian boys surrounded it. The boys pleaded to the passengers to toss coins from the deck, 100 feet above the blue water. As the coins sank into the harbor, the boys dove to retrieve them before they sank to the sandy bottom. Meanwhile, a boat packed with the official welcoming committee and reporters came aside, unloading its enthusiastic cargo. The travelers were first welcomed in the traditional Hawaiian fashion as young women placed a lei around each neck. They then posed for numerous photographs before reporters cornered Mack, Ruth, and a few others for precious quotes to fill Honolulu's many newspapers.

About a half hour later the *Empress* docked. The ship had arrived late due to the violent storm off the northwest coast, so the official welcoming ceremony had been canceled to give the tourists more time to see the island. After a group visit to Nu'uanu Pali to see the breathtaking vistas of Oahu from 1,186 feet above the ocean, they had a few hours to sightsee and lunch before meeting at the ballpark at two o'clock. Batting practice would begin at two thirty and a game against the local all-stars at three thirty. As they drove through Honolulu's bucolic surroundings, Stuart Bell noted the fortifications "with guns concealed even from the natives" strategically hidden throughout the landscape.[13]

Most of the players and their wives spent the morning at Waikiki Beach. The spot looked nothing like it does now. Although hotels already lined the beach, with the exception of the lavish Royal Hawaiian and Moana hotels, most were modest two-story structures, not the gleaming high-rises of today. The beach itself was narrower. It would be expanded to its present width as tourism became more important to the economy after World War II. Trees covered Waikiki in the 1930s. Palm, coconut, and monkey trees lined the streets and filled the yards of the area's many bungalows. The biggest difference would have been the lack of crowds. Prior to the advent of commercial flights to Honolulu, only the very rich chose the isolated islands as a vacation spot. The players' time at the world's most famous beach was short, however, as the All Americans had to hurry off to Honolulu Stadium.

When people think of Hawaiian sports, few think of baseball. But Hawaii has a long baseball history, and prior to World War II the national pastime was the territory's great pastime. In 1845 Alexander Cartwright helped codify the rules for baseball and organize the Knickerbocker Baseball Club of New York. The following year the Knickerbockers faced the Nine York Nine on the Elysian Fields of Hoboken, New Jersey, in the first recognized true game of baseball. Cartwright worked as a clerk and bookseller before he heard that gold had been discovered in California. In March 1849 he loaded a covered wagon with provisions, prospecting supplies, and his baseball equipment and joined the California gold rush, leaving his wife and two young sons behind. Within a few months of arriving in California, Cartwright determined that he had made a mistake and decided to return to New York in 1849 by ship. Before the Panama Canal opened in 1914, just two routes linked California to the East Coast. One could sail east around the treacherous Cape Horn at the tip of South America, or one could take the longer but safer route west across the Pacific to China and hence around the southern tip of Africa to the Atlantic. Cartwright opted for the western route and set sail on the *Pacific* for China. When the ship stopped at Honolulu, the New Yorker decided to visit the island paradise.[14]

Arriving in Honolulu in August 1849, Cartwright must have been shocked to see his beloved game flourishing. Many histories credit Cartwright with introducing baseball to Hawaii, but a form of town ball had come over with New England missionaries and merchants perhaps as early as the 1820s. Native Hawaiians embraced the sport, renamed it *kinipopo*, and played it with fervor. When missionaries created the Punahou School (Barack Obama's alma mater) in 1841, baseball became a favorite pastime of many students—partly because the school's first principal, Daniel Dole, was an avid player.

Meeting a business acquaintance from his New York days, Cartwright decided to remain in Hawaii. A year later King Kamehameha III appointed the "father of baseball" the chief engineer of the Honolulu Fire Department. Cartwright's family joined him in 1851, and he remained in the islands as a prosperous merchant and community leader until his death in 1892. During his forty years in Hawaii, Cartwright was only tangentially involved in baseball. His obituary in the *Hawaiian Gazette and Pacific Commercial Advertiser* does not mention the sport at all. Nonetheless, oral tradition states that Cartwright created a field, laid out by the Knickerbocker rules, at Makiki Recreation Park (now Cartwright Field) in 1852. Two of Cartwright's sons became strong players, playing at Punahou during the 1860s and later for various clubs.

Punahou graduates, joined by other American settlers, created Hawaii's first league in 1866. The first teams consisted almost exclusively of whites, or *haoles* in the local lingo, but as the ethnic makeup of Hawaii changed in the late nineteenth century, so did the ethnicity of its ballplayers. Early European and American settlers realized the potential for large-scale sugar cultivation on the islands. At first plantations used native Hawaiian labor, but disease soon decimated the population, reducing the estimated precontact population of 300,000 to just 22,000 by 1920. Seeking laborers, plantation owners brought in waves of immigrants from countries across Asia, the Caribbean, and Portugal. In 1920 Hawaii contained 109,274 Japanese (including Jimmy Horio), 27,002 Portuguese, 23,507 Chinese, 21,031 Filipinos, 5,602 Puerto Ricans, and 4,950 Koreans as well as a smattering of people from nearly every region of the world.[15]

The immigrants learned baseball and in the 1890s organized their own teams. By the early twentieth century Hawaii had several thriving interethnic leagues. The top teams had names like the All Chinese, All Hawaiians, and Asahi. Other teams were multiracial, grabbing the best available players. Some teams toured the mainland. The Chinese Athletic Club, for example, barnstormed across California in 1912, defeating collegiate, semipro, and even some professional teams. A second Chinese team traveled the mainland in 1914, defeating the University of California twice. The *Sporting News* noted in 1914, "The islands are a hot-bed of enthusiasm over the game. Nothing else is talked of. Amateur and league teams play ball on every plot of ground large enough to permit of a field being laid out."[16]

In 1925 the top ethnic teams on the island of Oahu formed the Hawaii Baseball League. Each of its six original teams identified itself with an ethnic group—the Japanese Asahis, the Portuguese Braves, the Chinese Tigers, the Hawaiians, the Filipinos, and the Wanderers (the *haole* team). Despite Hawaii's diverse nature, the vibrant ethnic communities segregated themselves, and fans packed Honolulu Stadium to watch "their boys" challenge ethnic rivals. The Hawaii Baseball League soon became the island's top sports attraction.

Honolulu was the usual stop for the ships traveling between the West Coast and Japan. This allowed Hawaii's top players to test their skills against American collegiate and professional teams en route to Asia and Japanese and Filipino teams heading to California. Between 1905 and 1934 dozens of visiting ball clubs passed through, allowing locals to face Rap Dixon, Al Simmons, and Mickey Cochrane, among many others. As the All Americans sailed from Vancouver, a team of Hawaii Baseball League all-stars prepared to challenge the Major Leaguers.

The Hawaiian All Stars were probably the most diverse squad any of the visitors would ever face. During their Minor and Major League careers, the All American players rarely face nonwhite opponents—an unwritten rule barring African Americans from organized baseball had been in place since the 1880s. The rule, however, did not explicitly exclude Asians, and a handful of Asian Americans had played in the Minors. One Asian American had even reached "the Show." John Williams, the son of an English father and native Hawaiian mother, played briefly for the Detroit Tigers in 1914. During the off-seasons many Major Leaguers barnstormed across the United States, playing amateur and semipro squads as well as professional Negro League teams. The All Americans would, of course, play against Japanese, Chinese, and Filipino teams in the coming weeks, but with various forms of segregation the norm at this time, few of these opponents would look like the Hawaiian All Stars. Johnny Kerr of mixed native Hawaiian and Chinese ancestry, coached and pitched for the All Stars. Behind him in the field stood four Chinese, a Japanese, two Portuguese, and a Hawaiian. The bench included a similar mixture of Chinese, Japanese, Portuguese, Hawaiian, and Caucasians, as well as Ted Shaw, a former Negro Leaguer who had pitched for the 1927 National Negro League champion Chicago American Giants.[17]

By two thirty enthusiastic fans filled Honolulu Stadium to capacity. The Hawaiian newspapers had been promoting the game since the All Americans had left Vancouver five days earlier. Tickets had been on sale all week at E. O. Hall & Sons store in Honolulu—$1.50 per box seat, a buck for reserved seats, and $0.50 for general admission.[18]

The stadium was a magnificent venue for a ball game. Located at the corner of King and Isenberg streets, it stood just outside the bustle of downtown Honolulu. Diamond Head rose majestically above the center-field wall. Beyond the left-field wall stood Dreier Manor, a tiered white Victorian mansion complete with finials and cupola that resembled a wedding cake. The stadium had been configured for the fall football season, so workers had spent the past week removing the temporary football stands and goalposts and re-creating the diamond. The gridiron ran from the first-base foul line to left field, so permanent large grandstands, designed to seat the fourteen thousand football fans who packed the stadium each weekend, stood along the third-base foul line and just behind the right-field wall.[19]

The players took the field at two thirty to warm up, and nine thousand fans settled in, in anticipation of the All Americans' batting practice. The Hawaii Baseball League had a handful of power hitters—Johnny Kerr had belted a 451-foot home run against the Negro League Philadelphia Royal Giants in 1932 and was also the first player to hit one out of Honolulu Stadium—but few Hawaiians could compare to the visitors' lineup of Ruth, Gehrig, Fox, Averill, and Gehringer. The fans had come to watch the ball soar over the stadium's walls.

The All Americans did not disappoint. The bleachers in right field were a tempting target, and the big leaguers seemed to be aiming for them. The Bambino sent two into the right-field stand, while his rival Gehrig smashed a mammoth drive off the ceiling of the press box located at the uppermost reaches—475 feet from home plate and 50 feet above the playing field. Earl Averill, with his unusual lowball swing that resembled a golfer driving, clouted the ball into the upper portion of the stand. Even second baseman Charlie Gehringer, who had only moderate power for a Major Leaguer, joined in on the fun with a homer of his own. Among the stars only Jimmie Foxx—looking tired and wan—failed to hit a blast. At the end of the show the fans felt sure that mighty feats awaited them in the game to come.

At first they were disappointed. Johnny Kerr was determined that the Hawaiian All Stars would not be embarrassed. He had chosen his squad several weeks earlier, and they had been practicing daily. Fans congregated at Fort Armstrong Diamond to watch the local heroes practice, and a knowledgeable sportswriter concluded that the team was in top condition and "capable of playing a brand of the ball which ranks with that of the Pacific Coast [League]."[20]

The game began as a pitchers' duel. Kerr overpowered the rusty Major Leaguers, allowing just a single and striking out three in the first four innings. Racked with nervousness, however, Kerr was wild. He walked three, threw a wild pitch, and plunked Gehrig. The harder he tried to get the ball over the plate, the more unnatural it felt and the wilder he became. But somehow Kerr escaped each inning without giving up a run.[21]

Lefty Gomez, starting for the All Americans, dazzled the Hawaiians with sharp curves and fastballs that "virtually shaved the whiskers off our local boys."[22] He faced the minimum twelve batters in his four innings, striking out seven. By the end of four scoreless innings, Ruth had become grumpy, loudly cursing the long voyage and his players' anemic hitting.

The All Americans broke through the next inning, driven not by Ruth's pep talk but by a complete breakdown of the Hawaiians' confidence. One can imagine the giddy feeling of matching the great All Americans for four innings—that strange combination of relief and intense pressure to not make a mistake. A Gehringer single, two walks, and two errors led to three unearned runs and broke the Hawaiians' morale. With their confidence gone, the outcome was decided. The All Americans tacked on five more runs in the next few innings, as the Hawaiians committed three more errors and another wild pitch.

The fans coming to watch the Major Leaguers hit home runs had to wait until the seventh inning, when Lou Gehrig settled into the box against Ted Nobriga, a half-Portuguese and half–native Hawaiian, who had pitched in the St. Louis Cardinals organization. Nobriga threw his best, but the Iron Horse turned on it, driving the ball toward the top of the football stand in right field. At the last moment the ball sliced foul. Probably a little shaken, Nobriga tried again. Like an instant replay, Gehrig brought his hips around, hitting the ball squarely with a loud crack. Once again the ball flew in a majestic arc toward the top of the football stand—this time landing fifteen feet to the left for home run.

By the eighth inning the Babe was in a much better mood. He joked with fans and came onto the field wearing galoshes. Thus clad, with two outs in the ninth, the Bambino drilled a Ted Shaw pitch off the wall in right-center and slowly jogged to second as "souvenir hunters fought police and fielders for possession of the ball."[23] Immediately after the final out, the players hustled back to the ship. The game had taken an hour and forty minutes. To make up for the time lost during the storm, the *Empress of Japan* would embark at six o'clock, and it was now ten minutes past five. Suzuki had explained to Capt. Lionel Douglas the importance of arriving at Yokohama on schedule. The players needed to be in Tokyo for the welcoming ceremony on November 2 and to pay their respects at the Meiji Shrine the following morning. Douglas assured Suzuki that he would do his best.

Most of the squad boarded the ship in good humor. They had fun, faced live pitching for the first time since the soggy day in Vancouver, got some of the rust out, and, most important, returned with $2,019.54 as their share of the gate receipts.[24] Jimmie Foxx, however, must have been concerned. He went 0 for 4 and had not even made contact with the ball. Reporters noted that he looked tentative at the plate. After a serious beaning, many players return with a justified fear of the ball. Most overcome this fear, but others never reestablish their confidence and soon leave the game. Foxx told Mack and the reporters that he felt fine, but he obviously was not. It would be nearly seven more days before the *Empress* would arrive in Japan. With his career in jeopardy, would he be able to relax and recuperate? Or would the worrying combined with inaction only exacerbate his uneasiness at the plate?

On the dock, before boarding the *Empress*, reporters cornered

Mack. They warmed up by asking the manager's opinion of local favorite Johnny Kerr. Mack had watched the game from the stands, leaving Ruth in control of the dugout. When the manager was not signing autographs—according to the *Hawaii Hochi,* he signed more than a thousand balls, "refused no one [and] talked to every man . . . with a smile and a cheery greeting for every well-wisher"—he focused on Kerr. "He's a good ballplayer," Mack responded. "He's a better ballplayer than he is a pitcher. He can develop into a great infielder or an outfielder. And I like his spirit."[25] Kerr's outing nearly changed his life. Two years later Lefty O'Doul, whom Kerr had retired to end the disastrous fifth inning, invited the Hawaiian to the San Francisco Seals' spring training camp. Kerr pitched well at first and was called the best Seals pitching prospect in years but in the end failed to make the roster.[26]

After discussing Kerr, reporters got down to business. They confronted Mack with the rumor that he planned to retire and name Ruth his successor. Mack emphatically denied the rumor. "The only time that I'll quit is when they cart me off the diamond. Seriously, I hope to be still manager of the Athletics for ten more years." He did, however, admit that he was assessing Ruth's ability to manage and had been asked to make a report when he returned from Japan. Mack did not reveal who had requested the report.[27]

The following day as the *Empress of Japan* steamed across the Pacific, Bell spoke with Mack about Ruth's prospects as a manager. "He would make a fine manager. Ruth is very capable, he is smart and he has a fine way with young players. I hope he gets placed somewhere. Even on this trip he has shown a high sense of direction and an aggressive spirit that stamps him as a leader." But Mack reiterated that the Babe would not be managing the Athletics.[28]

Had Mack already determined that Ruth was unsuitable to take the Athletics' helm? Or were the denials mere subterfuge? The explanation that he was assessing Ruth for another party was probably false or at least deceptive, as Mack had to report to Landis on all aspects of the tour. A few years later Mack would tell Joe Williams, the sports editor of Scripps-Howard newspapers, that he had indeed considered turning the Athletics over to Ruth but that he rejected the idea once he saw how Claire made every decision for the Babe. "If

I gave the job to him, she would be managing the team in a month," Mack told Williams.[29]

Ruth, or more likely the astute Claire, must have heard the rumors about the possible job with the Athletics. Yet the Babe seemed genuinely unconcerned about his future. "Aw, let's forget next year," he told Bell when asked about his prospects. "I'm out for a good time. I'm going to shoot grouse in Scotland and shoot the shoots in Switzerland. Of course, I want to stay in baseball and want to manage a team, but I am not going to let the future interfere with the first real vacation I have ever had."[30] The words were pure Ruth—why worry about the future when you could have fun? The attitude had cost him the Tigers' helm the previous year and helped him lose the job with Mack.

Sometime during the trip to Japan, probably after the ship left Honolulu, an incident occurred that would ensure that Ruth would not manage the Athletics and erased any chance he might have had with the Yankees. Rumors of the event reached the clubhouses and sportswriters over the following season, but the only person to record it was the primary participant, Eleanor Gehrig, who wrote about it a half century later in her autobiographical *My Luke and I*.[31] We must, therefore, take her narrative skeptically—she had a strong motive for downplaying the incident as just a misunderstanding.

After spending most of the trip cocooned with her husband, Eleanor decided to take a walk alone on deck. She passed Claire Ruth, lounging on a deck chair, and although the families still feuded, the women casually said hello. The pleasant exchange must have started Claire thinking about the silly rift, for when Eleanor strolled by again, Claire invited her to the Ruth suite to talk about the situation. Opening the cabin door they found the Babe "sitting like a Buddha figure, cross-legged and surrounded by an empire of caviar and champagne." Unlike her husband, Lou, who grew up in a frugal, working-class German household, Eleanor had been wealthy for a short period before the Depression. Her father had made a fortune running concession stands in Chicago's parks, and Eleanor learned to enjoy the finer things in life. Enticed by the caviar and champagne, Eleanor joined the Babe in the expensive feast, staying for about two hours.

Topside, Lou Gehrig was frantic. The couple had been together constantly since they had left New York. He found her prolonged absence inexplicable and concluded that she may have fallen overboard. Gehrig organized the crew into search parties as a final measure before scouring the surrounding ocean. Eleanor's eventual appearance calmed her husband, but his joy gave way to cold anger when she revealed where she had been. The couple dressed and dined in a stony silence that Lou maintained for days.

Eleanor's version of events was that her love for caviar and champagne led her to lose track of time and that her husband overreacted. But the rumors said that the encounter in Ruth's cabin was not so innocent. Gehrig had met Eleanor at a party in Chicago, where she was a regular at the ballplayers' after-hours bashes. She had met Ruth at these parties, and in author Leigh Montville's words, the Babe "didn't suffer many platonic relationships with women."[32] The rumors stated that Claire was not in the cabin during the event but that Eleanor remained in the cabin alone with the Babe for the two hours and had been drinking heavily. Certainly, Gehrig's reaction to the incident seems extreme if Claire had been in the suite. The event sealed the players' rift. They would not speak to each other about nonbaseball matters until July 4, 1939, minutes after Gehrig delivered his famous "luckiest man" speech.

Four days after the ship left Hawaii, a wireless message reached the *Empress of Japan*. A crew member rushed it to the Bambino, for it contained a job offer. Ray L. Doan would match Ruth's 1934 salary of thirty-five thousand dollars if the Babe would play the 1935 season for the House of David—the bearded, independent barnstormers whose players were forbidden to shave or cut their hair. As a concession to the Sultan of Swat, Doan noted that "the Babe won't be required to wear whiskers." The Babe declined.[33]

As the All Americans approached Japan, headlines across the globe brought worrisome news. The American-British-Japanese naval talks had broken down. In 1922 and 1930 the Washington and London naval treaties had restricted the sizes of the great powers' navies. The three most powerful maritime powers—the United States, Britain, and Japan—had agreed to limit their fleets by following a 5:5:3

ratio. For every five tons of ships owned each by the United States and Britain, the Japanese were entitled to three. The rationale behind the proportion was that both of the Western powers needed Atlantic and Pacific fleets to protect their interests, while Japan needed only a Pacific fleet. Most Japanese found the unequal ratio insulting. Shortly after Prime Minister Osachi Hamaguchi authorized the London Naval Treaty over the Imperial Navy's protests in 1930, he was assassinated by a twenty-three-year-old ultranationalist.[34]

With the Washington treaty due to expire in 1936, the British had invited the Japanese and Americans to London to discuss the terms of renewal. The nations' representatives met for two weeks before the Japanese made their position clear. They would refuse to sign any treaty prescribing an unequal ratio. Instead the Japanese called for parity in global tonnage and a ban on constructing battleships and carriers. The proposal would help Japan overcome its lack of native steel. It would allow the Japanese to concentrate on building smaller vessels, such as submarines, cruisers, and destroyers, while avoiding the steel-intensive battleships and carriers. The United States and British rejected the proposal outright, noting that overall parity would give the Japanese a numerical advantage in the Pacific, as the western fleets would be divided between the Pacific and Atlantic. Their proposal rejected, Japan was now expected to withdraw from the Washington Naval Treaty by the end of the year. The result would be a naval arms race.

As the talks broke down, the Japanese also announced a new domestic policy. All oil companies in Japan, even foreign-owned corporations, would be required to keep a six-month supply of oil in stock—a reserve that could be seized by the military in times of crisis. Japan was preparing for war.[35]

PART 2

"Babe Ruth . . . is a great deal more effective Ambassador than I could ever be."

AMBASSADOR JOSEPH GREW, November 6, 1934

10

Joseph Grew stretched out his long legs and put the final touches on the speech he would give the following evening at Hibiya Park to welcome the All Americans to Japan. He was constantly writing and giving speeches, thirty-five in his first year alone as the U.S. ambassador to Japan. His favorite was probably for the eightieth anniversary of Commodore Matthew Perry's initial treaty with the Land of the Rising Sun—his wife, Alice, was Perry's cousin, a fact Grew enjoying telling Japanese. Tall and thin, with gray hair, a mustache, and dark, bushy eyebrows, Grew was a Boston Brahmin—Groton, class of 1898, Harvard, class of 1902. His fussy sense of etiquette made him comfortable and popular with Japan's aristocracy, but he had little understanding of most of Japan's population or of the American ballplayers arriving the next day.

Although Grew was probably pleased with the speech, it read like most of his speeches—banal and pompous. "I am a 'fan' myself, decidedly so, and you may be sure that it is to me a great privilege, and it gives me one of those good old-time thrills that I used to get in exuberant youth, to find myself on the same platform with some of the doughty warriors whose names and valiant achievements have been just as familiar as those of the old Greek heroes of whom I learned at school but who could never quite compete in my youthful estimation with our own heroes of the diamond." At least it was short and ended with an appropriate message of goodwill: "I am confident that the result of your visit here will be a further contribution to the ideal of mutual understanding, mutual respect and mutual friendship between our two countries."

Grew hoped that the baseball tour would accomplish these modest goals. In general, he found that goodwill tours and cultural exchanges did little to help international relations and at times actually hurt them. The Japanese tended to overschedule American visitors, seeing historical sites, museums, and industrial centers and filling in the remaining time with banquets, receptions, and formal speeches, all the while spouting transparent propaganda. Visitors often left exhausted and suspicious of Japanese intentions. Grew had spoken to the Japanese about tailoring the tours to the American temperament, but he found habit and custom too entrenched, and the pattern continued.[1] Japanese-American mutual understanding, respect, and friendship could use a boost at the moment.

Lying on his desk was a disturbing memo he received the day before from Kobe. A Lieutenant-Colonel Matsumoto had recently made an inflammatory speech concerning the failing naval conference at the Young Men's and Ex-Soldiers Association. The colonel argued that the terms of the naval treaty were immaterial, as Japan's smaller navy was superior in quality and spirit to the American navy, but that the treaty itself was an insult to Japan that must be avenged. It was time, the colonel implored, for young men and ex-soldiers to ready themselves for the inevitable war, "which will probably be by the end of the year, or early next year." "To establish Japan as the just ruler of the world, America must be crushed!"[2]

Since arriving in Tokyo on June 6, 1932, Grew had seen Japanese-American relations swing back and forth, as moderates or militants gained the upper hand in the Japanese government. He had arrived nine months after Japan had invaded Manchuria and faced international condemnation, three months after Japan attacked Shanghai, and just three weeks after the May 15 attempted coup. Nine months after Grew took his post, Japan withdrew from the League of Nations. Grew wrote to Secretary of State Cordell Hull, "The cabinet's decision to secede from the League of Nations [is] . . . a basic defeat for the moderate elements in Japan and [establishes] the complete supremacy of the military. . . . The Army and a large section of the public have been led by propaganda to believe that eventual war with the United States . . . is inevitable. . . . In the present temper of the country any serious incident tending to inflame public opinion might lead Japan to radical action without counting the cost."[3] Japanese-American relations were probably at their lowest point since Perry arrived in Japan sixty-six years earlier.

But on June 8, 1933, a year after arriving, Grew telegrammed the State Department to report a noticeable improvement. There was less anti-American rhetoric in the press, and moderate Japanese, who had been avoiding their American friends, began to reestablish their relationships. The new foreign minister, Koki Hirota, seemed to be "genuinely doing his best to improve Japan's relations with foreign countries . . . by keeping the military comparatively quiet and by exerting a calming influence on the press." The good feeling continued throughout the year, causing Grew to write in his diary on February 8, 1934, "The pacifist tendencies latent in Japan have in the past few months been able to make themselves felt and heard to a greater degree than at any time since September 18, 1931 [the start of the Manchurian Incident]."[4]

Unfortunately, what Grew would call "the perfectly normal swing of the pendulum as has happened throughout Japanese history" went the other way with the opening of the naval conference.[5] Conservative newspapers ran more anti-American articles, while talk of an inevitable war increased. In late July three major department stores in Kobe ran exhibitions on Japan's military strength, complete with weapons and even a fighter plane hanging from the facade of the Daimaru department store. The exhibits pointed to the United States and Russia as the two most likely enemies and contained maps and diagrams showing how the Western powers threatened Japan. On October 30, just a few days earlier, another memo from Kobe reported the sale of nationalistic kimonos for women and children throughout the city. Most of the kimonos just depicted tanks, battleships, and other weaponry, but one depicted a large Japanese flag raised over smaller American and British flags with the captions "Conquer" and "1936 *hinomaru* (the Japanese flag) outshine the world." The 1936 referred to the expected date for the future war against the Western powers.[6] A member of the Tokyo Metropolitan Police Board told Grew, "The situation in Japan is very serious. It appears quiet on the surface, but underneath there is great discontent among the people. . . . When something serious will occur it is very hard to say. It might happen at any time. The young Army officers are out of hand."[7]

11

Massive, sleek, gleaming white, the *Empress of Japan* glided into an equally immaculate Yokohama Harbor. Once a vibrant hodgepodge of East and West, Yokohama combined European-style brick structures mixed with American clapboard homes and traditional Japanese cedar shops and dwellings. Japanese clad in loincloths and cotton jackets pulled rickshaws carrying white-gloved Western belles and top-hated beaus dressed in Victorian finery. That Yokohama died on September 1, 1923. The Great Kanto Earthquake leveled the city of 434,170. Fire consumed 85 percent of the city's homes, killing 30,771. With millions of dollars of international aid, Yokohama rebuilt. Rubble from the destroyed buildings was used as fill to create the new harbor, featuring Yamashita Park with its formal gardens and tree-lined walkways.[1]

Captain Douglas slid the *Empress* into Pier 4 at eight in the morning. Running at top speed since leaving Honolulu, the ship had covered the 3,385 nautical miles in just six days, sixteen hours, and fifty-three minutes—a new world record.[2] They had made up the time lost in the storm so the players would be able to attend the celebration at Meiji Shrine after all.

Five thousand fans lined Pier 4. Many waved American or Japanese flags, a few others "Welcome to Yokohama" banners. A special train chartered by the *Yomiuri Shimbun* had brought them to the pier from Tokyo. The train now sat idle, waiting to bring the ballplayers to the capital. The All Americans, dressed in somber suits, and their wives, sporting stylish furs and feathered hats, gathered on deck for the initial welcoming ceremony. Ruth leaned over the railing, waved, and shouted, "Banzai!"

"Banzai! Banzai!" five thousand shouted back.

The health and customs inspectors boarded the *Empress*, along with a small delegation from *Yomiuri*. Three young girls led the way, followed by a contingent that included Tadao Ichioka, the *Yomiuri* sports editor and organizer of the All Nippon team, and Hidetoshi Shibata, the newspaper's chief editor. The girls presented bouquets to the female travelers as the *Yomiuri* officials gave each player a red-and-white-striped ribbon topped by a medallion of crossed American and Japanese flags under a silver baseball. "All American Baseball Player" was written in kanji down the white center stripe. Health and customs inspectors cleared the passengers for arrival, and soon those who did not hit a small ball for a living disembarked, fighting their way through the crowds of fans.

Around nine thirty, the official welcoming ceremony began. The *Yomiuri* airplane circled the ship as the governor and mayor of Yokohama strode on board to greet the players. Following the officials came a group of boys who played baseball for a school for the blind. Each boy read a line of welcoming off a Braille card. Perhaps seeing a little of himself in the disadvantaged boys, the Babe abandoned the ranks of ballplayers and hugged each child.

Next a group of young women presented each player with a customized *happi* coat—a thin cotton knee-length robe traditionally worn at festivals. The coats were blue above the thighs, white below, with each player's name embroidered down the lapels. The women helped the players into their ceremonial jackets, tying them in front with their satin belts.

Yomiuri photographers, many armed with two cameras, swarmed over the deck, snapping candids and herding the players together for group shots. The photographers focused on Ruth, shooting him "in the lounge, on the sports decks, on the promenade deck, in the salon, at the bow, at the stern, in the middle, on the rail and off the rail. He was snapped in shirt sleeves, and with his coat on, in kimono and without, with Mrs. Ruth, with Miss. Julia Ruth, with the captain, with fellow players, with policeman, soldiers, editors, mayor, stevedores and everybody who came within range."[3] Their film spent, the photographers attached the canisters to carrier pigeons and released them off the ship. The pigeons would have the film back at their Tokyo headquarters in twenty minutes—in time to carry the photos in the afternoon edition.

Throughout the photo shoots, Japanese besieged the All Americans for autographs. The Babe "autographed everything held before him, hundreds of baseballs, handkerchiefs, plain sheets of paper, menus, hats, caps, neckties, shirts, every conceivable article thrust at him in feverish excitement." He responded to all salutations with the only Japanese word he knew, "Banzai!"[4]

When the pandemonium died down, the All Americans lunched on board the *Empress* and answered the reporters' banal questions.

"How many home runs are you going to hit in Japan?" a reporter asked Ruth.

"I don't know but I am going to try to knock out as many homers as I can."

"How is your physical condition?" one asked Gehrig.

"Swell," the Iron Horse responded.

"What was the matter with the New York Yankees this year?" another tried, referring to their second-place finish.

"They just couldn't win" came Lou's terse reply.

Perhaps frustrated by the closed-mouthed Gehrig, a reporter followed the old standby that has been asked of all foreign ballplayers visiting Japan since time immemorial: "How many homers are you going to get in Japan?"

This at least gained more than a phrase from Gehrig. "I don't know but I am going to swing at everything and I am going to try. They can't condemn me for trying."[5]

At 1:18 the All Americans and their hosts from *Yomiuri* boarded the chartered train to Tokyo. As the countryside rushed by, Eleanor Gehrig stared out of the window, inhaling her first images of Japan. "[I] began to notice the population problem, every inch of ground was under cultivation right up to the tracks, and the farmers and their wives were bending knee deep in the rice paddies, with the women often carting their babies strapped papoose-style to their backs."[6]

The train arrived at Tokyo Station with its monumental three-story brick facade and twin glass domes at 2:12 p.m. The solid mass of people packing the platform began screaming, "Babe Rusu! Babe Rusu!" for that was how he was known in Japan, as the language has no *th* sound. Others shouted, "Banzai!" and waved American and Japanese flags as the train rolled to a stop. Police pushed the crowd away from the train, to no avail. The sheer numbers made it immobile. Finally, the authorities decided to clear the platform. Ten minutes later the ballplayers emerged into the empty space.

Police escorted them down the stairs to the concourse. Thousands awaited, belting out a deafening cheer that echoed off the station's masonry walls. More shouts of "Babe Rusu! Babe Rusu!" Ruth smiled and waved, relishing the attention. He reached up and turned his beige flat cap backward so that the brim would not cast a shadow on his face.

The police forced the crowd apart and led the line of Americans toward the main exit. As the Babe passed, fans jostled and pushed to keep him in view. Finally, the dam broke. "The crowd burst through in a mad wave that broke the small American contingent into helpless atoms of humanity who had to make their way to waiting autos as best they could," Stuart Bell told his readers. The Americans reformed outside Tokyo Station's west entrance and boarded open limousines for what Bell called "the wildest motor parade in history."[7]

Yomiuri representatives ushered Ruth into the backseat of the first car. He removed his cap altogether and perched on top of the backseat to make himself more visible. His close friend Lefty Gomez and Sotaro Suzuki slid in beside him. Gehrig took the front seat next to the driver. The other players filled the remaining five cars. Closed sedans, bearing the rest of the party, brought up the rear of the motorcade. A policeman accompanied each car, sometimes riding on the running board, more often forging ahead to clear the way.

The cars drove west through two blocks of Tokyo's Marunouchi financial district before reaching the outer grounds of the Imperial Palace. They paused at Nijubashi (the famed twin bridge that leads to the inner palace grounds) in a symbolic greeting to his Imperial Majesty, Emperor Hirohito. Hirohito did not come to meet the players, as later baseball writers would claim.[8] The emperor made few public appearances, and rigid etiquette governed these occasions. Ancient custom, for example, dictated that nobody could be on a higher elevation than the emperor. In the premodern world this law could easily be enforced, but in the twentieth century, where large office buildings lined Tokyo's streets, enforcement was problematic. The imperial household devised a solution. When the emperor left the palace, all window shades along his route must be drawn so that no one could look down upon him.⁹

On November 2, 1934, the emperor remained inside the formidable Imperial Palace, the 842.5-acre former castle of the Tokugawa shoguns surrounded by moats and massive stone walls. Had the players looked left, they might have glimpsed the Maya Revival facade of the Imperial Hotel—their home base during the tour. But the motorcade turned right, away from their destination, to parade through the wide streets of the Ginza shopping district.

Known as the Broadway of Japan, Ginza was the most opulent shopping district in the country and probably all of Asia. It contained the top department stores, Matsuzakaya and Matsuya, as well as specialty shops carrying the latest Western fashions and finest traditional crafts. Even the name meant money. Soon after uniting Japan, shogun Ieyasu Tokugawa established a mint, or *ginza*, in the area immediately east of his fortress in 1612. Although the mint was moved in 1801, the name for the neighborhood stuck. The streets were wide, with proportionally wide sidewalks, brightly lit with gas lamps adorned with bronze phoenixes. After dark thousands converged for the area's carnival-like atmosphere. Neon signs directed patrons to the area's numerous bars, cafés, and restaurants. Venders erected stalls or spread mats on the sidewalks to sell curios and secondhand goods. Wandering aimlessly through Ginza, just to experience the spectacle, had its own verb: *ginbura*.¹⁰

The streets of the financial district had been lined with fans, waving flags and shouting "Banzai," but they were just an opening act for the crowd in Ginza. Here hundreds of thousands packed the sidewalks, spilling into the streets, blocking traffic and trolleys. With nowhere to go, passengers disembarked, joining the throng. The crowd included businessmen, old and young, dressed in suits and fedoras; students in the military-style black uniforms and peaked hats covering their nearly shaved heads; workmen in their jackets and baggy *tobi* trousers with their thick bifurcated socks called *jika-tabi* that they wore instead of boots; soldiers in their khaki uniforms and narrow caps; street urchins in mismatching shirts and pants; young women in kimonos with their hair pulled back into tight buns; and women in Western dresses, their hair cut in a bob. They were all there, jostling, pushing, shouting, trying to get a better view of Ruth—the God of Baseball.

"Banzai! Banzai, Babe Ruth!" they screamed. Reveling in the attention, the Bambino grabbed American and Japanese flags from the crowd and waved one in each hand as he stood in the rear of the limousine. Confetti and streamers, thrown from the office buildings lining the avenue, showered the procession.

At the Kyobashi intersection the crowd surged forward, breaking police lines. Fans mobbed the cars, stopping the parade. They ran to Ruth, surrounding the limousine, climbing the bumpers, eager to touch. Nonplussed, Ruth grinned, gave another hefty "Banzai," and shook the outstretched hands—thousands of them.

Driving became impossible. Clearing the crowd became impossible. To move the parade along, police and fans began pushing the cars slowly forward. They passed Matsuya department store, then Mitsukoshi at a crawl. Ruth's voice was nearly gone. His hand ached, and sweat poured down his brow and across his back. But his grin never subsided. The final few blocks took nearly an hour, but at last they reached the entrance of the Imperial Hotel.

By four o'clock the All Americans had checked into their rooms on the third floor of the hotel's north side. Exhausted, soaked with sweat, most collapsed on the couches, sipping cold tea. The rest, however, would not last long. They needed to be at Hibiya Park for the official welcoming ceremony at five sharp.

Luckily, the trip to Hibiya Park was short—it was across the street. During the rule of the Tokugawa shoguns, both the park and the site of the Imperial Hotel were part of lands set aside for the samurai lords, known in Japanese as daimyo. Japan had been at civil war for more than 150 years before Ieyasu Tokugawa defeated his rivals at the battle of Sekigahara in 1600 and seized control of the country. Rather than banish his former enemies to remote areas, Tokugawa decided to keep them close. He set aside an area immediately outside the Edo castle walls for the daimyo's residences. Daimyo were required to spend every other year in Edo and leave their families in the capital when they returned to their home provinces. The plan had two effects. First, it kept rivals in the capital where Tokugawa could monitor them. Second, it forced the daimyo to maintain two residences. Social standing, pride, and competition between daimyo drove the samurai lords to create and maintain magnificent residences in the capital and entertain lavishly. The cost of this lifestyle left little money to fortify provincial castles or raise armies. In essence, Tokugawa subjugated his rivals with economic warfare. When the descendants of Ieyasu Tokugawa were overthrown in 1867–68, Emperor Meiji left the Imperial Palace in Kyoto and commandeered Edo castle. The residences of the daimyo were razed and the land divided to form the Marunouchi business section and public parks.

The doors of the amphitheater in Hibiya Park opened in midafternoon to avoid a dangerous rush for seats. By three thirty half of the seats were filled. An hour later more than six thousand people, mostly "roughnecks," according to Ambassador Grew, had jammed themselves into the small theater as police turned thousands away. The All Americans entered promptly at five and sat in an arc of chairs on the white stage. Their wives sat behind in a second row, followed by an army band. A large sign in kanji proclaiming "Welcoming Party for American Baseball Players Sponsored by the *Yomiuri Shimbun*," flanked by Japanese and American flags, hung from the backdrop. Red-and-white-striped bunting surrounded the stage as smaller flags fluttered in the mid-November breeze from lines running above the crowd. A single microphone stand stood at center stage.

The army band opened the ceremony—most likely with the national anthems. Next the general manager of the All Nippons and the head of *Yomiuri*'s sports department, Tadao Ichioka, approached the only microphone and welcomed the All Americans, dignitaries, and fans. Hidetoshi Shibata, *Yomiuri*'s chief editor, gave a short speech before Sotaro Suzuki introduced each player in turn. When introducing Gehrig, Suzuki's comments made the crowd laugh. Lou smiled, nodded politely, and sat down a little confused. The ever-helpful Moe Berg leaned over to explain that Suzuki had told the audience that the trip was the Gehrigs' honeymoon. Beet red, Gehrig spent the next part of the ceremony staring at his feet. Minutes later Suzuki introduced Ruth. The six thousand fans, who had previously just been enthusiastic, began thumping and screaming. Ruth smiled, waved, and sat down, but the noise continued. At length Suzuki finished the introductions, and the politicians began their speeches.

A tiny man with a neatly clipped mustache and large ears came to the mike. Foreign Minister Koki Hirota looked vaguely familiar to the ballplayers, as he had been on the cover of *Time* just a few months before. A former member of the ultranationalist secret society Genyosha, Hirota was committed to Japan's policy of expansion in China, but even so was considered too moderate by Japan's military leaders. He would nonetheless later serve as prime minister and eventually be executed as a Class A war criminal in 1948. Hirota's speech was short but to the point. The forthcoming games would bring Japanese and Americans together, and this friendship, forged on the diamond, would, he hoped, transcend the game and help solve diplomatic differences.

At ten past six the ceremony ended. Most of the Americans returned to the Imperial Hotel for a couple of hours of rest, but Suzuki whisked Mack and Ruth a few blocks west to the JOAK broadcasting bureau on Atago Hill. Even here, fans mobbed the entrance. At seven thirty Mack and Ruth addressed an estimated audience of several million listeners for about ten minutes as Suzuki translated. "Hello, my dear Japanese baseball fans, I am very happy to have a chance to be in Japan," Ruth began. He explained that the Japanese would have a chance to watch "the strongest team in the world" and ended with advice to young boys: "Whatever you want to be an expert at, you must work hard and make a great effort. *Oyasuminasai* [Good night]." Mack explained how the American League began and noted that the time was ripe for Japan to begin professional baseball. He hoped that soon the United States and Japan would compete in a true World Series.

Ruth, Mack, and Suzuki met the rest of the group at eight o'clock at Koyokan (the Maple Club), a traditional restaurant near the Japanese Diet, for a private welcoming dinner thrown by Matsutaro Shoriki. The guests removed their shoes at the entrance and donned slippers before being escorted to the dining room. Most of the Americans had never seen a restaurant like the Koyokan. The dining room was nothing but a large empty chamber. Tatami, woven straw mats, covered the floor; shoji screens sealed the dining area. There were no tables, no chairs, no furniture of any kind.

Shoriki, Ichioka, Suzuki, and special guest Marquis Nobutsune

Okuma, the president of the All Nippon team and the future president of Shoriki's professional baseball squad, showed the Americans how to sit on the floor Japanese style, with their legs tucked underneath their rears. Connie Mack, with his long seventy-one-year-old legs, and the women in their formal dresses had particular trouble with the position. But eventually, all were ready for the meal.

More than a dozen geisha entered with tiny steps, their close-fitting silk kimonos swishing. Their faces were painted white, their plucked eyebrows painted black, and following the style of the times only their upper lips bore red lipstick while their lower lips remained unadorned. Each wore her hair up in the traditional geisha style, kept in place and gleaming from being combed with hot wax. The women carried in small tables with three-inch legs, holding the dinner of tempura, sashimi, and rice served on the finest porcelain dishes. The geisha placed the food in front of the guests and sat opposite the diners ready to pour beer and sake as needed.

The Americans, struggling with chopsticks, ate the best they could. Chio-san, the geisha serving Ruth, told the press that the Babe was "quite handy with chopsticks but he had some difficulty in carving the fried lobster so I assisted him." Lou Gehrig had told the team about tempura, and most agreed that it was delicious. The sashimi, however, received mixed reviews. Few Americans in 1934 were willing to try raw fish. Most agreed with Julia Ruth, who wrote with disgust in her diary, "Tonight we were served about 50 kinds of raw fish!"[11]

As the players enjoyed and struggled with their meals, the geisha performed traditional dances and songs. Full of sake, Ruth became enamored with a young *maiko*, or apprentice geisha, and stared at her.[12] Next to the Bambino she seemed so tiny that Ruth announced that he could pick her up in one hand.

Contrary to what most Americans believed in the 1930s, geisha were not prostitutes. The word *geisha* means "artist," Moe Berg correctly told his parents in a letter written during his 1932 trip. The young girls, often indentured by their families to a geisha house, or *okiya*, studied to become geisha for years. They went to school to learn music, dance, storytelling, and deportment. Only when they had mastered these arts would they graduate to become *maiko* and be allowed to accompany a geisha on engagements to learn the art of entertainment. Most engagements consisted of serving meals and alcohol, making small talk, performing dances and songs, and running drinking games. Their job was to make their clients relax, forget their worries, and have a good time. Sexual favors were rarely included, although geisha were encouraged to become mistresses of wealthy clients.

Ruth, however, misunderstood the subtleties of the geisha's position. At some point during the tour, although probably not during this first evening, as both Claire and Julia were present, the Babe began fondling the geisha assigned to serve him. Noticing the girl's embarrassment, Moe Berg wrote four words in katakana (the Japanese phonetic alphabet used for foreign words) and passed the note to the woman. Understanding Berg's intentions, she read the note aloud to Ruth: "Fuku u Babe Rusu." This the Babe understood and thereafter kept his hands to himself.[13]

After dining Shoriki stood up and gave a welcoming speech. Ruth followed on behalf of the All Americans and promised to play hard to repay the Japanese fans and the *Yomiuri* newspaper for their hospitality. At eleven o'clock, after fifteen straight hours of ceremonies and facing frenzied fans, Marquis Okuma gave the ending banzai toast. The weary players, glad that the day was finally at a close, made this the most heartfelt banzai of the day.

"Tokyo Gives Ruth Royal Welcome" blared the *New York Times* on November 3. The Associated Press article, picked up by newspapers across the globe, continued, "The Babe's big bulk today blotted out such unimportant things as international squabbles over oil and navies." Many observers considered the all-stars' joyous reception proof that the two countries' differences could be reconciled. The *Chicago Daily Tribune* neatly summed up this argument in its lead sentence: "Diplomats and admirals are arguing over oil and navies, but the Japanese populace found a common ground of agreement today with Americans—baseball and Babe Ruth." Umpire John Quinn, writing in the third person, remembered that the fans' "enthusiasm for baseball astounded the [American] visitors. . . . On the day the tourists arrived there was war talk, but that disappeared after they had been in the empire twenty-four hours."[14]

12

Stuart Bell lay in bed, his head pounding. Light seeped through the curtains, and he knew that he had overslept. He cursed the sake that had been "poured in an uninterrupted stream" the night before. Today was a national holiday, Emperor Meiji's birthday, and the team was expected at Meiji Shrine at ten o'clock.

The All Americans ate breakfasts of oatmeal and ham hocks in the Imperial Hotel dining room before climbing into cars for the trip to the shrine. The motorcade made it easily to Aoyama, just east of the shrine, but there twenty to thirty thousand people gathered for the twin spectacle of the birthday celebration and the ballplayers' visit. The cars inched forward until discharging their passengers at Jingu Bridge. Police tried to clear a path but failed, as the mob pressed around the players, begging for autographs. They signed and signed, but the insatiable fans kept pushing closer. Ruth "was mauled," wrote a reporter. "When one particularly energetic contingent of boys tried to climb up his huge body and stuck their fountain pens and papers under his nose in a mass attack, he got out a big black cigar, lit it and puffed the smoke into their eyes." The malodorous smoke cleared the area, and under a re-formed police escort the players entered the shrine.[1]

Roughly one hundred yards down the path they passed through the second of the three *torii* that mark the entrance to Shinto shrines. The symbolic gates, formed by pillars on both sides of a path and topped by double crossbeams, are believed to purify the soul before visiting the enshrined spirit in the sanctuary. The pressing crowd obscured the first *torii* that stood at the shrine's entrance, but it would have been hard for the visitors to miss Meiji Shrine's famous second *torii*. The thirty-six-foot-tall gates with four-foot-thick pillars had been made from Taiwanese cypress supposedly 1,908 and 1,096 years old.[2]

A short walk brought the All Americans to the main shrine complex marked by a smaller *torii*. Here, the monk Tada, dressed in a white kimono, met the group. He welcomed them and explained that the shrine was built between 1915 and 1921 to honor the great emperor. The future emperor Meiji was just two years old when Commodore Perry's black ships entered Tokyo Bay in 1852 and broke 220 years of near isolation. Since the 1630s the Tokugawa shogunate decreed that no foreigner could enter Japan nor could a Japanese leave the country without permission. Violators, including luckless shipwrecked European sailors, were put to death. During these years Japan had remained technologically and socially static. But Perry's arrival brought on an influx of Western technology and culture, causing rapid change and exasperated dissatisfaction with the reigning shogun, Yoshinobu Tokugawa. Rival daimyo overthrew Tokugawa in 1867–68 and, in a radical move known as the Meiji Restoration, placed the fourteen-year-old emperor at the head of Japan's government. Meiji himself had little direct influence over the nation's affairs, but a group of advisers, known as the genro, modernized Japan under his name by abolishing feudalism, creating a Western-style constitution, and revamping the economic infrastructure. Japan became a world power during Meiji's long reign. By the time the emperor died in 1912, Japan had fought and defeated China and Russia and had colonized Korea and Taiwan. Its economy had become the strongest in Asia. Its subjects enjoyed more economic opportunity, a higher standard of living, and more political freedoms than they had in their entire history. Each year millions came to the shrine to thank Meiji for his many gifts to Japan.[3] Tada brought the Americans to the inner shrine and showed them the proper way to pay their respects, by clapping, bowing, and making a wish.

As the players and their wives left the shrine, autograph seekers besieged them again. The All Americans rushed to the cars and quickly closed the windows. Fans mobbed the automobiles, pounding on the windows until one broke. The drivers accelerated as people jumped on the running boards. Several fell under the cars and needed to be pulled free before the ballplayers could escape.

The motorcade dropped the All Americans at the home of Marquis Nobutsune Okuma, who was not only the All Nippon team's president but also the son of Shigenobu Okuma, founder of Waseda University and a former prime minister, who had his leg blown off by a would-be assassin. The marquis, dressed in a formal morning coat, met his guests in a reception room furnished in the Louis XIV style. After the welcoming he invited the Americans to enjoy the reception in the gardens. The players wandered the acres of formal gardens and met their opponents—the All Nippon baseball team.

Tadao Ichioka and the team's manager, Daisuke Miyake, had spent the summer recruiting Japan's top players. Many were recent graduates of Waseda or Keio who had been playing for one of Japan's amateur clubs or company teams. Some of these, such as Masao Date, the great Waseda hurler, and Keio's slugger Minoru Yamashita, had already played against Major Leaguers during the 1931 tour and were anxious to face them again. Others, however, were still students, and that posed a problem. The Ministry of Education's 1932 ordinance forbidding students from playing with, or against, professionals was still in effect. Students who joined the All Nippons would be banned from interscholastic play and might also be expelled from their schools. The most prudent course would have been to create a team of college graduates, but Shoriki and his staff rarely played it safe. They wanted a team that would not only challenge the Americans but also help bring fans to the ballpark. As the current collegiate stars were among Japan's most popular celebrities, their inclusion on the team would generate interest. Of course, the *Yomiuri* group had another reason for recruiting the students. Once banned from scholastic baseball and already affiliated with *Yomiuri*'s team, the players would be easy to recruit for the still secret professional league.

Sotaro Suzuki introduced the All Nippon and All American players, making sure that the Major Leaguers met their Japanese namesakes. Japanese often nicknamed their top players after Major League stars. Katsuo Tanaka, a slugger from Waseda during the early 1920s, for example, was known as the Japanese Babe Ruth; thirty years later 1950s star center fielder Makoto Kozuru was called the Japanese Joe DiMaggio. Suzuki introduced seventeen-year-old Eiji Sawamura to Lefty Gomez, telling the goofy American that the kid was known as the Japanese Gomez. Just two months earlier Sawamura had been pitching for Kyoto Commercial High School at the national championship tournament at Koshien Stadium. Although his team was eliminated in the first round, Sawamura was still considered the best young pitcher in Japan. In August Tadao Ichioka had approached his grandfather and explained that the *Yomiuri Shimbun* was sponsoring a team of Major League stars, including Babe Ruth, to play in Japan that fall and that he wanted the seventeen-year-old pitcher on the staff. The newspaper would pay 120 yen ($36) per month, more than most skilled artisans made. The Sawamura family needed the extra income to support Eiji's siblings, but the invitation carried a price. If Sawamura played against the American professionals, he would be expelled from high school and would forfeit his chance to attend Keio University the following semester. But to pitch against Major Leaguers! To pitch against Babe Ruth! The boy accepted. Now, several months later, he was shaking Gomez's and Ruth's hands. He felt dazed.

Shinji Hamazaki always amused American ballplayers. The graduate of Keio stood only five foot one and weighed just 110 pounds. The cover of a 1930 issue of the magazine *Yakyukai* depicted the miniature Hamazaki next to Neil Pullen, the six-foot catcher of the visiting Negro League Philadelphia Royal Giants (the catcher is often misidentified as Biz Mackey). Hamazaki, however, could pitch, and Suzuki assured the Americans that he could throw as well as their own Joe Cascarella. One All Nippon player, however, stood nearly as tall as the visiting Americans and needed no translator. Jimmy Horio had made the Japanese team. The first part of his wild plan had succeeded.

Luck had been with Horio. On the trip to Japan he befriended a nisei sportswriter named Wallace Hirai. Intrigued by Horio's story, Hirai published an article about Jimmy's baseball career in Honolulu's bilingual newspaper, *Nippu Jiji*. Upon reaching Japan in October Horio wrote to Daisuke Miyake and included a picture of himself in a Sioux Falls uniform and a copy of Hirai's article. Miyake, who had umpired a game during the LA Nippons' 1931 trip and perhaps remembered Horio, allowed him try out for the All Nippon team and even lent the Japanese American his own cleats for the workout.

Impressed with Horio's speed, power, and defense, Miyake asked Jimmy to join the squad after a single short workout. Horio agreed and, with a directness that surprised Miyake, asked what his salary would be. Miyake explained that the All Nippon would be an amateur squad so that they could use Meiji Jingu Stadium, but if Horio was willing to remain in Japan until they organized the professional league, *Yomiuri* would pay him retroactively.[4]

Soon the marquis reappeared, now dressed in a formal black kimono, and the festivities began. On a stage erected for the occasion, seventy young women in identical kimonos played "Hail Columbia!," the unofficial American anthem until Congress declared "The Star-Spangled Banner" the national anthem in 1931, and other songs on the three-string *shamisen*. Bell found the music without melody and did not even recognize the anthem but like the other Americans "listened attentively."[5]

Next came the food. Many of Tokyo's top restaurants had set up tents in the garden for the Americans to sample their specialties. Ruth first tried *oden*—a soy-flavored broth packed with various vegetables and fish cakes—but, finding the *konnyaku* (gelatinous cubes made from a tubular vegetable) not to his liking, moved on to the tempura tent, where he went through ten shrimp in a matter of seconds before visiting the sushi stall.

The guests who were not fond of Japanese food did not go hungry. Dozens of luncheon tables, complete with white tablecloths and fruit baskets, stood at the center of the garden. Seventy of Tokyo's most beautiful waitresses, selected from the city's top restaurants, served platters piled high with sandwiches and bottled beer.

The inevitable speeches and toasts came next. The highlight was the introduction of Hige no Tempei (the Bearded Tempei), considered Japan's greatest fish chef. Gehrig must have instantly recognized him; there would be no forgetting the odd-looking man that he had met during the 1931 tour. Dressed in a white chef's kimono, he stood about five foot two from his geta to his bald dome. Long, snowy whiskers covered his face and hung below his neck. In sharp contrast with his white beard and bushy white eyebrows, he wore round black-framed glasses. The thick lenses made his twinkling eyes appear unnaturally large. There was something endearing about the old man, and Ruth could not contain himself. Approaching the chef with a loud "Hello, Santa Claus!," he pretended to pull a rabbit from Tempei's long whiskers as they posed for dozens of photographs.

The party lasted just under two hours. The All Americans left at a quarter past one, changed into their uniforms at the hotel, and, as Tokyo's only large ball field was in use that day, boarded a train to ride to their first practice.

An hour train ride to the east brought the players to the town of Narashino in Chiba Prefecture.[6] They arrived at Yatsu Stadium to find that they would not be practicing alone. Twenty thousand fans filled the stadium's bleachers. Before practice could start the players had to endure another ceremony—more welcoming speeches, followed by a gift of horseshoe-shaped flowered wreaths for each player. The hosts would have been mortified to know that Ruth detested horse-shoe wreaths. He later told Japan's baseball magazine *Yakyukai* that he considered them bad luck, as he had never hit a home run after receiving one.[7]

At last the All Americans held their first practice on Japanese soil and the first workout on land in eight days. For nearly two hours the fans screamed themselves hoarse, yelling Ruth's name again and again. To get closer to the players they pushed against the flimsy wall separating the bleachers from the field, splintered it "with one wood-rendering crash and rushed to get better vantage points." The Babe, overwhelmed by the cheers, thanked Suzuki over and over for insisting that he come to Japan.[8]

After practice, the players boarded the train for the hotel. Waiting for them in their cars were apples, bananas, and beer, just in case they were too hungry to wait for the evening banquet and "Gala Dinner Dance" being thrown in their honor by the Imperial Hotel.

Stuart Bell summed up the prevailing thought: "Boy, what a league!"[9]

13

As the All Americans dined at the Imperial Hotel on *crème de tomate Chantilly*, *Dame de Saumon à la Victoria*, and *contrefilet pique sauce Chasseur*, fans began lining up outside the entrance to Meiji Jingu Stadium. These fans all held small 50-sen tickets printed on thin gray paper, good for an unreserved outfield seat. Sleeping the night on the ground before the stadium gate should guarantee them a good seat. The fans bearing the bright-orange, 1.50-yen tickets would arrive tomorrow to take their reserved infield seats. The tickets bore the game number, not the date of the match, in a large red box in the upper-left corner. *Yomiuri* officials realized belatedly that this might cause confusion and ran announcements in the newspaper all week warning patrons to check their tickets and the schedule to ensure that they arrived on the correct date.

The atmosphere outside the stadium gates resembled a summer festival, despite the temperature dipping into the low forties. Men had brought mahjong and go boards, and many played late into the night before falling asleep on makeshift beds of cardboard or ratty blankets. A *Yomiuri* reporter arrived to interview these true fans. Most felt that the Japanese had a fair chance against the All Americans. Kikuo Nakamura came with a large banner supporting the All Nippon team. The young man was a childhood friend of Eiji Sawamura and had come to cheer him on. One man in particular caught the reporter's eye. He was middle-aged, with legs so malformed that he needed crutches. His rough, blue-tinted hands identified him as a textile dyer. He had arrived at six o'clock to ensure a good seat, and a fellow fan had laid a sheet on the ground to make his wait more comfortable. He eagerly told the reporter his plans. A designer of kimono and textile patterns, he planned to study Babe

Ruth during the game and memorize his features. When he returned to work he would design a Babe Ruth pattern for underwear.[1]

When the gates opened at nine thirty the next morning, the line outside Meiji Jingu Stadium had swollen to thousands. The horseshoe-shaped ballpark held sixty thousand, and every ticket had been sold weeks before. As expected, several patrons holding tickets to Game 4 of the series and not to this game on November 4 tried to gain entry. One man had traveled through the night from Osaka, only to discover his error at the turnstile. He, like the others, was turned away.[2]

The fans with unreserved tickets hastened to the grandstands, jumping down into the best seats. Despite the rush, the newspapers recorded no injuries or incidents of note. The third-base seats behind the All Americans' dugout filled quickly, as most fans wanted to be close to the great Bambino. Soon the fans resumed their games of mahjong, go, and dice to pass the two and a half hours before the start of the ceremonies at noon.

Entering with the unreserved ticket holders at nine thirty were five geisha from Yoshiwara dressed in splendid kimonos. The young ladies took their assigned seats in the still-empty reserved infield section. Teahouses featuring geisha were expensive and often allowed only patrons with proper references. Thus, they served only the rich and connected. Most Japanese would never enjoy their company. With more than two hours to wait, some members of the infield bleachers relieved their boredom by making catcalls and lewd comments at the geisha. The abuse soon became unbearable, and the young women retreated. Whether they returned for the game is unknown.

The reserved seats slowly filled with wealthier fans, "the daughters of rich families," celebrities, and the seventy waitresses who had served the players the day before at Marquis Okuma's garden party. All the girls held American and Japanese flags that they waved frantically at any excuse. Asked which team they were rooting for, they diplomatically answered, "Both."

As the sun hit its zenith, the seats were all filled. Nearly sixty thousand fans waited for Babe Ruth and the All Americans to arrive. At twenty past twelve a naval band struck up the All Nippons' fight song, "Pacific Ocean":

Over the Pacific Ocean where the giant waves are reaching
   to the sky
Men and men are face to face

The gorgeous picture scroll of strong figures simultaneously
   striking each other

Spirits of men from a god country will dance

Go in and win! Go in and win! Japanese players!
Knock them to pieces!

Jingu under the clear autumn sky
Beautiful sacred shrine smiling at us
The elite players, bearers of homeland shrine
Capture the crown of the world now

Go in and win! Go in and win! Japanese players!
Knock them to pieces!

As the band played, Sotaro Suzuki, dressed in a light three-piece suit and his usual fedora, led the All Americans through the tunnel behind home plate and onto the field. Behind Suzuki strode Connie Mack, wearing his ever-present dark three-piece suit and high collar. Unlike most Major League managers, who dressed in their teams' uniforms, Mack had worn business attire since taking over the Athletics' helm in 1901, as he knew that his tall, skinny frame looked ridiculous in baseball flannels.[3]

Next to Mack sauntered Ruth, hands stuck in the pockets of his red woolen All American team jacket. According to *Yakyukai* writer Fujio Naoki, in contrast to the tall, stately Mack, the Babe "looked like an elephant." No matter. The crowd thundered when they recognized the God of Baseball. Ruth's solemn face broke into a wide grin as he pulled his hands free to wave and doff his cap. The rest of the All Americans marched behind in double file, each looking splendid in his red jacket, light-gray uniform pants with blue-striped socks, and navy-blue cap.

After the Americans came the Japanese, "looking like children" by comparison.[4] First, the Tokyo Club entered, dressed in white flannel with dark socks. They would oppose the All Americans in this first game. The squad consisted of former players from the prestigious Tokyo Big Six University League, but only those who had not been invited to join *Yomiuri*'s All Nippon team. These elite players filed in last. Led by organizer Tadao Ichioka and manager Daisuke Miyake, the All Nippon roster contained the best and most popular ballplayers in the nation. Besides seventeen-year-old Sawamura and Hawaiian Jimmy Horio, the team included Waseda University star hurler Masao Date, who prior to becoming a pitcher had won the Big Six batting crown; Keio slugger Minoru Yamashita, who had led the Big Six league in home runs and batting; the slick-fielding Hisanori Karita from Hosei University; fiery Keio third baseman and national idol Shigeru Mizuhara; and his rival from Waseda, Osamu Mihara—known to O'Doul, Gehrig, and the 1931 tour players as "Nosey." But these stars would have to wait another day before testing their mettle against the Major Leaguers.

The three teams paraded down the first base line as a *Yomiuri* airplane circled overhead, pulling a banner extolling the virtues of Chiyoda Pomade (a particularly greasy and smelly hair-styling product that helped underwrite the tour's expenses). Once the naval band had finished the national anthems and the teams posed for photographs, pregame practice began.

Ruth dragged a bulging sack of baseballs from the dugout, and the Americans took their practice swings. Meiji Jingu Stadium was larger than most American ballparks. Completed in 1926 and home to the Big Six University League, the outfield walls stood about 330 feet away down the lines and 390 feet in center. Few Japanese could reach the outfield stands, but the All American sluggers sent ball after ball arcing into the packed bleachers. Fans rushed to grab each souvenir. Not content to wait for a Ruthian blast to come their way, several enterprising fellows jumped the fence to grab a ball that landed in the outfield grass. Soon the balls were exhausted, and the announcer pleaded over the stadium's loudspeakers for the fans to return their prizes.

Nearly all of the sixty thousand seemed to focus on Ruth. Naoki told the readers of *Yakyukai*, "The fans went crazy each time Ruth did anything—smiled, sneezed, or dropped a ball." One old man brought a pair of high-powered binoculars, amusing himself and neighboring fans by focusing on the Bambino's famous broad nose, making his nostrils fill the lens. The Babe relished the attention and transformed into a comedian. During batting practice he purposely missed some pitches—twisting himself around like a pretzel before falling over. In the midst of hitting his infielders practice grounders, Ruth began a game of shadow ball—hitting an imaginary grounder to Eric "Rabbit" McNair at shortstop, who fielded it convincingly and started a double play, timed with perfect realism. The antics, according to Ambassador Grew, brought "roars of laughter from the grandstands."[5]

The Americans soon conceded the field to their hosts, who looked like schoolboys by comparison. Even before the first pitch, the outcome of the contest was obvious. As Nobumichi Katada of the Tokyo Club stepped to the plate to take his practice swings, Ruth bounded from the dugout. With a flourish he handed the small, bespectacled center fielder his bat and indicated that Katada should try it. Katada could not refuse such a great honor, but he was undoubtedly aware that he was the butt of a practical joke in front of sixty thousand witnesses. The Babe's bat was a famous club, thirty-six inches long and a hefty forty-four ounces. Many Major Leaguers had trouble swinging it with authority, but at least it was lighter than the fifty-two ouncer the Bambino used as a rookie.

Katada attempted a swing, but, according to *Yakyukai*, "it was so heavy that his body moved instead of the bat," and the center fielder tumbled over. Katada handed it to Takeo Nagai, who was waiting on deck, but not wishing to be humiliated, Nagai just handed it back. Ruth sauntered over, asked in a loud stage voice if the bat was too heavy, and took it from Katada with two fingers. The crowd, meanwhile, roared with laughter.[6]

At last officials cleared the diamond for the ceremonial first pitch. Marquis Nobutsune Okuma, by now well known to the American ballplayers, took the mound. Although president of the All Nippon Baseball Club, Okuma had not been the first choice for the honor. Shoriki had asked Foreign Minister Koki Hirota and Ambassador Grew to each throw out the first ball as a symbol of the two nations' goodwill toward each other and ability to cooperate. Hirota, however, declined, as he had never played baseball before and did not want to embarrass himself or by extension his country. Grew, although named a great fan of the game by the press, displayed his skill as a sportsman on the golf course and with the rifle. After graduating from Harvard in 1902, he had spent the following year traveling the Far East hunting tigers, wild boar, and other big game. He recorded his adventure in *Sport and Travel in the Far East*, a book that became one of Teddy Roosevelt's favorites. Not wanting to "make a spectacle of himself," Grew also declined to throw out the first pitch. The task then fell to Okuma, who also had no experience with the game. Connie Mack settled in behind home plate with a catcher's glove as the white-haired Okuma attempted to put one over. The ball made it about fifty feet before falling impotently to the earth. Ruth boomed out, "Ready Fellows? All set? Come on, let's go!" and lumbered out to his position in left field as the All Americans took the field to "cheers, the likeness of which has seldom been heard in the country."[7]

Left-hander Earl Whitehill took the mound, as the Tokyo Club would bat first in this exhibition. Stocky and darkly handsome, the thirty-five-year-old Whitehill had "an explosive temper and a vocabulary to keep it rich accompaniment."[8] His overriding desire to win pushed him to berate teammates for errors and poor play. He began his Major League career with the 1924 Detroit Tigers, winning seventeen games as a rookie, but soon clashed with star and manager Ty Cobb. The two hotheads rarely spoke to each other during their final two seasons together. After a winning season in '32, Detroit traded Whitehill to Washington while his stock was high. "The Earl" was a notorious beanball pitcher, hitting just over a hundred batters during his career. In April 1933 he came inside to Lou Gehrig, knocking him unconscious. A month later a fight with Yankees outfielder Ben Chapman escalated to a small riot involving both teams, police, and about three hundred fans, some armed with baseball bats. Despite the controversies Whitehill had his best season, as his twenty-two wins helped the Senators to the World Series.[9]

In the grandstands Whitehill's alter ego sat with the other players' wives. Violet Linda Oliver Whitehill was perhaps more famous, or at least more widely recognized, than her husband. Well educated, sophisticated, and beautiful, the redhead had been the California Raisin Girl. In 1921 and '22, she had toured the United States to promote the product and model for amateur photographers.[10] By the end of the tour Violet was advertised as the world's most photographed woman. On this trip to Asia Violet was more than a supportive wife; she would be covering the tour for the *Washington Herald*—wiring articles to the paper every few days.

Whitehill opened the momentous series with a fast one down the middle that, "to the amazement of the fans," leadoff batter Kaichi Masu cracked up the middle for a clean single.[11] The Japanese celebration was short-lived, however. After the second pitch of the game Whitehill snapped off a throw to first, catching Masu off the bag for the first out. A groundout and strikeout later, the All Americans were set to display their batting skills.

It took just a few minutes for the fans, and players, to realize the difference in skill level between the two teams. Tokio Takahashi, the former ace of Waseda University, looked nervous and lacked control of his pitches as he walked Rabbit McNair to start the inning. Charlie Gehringer, whose .379 average a few weeks earlier was not enough to stop the St. Louis Cardinals from topping his Detroit Tigers in the World Series, pounded a line drive off the right-field fence for a double. The crowd buzzed. The hit had sounded different—louder and more pronounced than when their native stars struck the ball. One of the Japanese outfielders later told the media, "Balls hit by Americans and Japanese are different. On a line drive, the moment I heard the sound, the ball was already there. I was very surprised by the strength of the ball."[12] With runners at second and third, Ruth strode to the plate. Fans cheered and cheered again. Takahashi reared back—ball. Then, another ball. The exact number of pitches was not recorded, but not seeing a pitch close to the strike zone, the frustrated Ruth swung at a low outside offering and grounded weakly to second for an out and RBI. Gehrig followed and also saw nothing he could drive. Finally, he managed to loft a sacrifice into center field to score Gehringer from third. The inning ended with the All Americans up 2–0.

Tokyo went down quietly in the second before the All Americans rallied again in their half. With one out, runners on first and third, it was the Babe's turn again. A ball. Then another, and another. Takahashi's plan was evident. He was not just nervous. Not wanting to embarrass himself by giving up a long ball, he was pitching around Ruth, Gehrig, and Foxx and concentrating on the other hitters. The cheers for Ruth turned to jeers at Takahashi. The Babe walked to load the bases. Takahashi focused on Gehrig, pitching him carefully—nothing over the middle of the plate, but there was no place to put him. Gehrig swung at one close to the strike zone and sent a towering fly ball into center field, but outfielder Masa Kataoka, taking advantage of Meiji Stadium's large dimensions, settled under it as McNair scored after the catch. Now with two outs and runners on first and second, Takahashi renewed the crowd's displeasure by walking Foxx before bearing down on Averill for the final out of the inning.

The All Americans scored in each of the first five innings and held a comfortable, perhaps insurmountable, 12–1 lead. Subsequent Tokyo pitchers continued Takahashi's strategy of pitching around Ruth and Gehrig, although by the fourth they had begun to challenge Foxx, who looked unsteady at the plate. In both the seventh and the eighth innings Ruth and Gehrig were intentionally walked in succession. Struck by the Major Leaguers' skill and Tokyo's poor sportsmanship, most of the sixty thousand fans abandoned the local team and clamored for the All Americans to hit one out. The Japanese pitchers, in particular, became "the target of vociferous criticisms."[13] The game ended with a 17–1 All American victory, but the lack of home runs caused many fans to leave disappointed.

The Babe later apologized for not going deep, telling reporters, "I was a little tired today, but tomorrow I will do my best to hit a home run."[14] Nevertheless, he was pleased. He had gained a hit in three at bats, despite rarely seeing a strike, and had walked three times. Moreover, the fans' adoration thrilled him. There had been few standing ovations during the past injury-plagued season, and he missed them. The Babe craved attention, and the Japanese provided it. Forgotten was the emotional parting with the Yankees, the uncertain future, and possible retirement. For the moment he was still the God of Baseball.

Jimmie Foxx could not share Ruth's euphoria. Despite the lavish receptions, exotic atmosphere, and adoring fans, he was going through hell. Three weeks had passed since Barney Brown's inside pitch had knocked him unconscious, and he still was not quite right.

He felt lost at the plate. His teammates had pounded out thirteen hits off the weak Japanese pitching, but he had barely made contact. The Japanese had pitched around him in his first two at bats, but once they realized that he was not a threat, he had struck out twice, fouled out, and grounded to second. Not even a ball out of the infield! Would he regain his batting eye? His old teammate Chick Galloway had been hit in the head during batting practice and was never the same again. He left the Majors only a year after the beaning. Foxx hoped that he would not share Galloway's fate.

Later that night, after the players had returned to the Imperial Hotel and dined, the Ruths were lounging in their suite when someone knocked on the door. The Babe grunted a response and opened it. A small, wizened Japanese man wearing a kimono stood outside. He bowed in greeting before thrusting a baseball at Ruth.

"Sign, please."

The Babe smiled and, seeing that no pen accompanied the ball, retrieved one from inside the suite. His large hand signed the famous bold signature on the sweet spot, and he returned the ball with a smile and slight bow. The old man returned the bow as he accepted the ball and produced another ball from the sleeve of his kimono. "Sign, please," he repeated.

Graciously, Ruth did.

After another series of bows, a third ball appeared from his sleeve. "Sign, please."

They repeated the sequence, again and again and again, each time with an identical "Sign, please."

From the suite Claire and Julia watched agape before breaking into laughter as the man produced more than a dozen balls from his kimono, each time repeating the request and exchanging bows with the Babe. The amused Ruth took it in stride, signing and returning each one as if it had been the first and only request. At last, the man ran out of balls, and the Ruths could retire for the night.[15]

14

The All Americans awoke by eight the next morning. It would be another full day. After breakfast at the hotel they left at ten for the Matsuya department store in Ginza. Stuart Bell told his *Cleveland Press* readers, "We banzaied our way through the aisles and up elevators to the landscaped roof, where the overworked photographers went through their hourly act. And then we descended to a spacious dining room, where a lunch that included everything from soup to nuts was spread. The big shot of the store made a fine speech presenting Japan's protestations of peace and goodwill to Americans, pledged the love of Japanese for Americans, and sat down with the closing injunction that everybody should eat." The Americans eyed the mounds of food warily. Nearly every type of Japanese dish stood on the table—sushi, sukiyaki, noodles, rice, fresh fruit, and a huge cake shaped like Mount Fuji. At ten o'clock in the morning, having just finished breakfast, the spread was daunting. As the visitors sat, a troop of young women clad in "multicolored kimonos and clopping [geta] brought out beer—bottle after bottle!" Too full from breakfast to truly enjoy the feast, the guests snacked on the many dishes and drank the beer.[1]

After about an hour the All Americans piled into their cars and were whisked down the street to the rival Takashimaya department store. In conjunction with the team's visit Takashimaya threw a "baseball sale" from November 4 to November 11. All customers spending more than three yen (about one dollar but two days' wages for most factory workers) would get a complimentary ticket to a game. A large advertisement in the *Yomiuri Shimbun* invited fans to meet the players at the store that morning. The first three thousand through the door would receive a Babe Ruth bromide (a black-and-white photographic baseball card). No known copies of this card survive, making it the rarest of all Babe Ruth baseball cards.

After shaking hands and signing autographs, the All Americans were brought to a dining room with tables strewn with flowers and ferns and were served a more modest fare of sandwiches, fruits, candy, and beer. There was little time to relax or digest, however, as the team needed to report to Meiji Jingu Stadium at one to play the All Nippons. Bell noted that "for some reason or other, the All Americans didn't collapse because of full stomachs" and took the field on time.[2]

Once again, fans filled every seat when the All Americans took the field for batting practice. The Americans put on another show, pounding ball after ball into the seats. Fans prayed that the power would not stop once the game began, as it had the day before. Today's game would be more even—most fans were certain of that. At last Japan could showcase its best against the Americans.

The All Nippon lineup featured six future Hall of Famers. Leading off at third base was Motonobu Makino, the former captain of Keio University. Considered "rock solid but unspectacular," Makino could be counted on to make all the routine plays. Makino, however, was not Japan's top third baseman. That honor went to Shigeru Mizuhara, the former Keio star. Mizuhara was on the All Nippon roster but not with the team, causing rumors that he had quit when he learned of *Yomiuri*'s not-so-secret plan to start professional baseball. In fact, he was temporarily unavailable for personal reasons and would soon join the team.

Hisanori Karita, a scrappy, slick-fielding shortstop, hit second. Just twenty-four years old and a bit cocky, the Hosei University product would eventually play professionally for fourteen more years, becoming known as one of Japan's greatest defensive players. He would also become the first player in Japanese pro ball to pull off the hidden-ball trick.

Osamu "Nosey" Mihara hit third. Mihara had been Waseda's second baseman when he collided with O'Doul in the seventh game of the 1931 tour. A perennial .300 hitter, Mihara had little power but used his speed to leg out extra bases. His rivalry with third baseman Shigeru Mizuhara was legendary and would continue until their deaths. The two grew up on Shikoku Island playing for rival school-boy teams. Upon graduating Mizuhara attended Keio, while Mihara went to Waseda. In 1931 Mihara won a key game by stealing home as Mizuhara stood on the mound. In the future the two would compete for the same managerial job and then face each other multiple times in the Japan Series.

At cleanup was Jimmy Horio, who would get his chance to show the Major Leaguers that he belonged in their company. Horio had more riding on the game than any of his teammates. A few big hits, and he might be playing against these fellows next season.

After Horio came one of Japan's true power hitters, Minoru Ya-mashita. From Kobe Yamashita was one of the larger men on the All Nippon team, standing five foot eight and weighing 165 pounds. In 1925 he hit the first home run during a national high school championship at mammoth Koshien Stadium. He enrolled at Keio, batting .315 in Big Six play and creating a league record with six career home runs.

Kumeyasu Yajima and Isamu Fuma, two former Big Six outfielders who fell into relative obscurity after playing a few professional seasons, hit in front of the aging catcher, Jiro Kuji. A product of Hokkaido, Kuji attended Waseda from 1917 to 1922, overlapping with All Nippon general manager Tadao Ichioka, where he led the league in hitting in 1918. After graduation Kuji decided not to remain in Tokyo, where he could have played on a number of semipro or company teams. Instead, he made the unusual decision to return to his home prefecture and joined the amateur Hakodate Ocean. As one of the nation's top backstops, Kuji occasionally played for Waseda alumni teams, had played on a Yokohama all-star team against the 1931 Major League squad, and had agreed to represent Japan against the All Americans.

Masao Date, Japan's top pitcher, took the mound for All Nippon. Date had been a catcher in high school, leading his team to four straight appearances at the national championships. In 1928 he hit .469 as Waseda's first baseman, becoming the first freshman to win a batting title. A few years later, when the team's ace became ill, Date took the mound, winning two games against Keio and propelling Waseda to the Big Six championship. That fall he pitched in three games against the Major League All Stars. He was hit hard, but Lou Gehrig was impressed and warned his 1934 teammates that the Japanese pitcher would be no pushover.

Unlike the Tokyo Club's pitchers in the first game, Date challenged the Major Leaguers. He sent the Americans down one, two, three in the first, with McNair flying out and Gehringer and Ruth both grounding to first. The second inning did not go as well, as Gehrig led off with a walk. The slumping Foxx came next. Having watched the opening game, Date must have realized that Foxx felt uncomfortable at the plate. He bore down and fired two pitches in for strikes and missed with another. He came right back with another strike, but the burly third baseman, known as "the Beast," met it squarely. The ball left the stadium in an instant, landing in the left-field bleachers for the tour's first home run. Just what the fans had been waiting for. No matter that it put the Americans ahead, the Japanese crowd cheered and shouted until they were hoarse. Earl Averill stepped into the box next and repeated the feat, slamming a line drive over the right-field wall. Shaken, Date subsequently gave up a single and a walk but managed to get out of the inning without further damage.

Date's troubles continued in the fourth. Ruth led off. The Babe felt that he had let down his newfound fans by not going deep in the first game and had promised to make amends. Left fielder Isamu Fuma noticed a difference in the Bambino's mannerisms right away. He enjoyed Ruth's easygoing personality and was surprised how serious he looked in the batter's box—his face tense and his eyes focused in concentration.[3] Seemingly unconcerned with the home runs hit off him in the last inning, Date went straight after Ruth. The Babe responded with a mighty fly ball to right field. Up it flew. Right fielder Yajima drifted back and back as the ball carried deeper and deeper toward the wall. Back again until Yajima could feel the wall against his back. The ball had reached its apex and was descending. The crowd cheered. It would be close, but they would get what they wanted, a Ruthian shot. The wind blew—just a gust, but enough to spoil the fun. The ball tumbled down into Yajima's glove, a foot shy of the wall. A single groan from sixty thousand mouths. One out. Ruth looked up at the disappointed crowd, "pointed his finger up into the air [to show] that the ball was too high, wrung his hands to show his disappointment that it wasn't a homer," as the fans "roared" with laughter.[4]

Gehrig was luckier. Or perhaps luck had little to do with it, given he was eight years younger than his former teammate, in better shape, and at the top of his career. There was no doubt about Gehrig's drive. He "smote it high and dry into the right field bleachers," according to a reporter.[5] Behind Gehrig an error, a single, a ground-out, and a walk loaded the bases with two outs, but once again Date wiggled out of the jam.

On the mound for the All Americans, Joe Cascarella was dominating the Japanese. At twenty-seven years old, Cascarella had just finished his rookie season in the Majors. Joe grew up playing semi-pro ball on the sandlots of Philadelphia. By the time he was fifteen he earned ten dollars a game as a ringer for local clubs. Two years later he was charging twenty-five per game. He entered Temple University in 1924 but left after his freshman year to pursue a professional baseball career. But he got off to a rough start. For nine years Joe struggled in the Minors, making little headway. After winning ten and losing sixteen at Jersey City in 1933, he realized that his baseball career was going nowhere. For years he had entertained his teammates during long bus rides with his beautiful tenor voice, so he decided to begin professional voice lessons. He was about to announce his retirement and go into radio entertainment when Connie Mack purchased his contract and told him to report to the Philadelphia Athletics' 1934 spring training camp. Cascarella made the team as a reliever and spot starter, picking up twelve wins although losing fifteen. At times, however, he looked like a potential star, tossing two three-hitters. To give him more experience, Mack had asked Cascarella to come to Japan.[6] So far he was looking like a future superstar. Through the first three innings he had given up just a single and had struck out three.

Up four to nothing the All Americans decided to switch Ruth and Gehrig in the field. The Iron Horse moved to left, and the Bambino took first. Ruth took advantage of his new proximity to the stands to entertain the fans. He smiled and winked at the crowd, tossed a ball to a particularly "fair lady" in the bleachers, and posed for photographs between innings with his cap "turned backward like a schoolboy." His favorite gag came when a runner reached first. The six-foot-two Ruth would stand on the bag, making him seem even taller, and pantomime the height difference between the Japanese runner and himself. The crowd loved it.[7]

All Nippon's only run came from Jimmy Horio's daring. Horio had struck out in his first at bat, but made it to first with one out in the top of the fourth after being hit by a pitch. Determined to show the Major Leaguers his speed, Jimmy danced off first as Minoru Yamashita, the power hitter, dug in. Perhaps rattled by Horio's lead, catcher Frankie Hayes let Cascarella's pitch get behind him. Jimmy "dashed for second." Hayes panicked and heaved the ball wildly toward second base. Reading the off-target throw, Horio did not slide but kept going full speed past the bag and streaked safely to third. A deep fly ball from Yamashita scored Horio to put the Japanese on the board.

On the mound for All Nippon Date continued to pitch "courageously, refusing to be disheartened."[8] He shut out the Americans in the middle frame, allowing lone singles in each of the three innings, before Averill scored the final American run of the day with another line-drive homer. The Japanese hurler also impressed at the plate, lashing two singles into right field. Although Date had limited the Major Leaguers to five runs, the game's outcome seemed inevitable. Cascarella gave up just three hits and walked only two. The Japanese nearly scored a second run in the eighth, but amateurish play spoiled the opportunity. After Date had led off the inning with his second single, pinch runner Nobuaki "Pep" Nidegawa had moved to third on a sacrifice bunt and long fly out. With two outs, and a strike on pinch hitter Haruyasu Nakajima, Nidegawa surprised the Americans by darting toward home. The steal of home nearly worked, but at the last moment Nakajima inexplicably swung at the pitch, grounding it in front of the plate. Frankie Hayes pounced on the ball, ignored Nidegawa sliding home behind him, and calmly threw to first for the force-out, nullifying Nidegawa's efforts. Five-foot-one Shinji Hamazaki came in to finish the game for the Japanese, setting the Americans down in order but nearly allowing Ruth to circle the bases. Once again the Babe got just under the ball and sent Yajima back to the wall before the right fielder recorded the out.

Satisfied with four home runs, most of the Japanese fans left the stadium happy. Few expected their team to win, so the loss caused little heartache. Indeed, most were probably thrilled that their countrymen kept the score so close. They would have liked to have seen Ruth homer, but he had amused them with his clowning and the two long fly balls that would have been home runs in most American ballparks.[9]

Newspapers across the United States covered the two games. The *New York Times, Chicago Daily Tribune, Los Angeles Times, New York Herald-Tribune*, and other papers carried a nine-paragraph Associated Press article. In Philadelphia, home of Connie Mack and many of the All Americans, the *Inquirer* ran the article accompanied by two large photographs on the front page of the sports section. The article's tone furthered the tour's goodwill mission by praising the Japanese players despite the losses and noting the "courtesy and orderliness of the great Japanese crowd" as well as their enthusiasm. So far the tour had succeeded in bringing baseball fans of both countries closer together.

15

The following day, November 6, the players would leave for northern Japan from Ueno Station on the 2:35 p.m. express sleeper train. That left Tuesday morning open for shopping, sightseeing, or free time in Tokyo. For the Babe that meant tee time. Among the Ruths' twenty pieces of luggage were his golf clubs. He was an avid golfer and a good one with a three handicap. Ambassador Grew brought Ruth and Lefty O'Doul to the Tokyo Golf Club, where they were joined by the club's pro. For fourteen holes they talked baseball and a little golf, as cameramen pursued the Babe across the course. Although not a big baseball fan, Grew enjoyed the players' stories and perked up when Ruth revealed that the secret to hitting well in golf and baseball was identical—a nice, easy swing. If one tried to hit either ball too hard, one was likely to move one's head and take one's eyes off the ball. After the game the men sat on the clubhouse steps to pose for photographers and the newsreel cameras. They finished the morning with a light drink. Grew and O'Doul sipped beers, while the Babe quenched his thirst by gulping down a "boilermaker's highball . . . followed immediately by a whole glass of beer in almost one gulp." Grew noted in his diary that night, "All Japan has gone wild over him. He is a great deal more effective Ambassador than I could ever be."[1]

As the Americans enjoyed their free morning, the All Nippon team received bad, but not unexpected, news. The Ministry of Education announced that high schooler Eiji Sawamura and Waseda student Isamu Fuma would be expelled for playing against the All Americans. Hiraku Iwahara, head of the athletic section of the Ministry of Education, informed the president of Waseda that "the Education Office cannot tolerate students taking part in games against professionals, . . . and that two courses are open. One is to let Fuma leave school of his own accord or for the school to expel him."[2] Iwahara told the press that a similar letter had been sent to Kyoto Commercial High School where Sawamura was enrolled. Both players knew that this was the likely outcome of agreeing to play for the All Nippons, but it still must have been harsh news. Fuma would never graduate, and Sawamura was now officially prevented from attending Keio University. Their future baseball careers were now tied to Shoriki's proposed professional baseball league.

After lunch the American players said good-bye to their wives, who would remain in Tokyo with Connie Mack and most of the nonplaying members of the party, and rendezvoused with the Japanese team at Ueno Station, a large, modern depot in the northeast section of the city adjacent to Ueno Park, famous for its cherry blossoms and national museums.

The train was packed. Travelers filled every seat and the aisles. Harold "Rabbit" Warstler wrote in his diary that he could barely wade through the second-class cars because of the bundles and slippers littering the aisles. Luckily, the ballplayers traveled in special first-class cars with private two-person rooms. They were served steaks for dinner, and each player had a sleeper berth, albeit a small one, for the night. The rooms were tight. The washstand folded out of the wall, and there was only enough room for one player to dress at a time. The other needed to lay on his bed to make room for the dresser. The five-foot-seven Warstler did not mention the length of the bunks, but they posed a difficulty for the taller players. Writer Fred Lieb had warned the All Americans that the berths were constructed for the average Japanese, not six-foot American ballplayers. During the 1931 tour Lefty Grove "had to sleep with half his long legs dangling outside while George Kelly, even taller than Grove, tangled himself into a pretzel."[3]

The express train steamed to the northeast, soon entering the six rural prefectures known together as the Tohoku district. Despite the area's cold climate and poor soil, the district produced much of the country's agricultural products. Farming in the area was hard work, with little economic reward. Half of Japan's rice farmers cultivated less than one-and-a-quarter acres, and only 7 percent owned more than five acres. Farmers terraced rice paddies throughout the region's numerous hills and mountains. The poor volcanic soil required the heavy use of labor-intensive and often expensive fertilizers that were constantly leached away by the area's heavy rains.

In good years most farmers eked out a living, but a series of poor crops along with the global economic depression had reduced many to starvation. The 1934 crop was the smallest in thirty years—production had plummeted by 40 percent. As the crop yield fell, the price of rice rose. Farmers faced with high costs of fertilizer and high taxes were forced to sell their entire crop to urban centers and eat less nourishing barley imported from Korea supplemented by barnyard fodder and roots. Malnutrition rose. On November 1, the day before the All Americans arrived in Japan, Iwate Prefecture on the northeast coast announced that more than thirty-five thousand infants were on the brink of starvation due to the undernutrition of their mothers. Many farmers owed years of back taxes and had run up debts exceeding several years of gross income. It would take years of exceptional crops to pay off these debts. To save their families thousands of farmers sold their daughters into prostitution. High school girls brought 400 yen ($132) each, nearly the annual average income for a family farm. Even eleven-year-olds were sold, bringing in just 100 yen ($33). Some villages of Tohoku contained no unmarried women between fifteen and twenty-five. They had all been sold. The national government did little to help. Many urban Japanese were outraged and organized relief groups and charities, but the famine was too widespread. Young men fled the region. Unable to find work in urban areas, they joined the ever-swelling ranks of Japan's Imperial Army—one of the few institutions with money, as it sucked up about half of the country's annual budget.[4]

The train came to a halt at 6:20 the next morning in the town of Aomori, near the northern tip of Honshu. They had run out of track. The passengers gathered their belongings and transferred to a ferry to cross the Tsugaru Strait to the island of Hokkaido. In a private room the players were served breakfast during the crossing, but few could eat much. The ferry tossed and rolled as it pushed through high winds, driving rain, and rolling waves. Just before noon they docked at Hakodate, the largest city in Hokkaido, with a population of nearly two hundred thousand.

As they steamed into port passengers watched the smoke rise from Mount Esan, an active volcano about thirty miles east of the city. The players were unable to take photographs, however. When they had boarded the ferry, officials handed each traveler a small map of the straits with three coastal areas circled in red. Large cursive writing proclaimed "Photographing, sketching, surveying, recording, flying over the fortified zone, without the authorization of the commanding officer of this fortress are strictly prohibited by order. The War Office."[5] The handout was no mere threat. Japan was paranoid about espionage, and officials even inspected Ruth during the trip to make sure that he was not taking photographs.[6] But neither the proscription nor the officials stopped Moe Berg. Defying the warning, Berg whipped out his camera and filmed the area. At the time nobody noticed.

By the time the ferry docked the cold rain had slackened, but the 1:30 start time for Game 3 of the series looked doubtful. Fearing that they might lose their chance to see the Major Leaguers, local fans began arriving at the stadium with pieces of canvas—many measuring just a few square feet—and placed them over the dirt infield. Others carried wood from their homes to secure the canvas from the wind. With hundreds of fans helping, they soon had the field covered.[7]

Ruth, as manager of the All Americans, wanted to play as scheduled. They were on a tight schedule, he argued, and he needed to be back in Tokyo on Friday, the ninth, for an international radio broadcast on NBC. He had signed a contract with the King Freedom Syndicate to give updates from Japan and would not miss the date. The All Nippon team, however, favored postponing the game. The temperature was just above freezing, making the rain icy, just the type that leads to sickness and, a decade before the mass production of penicillin, could easily lead to a debilitating illness. Suzuki tried to convince Ruth to accept the Japanese's decision, but the Babe remained stubborn. Becoming angry, the Babe stated that he would return to Tokyo for his interview even if it meant missing the next game in Sendai. Suzuki decided to telephone Mack in Tokyo. After a brief discussion Mack promised to take care of the situation. A telegram for Ruth arrived soon after. Exactly what Mack told Ruth is unknown, but the Babe agreed to not only postpone the game but also remain with the team for the remainder of the northern excursion.

With the day free the players split up. Some explored the town. Although not the capital of Hokkaido, Hakodate was the prefecture's most important city. Its great port contained one of Japan's largest fishing fleets, as the surrounding waters teemed with salmon, herring, trout, and cod. A hundred million yen worth of fish went through the port each year. Rabbit Warstler probably supped at one of the city's many seafood restaurants, as he noted in his diary that his dinner was the best meal he had in Japan. Considering the banquets the players attended, it must have been a fine meal.

The port was also the conduit for much of Hokkaido's raw materials to the industrial centers on Honshu. Most of Hokkaido's 30,089 square miles remained undeveloped. Mountainous and covered in forests, the prefecture exported timber and minerals to the main island. These undeveloped regions were also the last refuge of the Ainu—Japan's indigenous population. Physically and culturally different from the Honshu Japanese, the Ainu are believed to have first settled Japan in the Jomon period, roughly sixteen thousand years ago. They produced some of the first pottery and ground-stone tools in the world before the ancestors of the modern Japanese invaded and conquered the southern portion of the islands around 500 BC. Portions of the original Ainu population intermarried with the invaders, but others fled north, eventually settling in Hokkaido, where they maintain a distinct culture to this day.

To the American ballplayers Hakodate felt like a frontier town. Instead of the modern, spacious boulevards of Tokyo, many of Hakodate's roads were unpaved and had turned to mud in the heavy rain. There were few Western-style buildings and no Western-style hotels. Most structures were traditional two-story wooden homes with thatched or tiled peaked roofs. If the players had looked closely, they would have noticed that most of these houses were new. About eight months earlier on a cold March night, gale-force winds had ripped an iron chimney from the roof of a public bathhouse. Flames from the stove leaped up toward the hole in the roof, igniting the ceiling. The fire jumped from the bathhouse to the thatched roofs of the closely packed neighboring homes. Pushed by the strong winds, the inferno drove through the city, destroying thirty thousand of Hakodate's forty thousand structures. The inhabitants ran before the fire to the port. Trapped, many threw themselves into the harbor, despite the storm waves. Firefighters could do nothing until the gale subsided twelve and a half hours later. At that point, the fire had already consumed most of the combustible material. Sleet, turning to snow, began falling the next morning, as nearly one hundred thousand homeless looked for shelter in the ruins. At the docks bodies of the drowned came in on the morning tide. Nearly fifteen hundred died that night. Another twenty-five hundred were seriously injured. It was the worst fire in Japan since the Great Kanto Earthquake in 1923 and still ranks as one of the most devastating fires in history.[8]

Most of the ballplayers sampled the town's famous *onsen*—baths drawing their water from the volcanic hot springs. Following custom, the players washed with soap prior to entering a communal tub, where they soaked in the steaming waters. The *onsen*, however, were not a huge success among the Americans. Most found the water too hot and quickly retreated from the tub.[9]

Some of the players may have been looking forward to this northern excursion as a chance to escape the supervision of their wives, Connie Mack, and the ever-present Tokyo press. Japan had a reputation for its nocturnal delights. Uninhibited by Christian-based taboos against sex, throughout Japan prostitution was legal and considered a normal aspect of society. Prior to the Great Depression, legalized brothels entertained approximately four million customers and brought in twenty million yen per year. Although the Depression had curtailed the pleasure industry, causing more than 600 brothels to close since 1929, there were still approximately 10,500 licensed brothels in Japan. An additional quarter-million women plied their trade outside of the licensed quarters, causing the government to require waitresses at resorts to undergo the same annual physicals as licensed prostitutes.[10]

O'Doul may have told the team about the distractions enjoyed by the 1931 squad during their trip north. The details were not recorded, but Fujio Naoki, writing for *Yakyukai*, noted that the players in '31 had fun with the girls and that the Americans were "not focused" during the games in Matsumoto and Sendai. Berg had also enjoyed the companionship of a Japanese professional during his 1932 visit. Movies, taken with his famous Bell & Howell camera, survive showing the future spy and pitcher Ted Lyons kissing and fondling a pair of kimono-clad young women. If some of the players misbehaved during the night Babe Ruth was left in charge, they did it discreetly, as Naoki assured his readers that unlike the '31 team, these All Americans were well behaved. Yet some of the players became more intimate with Japanese women than they desired.

It had been a tiring day, waking at six to transfer from the train to the ferry, the rough ride across the Tsugaru Strait, and the afternoon in the cold rain. Earl Averill was exhausted. He had tried a Japanese bath in the *onsen* but found the geyser-fed water too hot. The hotel was not what he had expected, even though he had been warned. With no Western-style hotels in town, the team stayed at a traditional Japanese *ryokan* called the Fukuikan. It was a typical wooden inn with large common rooms on the first floor and sleeping rooms on the second. Many of the interior walls were sliding paper doors, enabling the innkeepers to divide the space to suit their guests' needs. There were no Western tables, chairs, or beds. The players ate sitting on the floor, slept on futons placed directly on the tatami floors, and used a communal toilet and bath.

After dinner Averill trudged into his room, ready for sleep. The maid, the innkeeper's daughter, followed him. As he turned to face her she reached out and tried to unbutton his overcoat. Startled, the burly slugger, who Stuart Bell noted "hasn't the reputation of being exactly a shrinking violet with women, . . . brushed her hands aside." The young maid persisted, and eventually Averill "succumbed out of weariness." "The young lady took off his coat, his shoes and his socks and put them carefully aside," Bell writes. "Whether she took off his vest, Mr. Averill did not say. No doubt, he was too embarrassed to remember. The last thing he remembered was the young lady handing him his pajamas and standing discreetly aside while he donned them and got on to the thick mattress on the floor. Then the young lady placed two mattresses [quilts] on top of him to keep him warm, blew out the candle and left him to the lord only knows what kind of sleep." When morning came, she returned, raised the shades, and assisted with dressing. At breakfast Averill discovered that the other players had similar experiences.[11]

Japanese attitudes toward nakedness and personal privacy in the 1930s differed from those of Americans. Until the 1870s Japanese men, women, and children commonly bathed together in public baths. During the hot summer months, workmen would often strip to loincloths, while rural women would go topless. The naked body held little sexual intrigue. Indeed, mid-nineteenth-century Japanese pornography shows women mostly clad—not out of prudishness but because the fine clothing added some mystery.

Attitudes changed as Westerners settled in Japan. In the midst of the Victorian era, when even references to sexuality were taboo in polite society and a woman's bare ankle was titillating, many Westerners found the Japanese practices barbaric and immoral. Sensitive to criticism and wanting to be considered a modern nation, in 1872 the Japanese government banned public nudity, including partial nudity, urinating in public, and mixed-sex bathing in Tokyo. At first bathhouse owners complied solely with the letter of the law by stretching a string across the baths to create separate sections, causing the government to eventually require a solid barrier. Despite the ban the practice still continued in areas inhabited only by Japanese. By the 1930s mixed public baths were rare in Tokyo and other cities but still existed in rural areas. Many *onsen* continued to be coed. Those that separated the sexes often did so with a flimsy cloth, or a wall that blocked the view above the water, but not below. Virginia Cowles, an American who traveled throughout Japan in October 1934, told *Washington Herald* readers that during her visit to an *onsen*, a boy saw to the needs of both the female and the male bathers. Overcome by modesty, Cowles complained to her Japanese friend, but the woman assured her not to be embarrassed, as "nakedness means nothing to the Japanese mind."[12]

Back in Tokyo Stuart Bell found that the concept of privacy in restrooms was also not culturally shared. While dining at the opulent Maple Club in Tokyo, Bell excused himself to go to the men's room. To his surprise several young women clad in kimonos entered soon after and approached him, holding baseballs and menus. With bows and "smiling graciously . . . in an entirely innocent manner," they asked for his autograph. Red-faced, he "wrote the best signature I could under the circumstances."[13]

Thursday, November 8, was the first day of winter, and true to form the temperature had plummeted to just below freezing when the All Americans awoke. As soon as they left their snug futons they felt frozen. The inn, like most traditional Japanese houses, lacked heat. Inhabitants stayed warm by wearing layers and gathering around small tables placed above charcoal burners known as *kotatsu*.

They breakfasted on beer, sake, oatmeal, ham, eggs, toast, rice, goat milk, coffee, tea, and cocoa before readying themselves for the 1:00 p.m. game. Despite the cold all eight thousand seats of tiny Yunokawa Stadium were full when the players arrived for practice. The fans were unlikely to miss the game, as they paid the exorbitant price of two yen for an outfield seat or three yen to sit in the infield. Snow dotted the outfield, and both fans and players alike needed to pound their feet to keep the blood flowing to their frozen toes. Soon officials set up charcoal burners in the dugouts to help warm the players. Like most fields in Japan the infield was all dirt and still soft from the rain.[14]

The All Americans took control of the game minutes after the first pitch. With two outs, Ruth on third, Gehrig on second, and Foxx on first, Earl Averill hit a grand slam over the right-field bleachers to give the visitors a 4–0 lead. Just as it looked as if the Major Leaguers would rout the Japanese, pitcher Kenichi Aoshiba settled down and shut out the Americans for the next four innings. A line drive up the middle by Ruth plated McNair in the sixth inning for the Americans' fifth run, but Aoshiba continued to pitch well. By the end of the contest, the young Japanese gave up just six hits, walked three, and struck out four, including Ruth. But the five runs were more than enough for the Americans to win the game. Lefty Gomez, coming off his best season in 1934, dazzled the fans and opponents with both his speed and his control. He would have held the All Nippons scoreless had not Ruth, playing first base, blown an easy double play with a wild throw to second. Up 5–1, manager Ruth brought in third baseman Jimmie Foxx to close out the game. Once again Foxx had struggled at the plate, going one for three with a walk and a strikeout. He was now hitting just .182 since coming to Japan, and his three strikeouts led the team—nobody else even had two. As a pitcher, however, Foxx did well, preserving the victory by allowing just one run in the final three innings.

The game took an hour and twenty-five minutes, giving the players enough time to return to the hotel, change, and catch the 5:30 ferry back to the main island of Honshu. After another rough crossing and a special dinner for those with weak stomachs, the players arrived in Sendai, a city of 190,000 on Honshu's east coast. They spent the night at the Sakaiya Ryokan, a two-story traditional wooden house, tightly wedged between the neighboring homes.

The All Americans spent the morning of November 9 wandering about town and lunching with some of the city's sixty American residents before heading to Yagiyama Ball Field. Compared to the tiny park at Hakodate, Yagiyama Ball Field was cavernous, holding twenty thousand spectators and outfield walls more than four hundred feet from home plate. Despite the size of the park, fans in the center-field bleachers, remembering what happened during the 1931 tour, brought their ball gloves.

When the Americans arrived three years earlier on November 10, gale-force winds blew steadily all day. Nevertheless, the game went on as scheduled. Fred Lieb noted in *Baseball as I Knew It*, "In all my years of attending ball games I have never seen a game attempted under such conditions." The Americans jumped all over the Japanese pitcher and led 8–0 when catcher Mickey Cochrane came to the plate in the third inning. Cochrane pounded a line drive up the middle that kept going until it rocketed into the center-field stands. According to Lieb, "Ordinarily it would take a cannon to hit a home run into this bleacher, an estimated 450 feet away, and a monstrous swat against a gale. Since I could follow the flight of the ball all the way, I would think any bleacherite could have done so also and ducked or scrambled aside when he saw the ball headed in his direction. But this unwary fan was hit right in the mouth; his lips were bloodied and three teeth were knocked out." After a brief pause the game continued. Twenty minutes later a small ambulance drove onto the field, parking behind home plate. A doctor and two nurses emerged and, seemingly unconcerned that they were interrupting a ball game, "marched single file across the entire field from home plate to pitcher's box, second base, and out to the distant bleacher," only to find that the injured fan had already been removed to the stadium office and had received treatment. "The man who tried to catch the ball with his mouth received 100 yen [$33—nearly a month's wages] from the management and apparently felt that he had put in a good day."[15]

With their gloves to protect them from home runs, more than twenty thousand fans squeezed into Yagiyama Ball Field to watch the All Americans at 1:00 p.m. At the time it was the largest crowd to watch a sporting event in Sendai. The mitts came in handy, as the Americans belted five home runs. No injuries were reported.

Kaichi Takeda, a veteran pitcher for Nagoya Railways but not one of Japan's top hurlers, threw a complete game and surrendered just eight hits, but five of them left the park. Through the first three games Ruth had hit Japanese pitching well, batting .300, but had disappointed his hosts by not homering. At last, in the third inning, he pounded the ball over the right-field wall for his first home run on Japanese soil. In the next at bat the struggling Jimmie Foxx outdid the Babe by launching the ball over the distant outfield bleachers, completely out of the ballpark. Despite the mammoth blast Foxx still looked uncomfortable at the plate. He had picked up just three hits in fourteen at bats and had struck out four times. At least two of his hits were impressive home runs. In the eighth Ruth homered again.

On the other side of the diamond, All Nippon struggled against Earl Whitehill and later Clint Brown. The Japanese managed just four hits and struck out six times. American Jimmy Horio fared no better than his teammates, going 0-2. With his average at .125, Horio had to share playing time in center field with All Nippon's sole Korean member, Eibin Ri (Lee), who had attracted Ichioka's attention after hitting a mammoth home run off star pitcher Saburo Miyatake during Keio University's 1930 trip to Korea.

After the game, the players returned to the Sakaiya Ryokan, changed, dined, and boarded a sleeper train to Tokyo, eager to rejoin their wives, who were having their own adventures in the capital.

16

In Tokyo Connie Mack, Stuart Bell, and the nonplayers spent a quiet week visiting cultural sites and lounging around the team's hotel. The opulent Imperial Hotel designed by Frank Lloyd Wright to fit into the natural landscape nonetheless looked out of place in the neighborhood dominated by newer office buildings. Designed after a Mayan temple, and built with brick and shaped lava boulders, the hotel resembled an *H*, with a large lily-covered pool fronting the hotel's entrance.

After receiving the contract to build the hotel in 1916, Wright spent the next four years wrestling with the fundamental problem of how to build a Western-style hotel that would survive Japan's earthquakes on a land-filled swamp. Following his principle of unity between nature and structure, Wright decided to use the mud to his advantage by building a floating foundation. He reduced the superstructure's weight by building the walls with lightweight lava, and by using cantilevers and flexible joints, he designed the hotel to not fight an earthquake but to "sympathize with it and out-wit it." Wright even designed the large lily pool that stood before the hotel's entrance with Tokyo's earthquakes in mind. The pool was connected to the hotel's water supply and could be used if the city's supply was disrupted. Wright's design saved the building from destruction as well as the lives of hundreds of occupants during the Great Kanto Earthquake of 1923.[1] Since the earthquake the hotel had become the focal point for foreign residents.[2] Correspondents, diplomats, and businessmen met in its famous bar just off the main lobby and dined at the New Grill. It also became the favorite residence for visiting celebrities.

There was plenty to keep the rest of the travelers busy until the players returned. During their first free day most of the wives headed across the street to view the annual chrysanthemum show at Hibiya Park. Adopted as the crest of the Imperial family, the chrysanthemum, along with the cherry blossom, is one of the symbols of Japan. Hundreds of thousands came to view the flowers each November. The arrangements particularly impressed Julia Ruth, who remembered the exhibit seventy-five years later: "It was just breathtaking. They were so big and so beautiful." On subsequent days they visited the national museums at Ueno Park.

Stuart Bell disliked sightseeing. "What would I have done with the scenery?" he asked his readers. "I couldn't bring it back."[3] Unlike many of the other tourists who had used their free time to visit museums and nearby cultural sights, Bell decided not to stray far. Curiosity, however, did drive the close-minded sportswriter to visit Sengaku-ji temple, the resting place of the forty-seven *ronin*.

The tale of the forty-seven *ronin*, known as the Chushingura, is perhaps the most famous of all Japanese legends. Most Japanese of the 1930s would agree with the modern scholar who concluded, "If you study Chushingura long enough, you will understand everything about the Japanese."[4] The story, although often heavily embellished and romanticized, derives from a true tale.

In 1701 the Tokugawa shogunate ordered Yoshinaka Kira, a high-ranking official, to instruct two country daimyo, Muratoyo Date and Naganori Asano, on court etiquette. Animosity between the urban instructor and the rural lords ensued, perhaps because the two students had not offered adequate gifts to Kira in return for the instruction. Date's retainers, realizing the mistake, sent Kira a large sum of money, but the teacher received nothing further from Asano. Kira took revenge on Asano by insulting and humiliating him in public. At first, Asano bore the insults with dignity, but eventually tempers flared and Asano drew his sword in anger in Edo castle and attacked Kira. Kira escaped with a minor wound, but by drawing his sword within the shogun's castle, Asano had committed a capital offense. The shogun ordered Asano to commit seppuku, ritual suicide by slitting one's belly, and confiscated his lands.

Forty-seven of Asano's retainers seethed with anger at their lord's punishment and Kira's behavior. After burying their lord at Sengaku-ji, they vowed to take revenge. But Kira, foreseeing this possibility, surrounded himself with guards and sent spies to watch them. Asano's retainers, now masterless samurai known as *ronin*, formed a pact. They would disperse and create new lives for themselves until Kira lowered his guard. To confuse Kira's spies, the *ronin* began to drink heavily, frequent prostitutes, and engage in other improper behavior. By all accounts Asano's retainers had become a pitiful, dishonorable rabble. After two years Kira no longer feared retaliation. Now, the forty-seven *ronin* were ready. On December 14, 1702, they regrouped in Edo, attacked Kira's fortified home, beheaded him, and laid the head at the foot of their lord's grave at Sengaku-ji. Their duty complete, the *ronin* surrendered to shogunate officials.

The ronin had committed murder and by law would be put to death, but the public and the shogunate respected their loyalty to their master and conceded that the motive for the crime had been pure. Therefore, the shogun ordered that they could achieve honorable deaths by committing seppuku rather than being executed as common criminals. On February 4, 1703, forty-six of the forty-seven (one disappeared) took their own lives through the painful ritual of seppuku and were interred beside their lord at Sengaku-ji temple.

To reach the famous temple Bell, probably accompanied by other members of the group, traveled roughly four miles south of the Imperial Hotel. After climbing a small hill they entered Sengaku-ji through a two-story, double-roofed wooden gate, or *nijumon*, a sign of the Buddhist temple's importance. Bell probably continued straight though the small courtyard to the temple's main hall, a wooden building with a graceful hipped roof covered in blue-green tiles, but the main attraction was off to the left. There a path led past a small garden, past the spring where the *ronin* washed Kira's head before laying it at Asano's grave, up a stone staircase, and through a second decorative gate to the cemetery. The cemetery itself was a walled rectangle, containing thirty-six three-foot-high stone markers along its perimeter and two rows of five markers in its center. Stone braziers holding burning incense stood at the foot of each marker. Bell found the cemetery packed with Japanese visitors, who came, in his words, "to see the names on the stone tablets, to smell the joss sticks which always burn and to live in their own hearts and minds the steadfastness of Japanese who hundreds of years before went to their death willingly because they loved their master before all."[5]

Like the tourists visiting the graves in 1934, most eighteenth-century Japanese praised the forty-seven *ronin* for their loyalty. The story became one of the most popular in Japan, retold in kabuki theaters and puppet shows, around hearths, and eventually on film. With the rise of nationalism in the late 1920s and 1930s, writers transformed the story into propaganda, emphasizing the *ronin*'s unquestioning loyalty and self-sacrifice for their superior. Even the culturally insensitive Bell noted, "It is a rugged lesson in discipline and fealty which would not be practiced today, except, perhaps by the Japanese."[6] Yet even right after the incident, some believed that the shogun's decision to grant the *ronin* honorable deaths after committing murder just because their motives were pure condoned vigilantism and set a dangerous precedent—one that would be used many times by right-wing extremists during the 1930s.

During the week in Tokyo Moe Berg's old friend Frank Matsumoto joined the group as a guide and translator. When Matsumoto was not leading tours or solving all the little problems only a native could negotiate, he helped Mack answer fan mail. Mack received stacks of letters each day from Japanese fans. Many just wished him and his team success, but others asked interesting questions or gave advice. One young boy reminded Mack that he was seventy-one years old and needed to "take precautions against colds and influenza," as "the Japanese people would deeply regret any indispositions that befell [him]." Matsumoto translated each letter for Mack and helped him respond. Like Ruth and the other ballplayers, Mack was overwhelmed by the reception the All Americans received. By corresponding with the fans he felt "very close to the Japanese people." Indeed, after spending a week in Japan, he identified with his hosts and told a reporter from the *Yomiuri Shimbun* that he now tried to think about why Japan left the League of Nations and the Manchurian problem from their perspective.[7]

The group did occasional walking tours of Tokyo, visiting cultural sites and major shopping spots. Eleanor Gehrig concluded that "walking down the Ginza was like walking down Broadway, with record shops blaring away but with no hookers." But she added, "We also walked past clusters of 'sex stores,' the kind that became fixtures much later in Times Square or in the center of many cities back home. All sorts of fancy ticklers, colorful gadgets, miraculous 'get strong' salves. We weren't too shocked by it all, but it did seem kind of funny parading through this section behind the tall, spare and absolutely dignified figure of Mr. Mack, who saw no evil, spoke no evil and heard no evil."[8]

The traffic in Tokyo amazed them. Everywhere they turned there were people. Bikes, some piled high with boxes or lunches to be delivered to hungry clients, darting in and out, taxis speeding with abandon, buses and trucks rumbling along, and throngs of pedestrians, the women with infants strapped to their backs—all on the wrong side of the street. The Japanese, like the British, drove on the left-hand side of the road. Although Edo-period travelers were required to keep to the left on Japan's highways, urban traffic remained chaotic and unregulated until streetcar lines were established in the late nineteenth century. As the British advised Japan's railroads, the streetcars naturally followed British traffic patterns. Over time other forms of transportation followed the streetcars, and in 1924 left-hand-side traffic became law.

Stuart Bell told readers of the *Cleveland Press*, "Somehow or other members of the All American baseball party have survived the flow of motorcars, bicycles, ox-carts, motorcycles and rickshaws that pass over Tokyo's well-paved streets from early morning to late at night. The bicycles are the hardest to duck because it outnumbers every other conveyance." "The cyclists are . . . positively artists on wheels," contemporary tourist Katharine Sansom recalled. "They take chances as mere mortals draw breath. . . . I can think of no more exhilarating site than the youth on wheels who carries lunches from the restaurant which he serves to its various customers; he bears on one upturned palm a castle of lunch boxes and rice bowls, tier upon tier, and steers with the other hand, threading in and out of the motor traffic, bent to an angle sideways as he swirls round a corner, pulling up as suddenly as an arrow that has found its target."[9]

"There are a lot of cars, mostly taxis," Stuart Bell noted, "and the drivers honk their horns incessantly. No sirens are permitted and all cars are equipped with the old-fashioned bulb horns which emit sounds like those you might hear from bullfrogs." The taxi drivers plowed down the streets with an aggressiveness that even frightened the New Yorkers in the group. Sansom advised travelers to offer taxi drivers "a good tip to go slowly."[10]

Tokyo traffic patterns became so bewildering for foreigners that the Japanese government produced a pamphlet titled *Rules of the Road in English* that listed the eight basic tenets of driving in Tokyo. Besides five mundane rules, such as drive on the left and stop at stop signs, readers learned, "When a passenger of the foot heave in sight, tootle the horn. Trumpet at him. Melodiously at first, but if he still obstacles your passage, tootle him with vigor, express by word of mouth the warning, Hi! Hi!" Foreigners also needed to know to "give big space to the festive dog that shall sport in the roadway" and to "avoid tanglement of dog with your wheel spokes"—sound advice for drivers everywhere.[11]

As the group traveled around Tokyo Mack noticed familiar faces. The same men were everywhere they went—in Ginza, at the museums, in the shrines, on the streets. They were being shadowed. Mack also believed that the All Americans' rooms at the Imperial Hotel were searched during their excursions. Unfamiliar with Japanese politics, Mack assumed they were government agents, perhaps secret police, assigned to keep tabs on the Americans, but there were other groups interested in the Americans' movements. In his *Unofficial History of Japanese Professional Baseball*, Sotaro Suzuki wrote that members of ultranationalist groups visited him during his stay at the Imperial Hotel to complain about the All Americans' presence and warn him that their visit could have serious consequences. All bluff, he thought at the time.[12]

17

As the All Americans were enjoying their first week in Japan, Suke-yasu Atsuta, Katsusuke Nagasaki, Raisuke Kudo, and other members of the War Gods Society (Bushinkai) met at their dojo to put the final touches on the first issue of their newsletter, *Kyoka*. The word *kyoka* means "moral suasion," and it was often used to refer to propaganda upholding Japanese nationalism. It was a common term bandied around by ultranationalist groups such as the War Gods Society.

In an editorial Atsuta explained to readers that the War Gods Society published *Kyoka* to caution people who behaved selfishly as Japan faced international and domestic crises and to remind people not to pursue their own peaceful life influenced by individualism or liberalism in a time of emergency. The newsletter, he wrote, was intended to (1) enhance the Japanese mentality; (2) strengthen and cultivate the spirit of high integrity, loyalty, and reverence; (3) rebuild the nation through patriotism; (4) help shed sources of disease that could waste away the Japanese spirit; and (5) correct mistaken theories with strong logic.[1]

Most of the first issue of *Kyoka* focused on a pamphlet issued by the War Ministry in October 1934 titled *Principles of National Defense and Proposals for Strengthening It*. The tract, possibly written or at least directed by Gen. Sadao Araki, leader of the Imperial Way faction in the army, set forth the ideas of Ikki Kita. Japan, it argued, was facing both internal and external crises. Economic inequalities at home were weakening Japan's ability to defend its interests. To make Japan stronger economic and moral reforms were needed to limit the power of big business and bring prosperity to rural areas. The publication of such ideas from a government agency caused an uproar within Japan's financial and politically moderate communities.

Ten of *Kyoka*'s twenty-one articles focused on the pamphlet, while another four discussed Japan's socioeconomic crisis. By lifting articles from other sources the newsletter presented both sides of the debate, even through the editorials made it clear that the War Gods supported both the publication of the pamphlet and its message. All in all the first issue of *Kyoka* gave the impression that the War Gods Society was a legitimate, although ultraconservative, political organization. That, of course, was a deception.

Of the 160 ultranationalist groups listed in the Home Ministry's 1934 annual report, *Conditions for Social Action*, only a handful were legitimate political groups, and even these often relied on violence, intimidation, and blackmail to achieve their goals. The Dark Ocean Society (Genyosha), for example, advocated military expansion on the Asian continent and employed spies and assassins to achieve their goals. Formed in 1881 on the south island of Kyushu, the society's future leader Mitsuru Toyama fought against the newly formed Meiji government in the failed 1877 Satsuma Rebellion (the revolt that inspired the historically inaccurate Tom Cruise movie *The Last Samurai*). Unwilling to back the pro-Western central government, Toyama recruited other disenfranchised southern samurai and created the Dark Ocean Society to "revere the Imperial house, respect the Empire and protect the rights of the people." The society's name, however, declared its true mission. *Dark Ocean* referred to the Genkainada Strait that separates Japan and Korea, a barrier that Toyama believed needed to be crossed. Over the next several decades the Dark Ocean Society used violence and blackmail to encourage politicians to support their expansionist goals. Members attempted to blow up liberal prime minister and Waseda University founder Shigenobu Okuma (the assassin failed to kill Okuma but did take off his leg), probably arranged the assassination of Queen Min of Korea in 1895, and created an espionage ring in China to further Japan's interests.

The Black Dragon Society, the most famous of all the ultranationalist groups, split off from the Dark Ocean Society in 1901. The group's infamous name is actually a mistranslation. Kokuryûkai, the group's Japanese name, is better translated as the Amur River Society, as the society named itself after the river that separates Russia from China. The society's goal was to drive the Russians out of China, thus opening the area for Japanese expansion. Although closely tied to Mitsuru Toyama and the Dark Ocean Society, the Black Dragon Society tried to remove itself from the criminal elements prevalent in the parent organization. Its membership included high-ranking military officers, members of the Imperial Diet, and even Koki Hirota, the foreign minister who gave the welcoming speech to the All Americans at Hibiya Park. Despite its lofty ideals the Black Dragon Society soon became linked to organized crime and just like the Dark Ocean Society used espionage, intimidation, and blackmail to further its political goals.

Most of the groups listed in the *Conditions for Social Action*, however, did not have pure political goals. Instead, in the words of Hugh Byas, the *New York Times* Tokyo correspondent during the 1930s, they were "a mixture of ward politicians, poolroom loafers, gang leaders, and racketeers." These societies usually consisted of a boss, often with minor political connections, and a handful of *soshi*—a term that once meant "stout fellow" but by the 1930s was synonymous with "thug." To create a mask of legitimacy, most societies had an official headquarters and a lofty-sounding patriotic name. Yet a brief investigation by Byas found that the headquarters were often just the home of a member, an empty office in a cheap rental building, or a dingy hotel room, while many of the "high-sounding titles were but the trade names of enterprising rascals who lived by soliciting contributions and got them from people who would rather part with money than be haunted by bullies."[2]

The nationalist politics of these societies protected them from prosecution. At the time when socialist groups were hunted down by police and incarcerated, violent nationalist groups not only were tolerated but often had ties to local police. "Patriots" arrested for violent crimes, including assassination of elected officials, were often given short jail sentences once they explained that their actions stemmed from the love of country and emperor. Following the precedent of the forty-seven *ronin*, the perpetrators were often lionized if their motives were considered pure. American sociologist and Japan expert Harry Emerson Wildes wrote in 1934:

The most surprising latitude is granted to the reactionary ronin. He may, in the name of patriotism, commit almost any outrage with impunity. He stalks into an office to demand financial contribution, publicly threatening blackmail if payment is not made. He rushes, with drawn sword, into the largest Tokyo hotel and orders a fashionable crowd to disburse at once. He hurls live snakes at a famous actor and throws an audience into a panic. . . . He murders politicians of whose policies he disapproves. In none of these cases . . . was punishment severe. Three months' imprisonment, a reprimand, or absolute acquittal rewarded the hoodlums guilty of the acts. For, in each case, the violence was deemed directed toward a worthy end. The patriot to resorts to force to keep the status quo . . . is a public hero.[3]

Like most of the smaller ultranationalist groups, the War Gods Society was really a band of gangsters hiding behind a right-wing political agenda. Their leader, Sukeyasu Atsuta, was employed by the conservative *Tokyo Nichi Nichi* newspaper. He began by managing a distribution location in 1924 before becoming the supervisor of a special unit to expand the subscriptions, probably through intimidation and extortion. Atsuta also became a bodyguard and enforcer for *Nichi Nichi*. On July 31, 1927, Atsuta formed the War Gods Society. The dozen or so members met in a dojo in the working-class neighborhood of Okachimachi, Shitaya-ku, not far from Ueno Station. There they offered classes in kendo and judo, gave public lectures on various nationalist topics, and planned their crimes.[4]

Katsusuke Nagasaki was the group's leading enforcer. He did not look like a gangster. Although tall, he was neither burly nor tough looking. He had an intelligent, pleasant long face with a high forehead and neatly trimmed, thin mustache. He would have blended into any group of Japanese businessmen. Born about 1905 and raised in Kumamoto City on the southern island of Kyushu, in the spring of 1929 Nagasaki moved to Tokyo and joined the Metropolitan Police Force. He served as a foot patrolman in the Oji section of Tokyo from April 22 to August 29, 1929, before resigning due to poor health. Soon after he joined the War Gods. Officially, Nagasaki served as the group's youth manager and martial arts instructor. He was an expert at judo, reaching the rank of Fourth Dan, and was also an accomplished swordsman. His main job, however, was to threaten, extort, and punish rival newspapers. For this he became known as Shimbun Goro (newspaper thug). From 1930 to 1934 the police arrested Nagasaki several times—once for throwing sand in the presses of the *Asahi Shimbun* and threatening an executive—but he served little or no jail time.

With the newsletter nearly finished, Atsuta briefed the society on another problem. On November 4 he had met with his old friend and employer Yasuichi Marunaka, the sales manager at *Nichi Nichi*. Subscriptions at *Nichi Nichi* had fallen since the *Yomiuri Shimbun* had gained in popularity. Shoriki's latest stunt of bringing over the American ballplayers was sure to increase sales at *Nichi Nichi*'s expense. The paper was in crisis. Marunaka, an ultraconservative and supporter of the Showa Restoration, had asked Atsuta to disrupt *Yomiuri*'s progress, perhaps by damaging the presses as the War Gods had done to the *Asahi Shimbun* in 1932.

The society discussed the problem. Just damaging the presses would not be enough, Toshio Fukuroi, the group's secretary, concluded. Shoriki had enough capital to rebuild quickly. No, Shoriki was the problem. He ran the newspaper like a dictator, controlling all aspects of the business. Without him, the paper would collapse. Shoriki had to be the target. But not now. With the American ballplayers in the country the international press coverage was too great. Carrying out the attack would be difficult, plus a disruption of the baseball tour might lead to a close investigation that would endanger both the society and *Nichi Nichi*. They agreed to wait.

18

The All Americans returned to Tokyo on the 6:00 a.m. Saturday, November 10, train, bursting with enthusiasm for Japan. Cars met them at Ueno Station and, after a brief stop at the hotel, drove the team to the JOAK radio station for a live broadcast to the United States and Japan. Connie Mack began the speeches. "Hello, Philadelphia, Los Angeles. I never expected to have the pleasure of talking to the baseball fans of America from Japan."

Ruth spoke next:

Hello, folks. When I say good evening to you, this is morning in Japan. But let me tell you, friends, the time in Japan and America may be different by 24 hours [*sic*], but fair play and sportsmanship are no different. They are just the same as I find back home. The Japanese fans here are a serious lot. I was surprised by their attitude. They actually respect the umpires! That's one thing I don't find back home. You know what the fans here do, folks? They actually yell at their own pitchers to let us big leaguers hit home runs! The players here have all good form and they play for all what they are worth. They have plenty of courage too. They have as much enthusiasm for baseball as have our own big leaguers.[1]

He went on to gush about the fans' enthusiasm for the game, told listeners about the parade through Ginza and how fans in Chiba broke a fence at Yazu Stadium to get closer to watch a practice, and ended by telling Americans that they should visit Japan themselves.[2]

The Babe then introduced his teammates, who each delivered a short speech as Sotaro Suzuki translated for the Japanese listeners. Umpire John Quinn told the audience, "Hello to my American friends. Japan is one great country and talk about orderly people and respect for an umpire, these Japanese boys take their hats off and bow to the umpire. Did you hear that? Bow to the umpire! These Japanese youngsters, who want to be the future Gehrigs, Foxxes, Gehringers, and Ruths are playing the game hard. They love to play but they play it with the seriousness of a professor."[3]

Moe Berg touched on the more serious side of the visit: "It would be a revelation to you folks back home to see what a marvelous influence a representative All American ball team can have in cementing and furthering the good relations and overthrowing the barriers of race, language, politics and customs of our widely separated nations. . . . I hope an innocent adventure like ours will turn out to be a scoop of diplomacy without portfolio."[4]

Nearly all the players spoke about how well they were treated, the Japanese enthusiasm for baseball, and how the Japanese players were improving. Lou Gehrig noted, "I wouldn't be a bit surprised if our chief rivals in baseball would be the Japanese," and O'Doul added, "Before many years the World Series may be played across the Pacific Ocean."[5]

The English-language *Japan Times* summed up the prevailing message: "Their reception by the public in Japan has been almost unbelievable in its enthusiasm and . . . their present trip is the grandest event of their baseball careers."[6] Broadcast across the United States on NBC Radio on Friday night, just after dinnertime, millions heard the show. In contrast with newspaper headlines that depicted Japan as a belligerent nation, determined to strengthen its navy at the expense of world peace, the players portrayed the Japanese as gracious, friendly hosts who shared a love for the national pastime. It may have been the best publicity Japan had received in decades.

Later that morning, Billy Amos sat in the lobby of the Imperial Hotel. The thirteen-year-old student at the American School stared at the room's intricate brick and carved stone walls. He was bored. His father had asked him to wait while he met with one of the hotel guests. Billy looked around the lobby again, hoping to see his father return.

A tall, white-haired man in a dark suit with an old-fashioned starched white collar entered the hotel, soon after his father returned with another man. "Mr. Mack. Mr. Mack," the man called. Connie Mack approached. "Mr. Mack," said his father's friend, "I wish to introduce Mr. Harold Amos, and this is his son, Bill. Mr. Amos, meet Connie Mack."

After speaking briefly with the two men, Mack looked at the boy. "Billy, are you going to the game this afternoon?"

"No, sir. We weren't able to get tickets even a couple of months ago."

Mack gave Billy a thoughtful look and then asked his father, "Mr. Amos, will you leave Billy with us for the rest of the day? I think we can do something for him." The dad grinned and nodded.

Billy accompanied Mack to the dining room, where he was served lunch while Mack excused himself to make arrangements. After the meal Mack returned and told the lad to follow him. They went down a corridor, out the hotel's doors, straight into the back of a large limousine. Decades later Bill could recall what happened next: "Almost at once a huge and excitingly familiar figure wearing a gold cap and wrapped in a tan polo coat emerged from the hotel and climbed into the car, crushing the seat beside me. Babe Ruth looked down at me and held out a powerful hand as his tanned, round face broke into a smile. After a numbing introduction from Connie Mack, Ruth rumbled, 'Hiya, kid. Let's show 'em how to do it.'"

The motorcade took off, carrying the team to Meiji Jingu Stadium. Fans lined the streets to glimpse Ruth and the other players. They clapped, cheered, and shouted, "Babe Rusu! Babe Rusu!" The Bambino waved back, and Mack leaned over to tell Billy to wave to the fans—at the moment they were cheering for him, too.[7]

When they reached the stadium, parked bicycles crowded the streets. Fans milled around the entrances, unable to enter. As Billy knew, the tickets had all been sold out for months. More than sixty thousand fans packed the stadium, more than the ballpark's official capacity. People stood in the aisles, behind the bleachers, in every conceivable space. A writer for the baseball magazine *Yakyukai* exclaimed, "The stadium was so full that there was no room for an ant." Mack escorted Billy to the best seat in the house—on the bench in the dugout. As he sat on the hard bench watching the players take batting practice, a cold November wind blew across the diamond. Not expecting to spend the day at the ballpark, Billy had not dressed warmly enough. He shivered. A large hand gripped his shoulder as a deep voice stated, "Billy, you're cold." The boy looked up into "one of the strongest, kindest faces" he had ever seen. Lou Gehrig took off his red-flannel warm-up jacket, draped it around Billy, and told him to "keep this during the game." The lad sat back and watched.[8]

In the center of the large field stood another boy, seventeen-year-old Eiji Sawamura. He could feel the 120,000 eyes trained on him. He pawed the pitcher's mound with his spikes. He had pitched in front of large crowds before. Just three months earlier he had led Kyoto Commercial High School to the summer championship tournament at Koshien Stadium. Tens of thousands had watched as he held Tottori First Middle School to just four hits in a losing cause. But that was different. Then he had been facing boys his own age. Now he would be pitching to grown men, who just happened to be the greatest players in the world. Yes, he admitted to himself, he was scared. But he also felt energy pulse through him in a way he had never felt before. He took a deep breath to steady himself and began to throw.[9]

Rabbit McNair and Charlie Gehringer went down easily. Next came Ruth. Sawamura swallowed hard and went to work. The count went full. Determined not to give in, Sawamura decided on an inside curve at the knees. It was his most effective pitch and also the Babe's known weakness. The Bambino, however, was ready. He swung his massive body around, meeting the ball squarely, and banged it into the right-field stands for the Americans' first run.

In the bottom half of the inning Lefty Gomez, the man who claimed to have invented a rotating goldfish bowl to allow tired fish to rest, took the mound for the All Americans. He had pitched eight innings in Hakodate just two days before, so he was not at full strength. Jimmie Foxx crouched behind the plate. Mack had announced that he would use Foxx as a backstop during the upcoming Major League season. Today's game was ideal for acclimating him to his new position. Mack knew that his team should beat the Japanese so Foxx could concentrate on his catching duties, but the packed stadium and rabid Japanese fans would provide enough tension to test his mettle.

Foxx would get a workout. The tired Gomez was wild, and "time and again, [Foxx] made brilliant stops of bounded drops to curb his pitcher's number of wild pitches."[10] Despite his fatigue, or maybe because of it, Gomez's curves bit sharply, diving out of the strike zone and mystifying the Japanese batters. Nothing seemed to break the Yankee hurler's rhythm. In the third inning play was halted when Princess Kitashirakawa, the granddaughter of Emperor Meiji, and her husband entered the royal box behind home plate. Both teams lined up before the box, doffed their caps, and bowed. When play continued Gomez set All Nippon down hitless for the third consecutive inning. An inning later he struck out two batters and threw strike three by the third batter when Foxx dropped the pitch. The ball scampered away, allowing the batter to reach first. Gomez bore down to strike out the next hitter, thus fanning four in the inning.

In the fifth a frustrated fan heaved an apple from the stands toward Gomez. The unflappable pitcher caught the projectile in his glove and in a single motion whipped it toward home plate. It landed in Foxx's glove with a thud and a splat, apple sauce exploding over the catcher. Unaffected by the only hint of hostility seen on the trip, Gomez retired the side. The Yankee's no-hitter continued into the eighth inning, when with one out Mamoru Sugitaya looped a single into right field. By the end of the ninth Gomez had struck out eighteen Japanese and surrendered just two singles.[11]

Sawamura fared less well. The All Americans belted out eleven hits, including home runs by Ruth, Averill, and Warstler, to score ten runs off the young pitcher. Nonetheless, the *Japan Times* noted, "The score hardly does justice to the credible pitching by a youngster named Sawamura, who possessed a fast ball and a sharp breaking hook. He pitched courageously to the murderers' row of the visiting ball squad. He struck out the Bambino, Lou Gehrig, this year's home run king, McNair and Warstler."[12]

The Japanese bore their fifth straight loss with dignity. Although they played their hearts out, they had not really expected to win. Instead, they viewed the series as a learning experience and the Major Leaguers as teachers. Nonetheless, Ichioka suggested that they mix the squads in Sunday's match.

Another sellout crowd watched Bing Miller's stars take on the

Advertising poster for the 1934 All American tour. Courtesy of the *Yomiuri Shimbun*.

(*above*) Tadao Ichioka and Herb Hunter. Author's collection.

(*opposite*) Lefty O'Doul during the 1931 tour of Japan. Author's collection.

Matsutaro Shoriki greets Babe Ruth and Lou Gehrig upon
their arrival in Japan. Courtesy of the *Yomiuri Shimbun*.

(*top*) Sotaro Suzuki and Connie Mack. Courtesy of Sotheby's, Inc. © 2007.

(*bottom*) Jimmy Horio. Courtesy of the *Hawaii Hochi*.

The welcoming parade through Ginza on November 2, 1934.
Courtesy of the *Yomiuri Shimbun*.

Babe Ruth waves Japanese and American flags during
the welcoming parade. Courtesy of the *Yomiuri Shimbun*.

(*above*) November 3 visit to the Meiji Shrine. The event would later be used to justify an attempted murder. Courtesy of the *Yomiuri Shimbun*.

(*opposite top*) Babe Ruth with the famous tempura chef Hige no Tempei and his assistant. Author's collection.

(*opposite bottom*) Matsutaro Shoriki, U.S. Ambassador Joseph Grew, Marquis Nobutsune Okuma, and Babe Ruth prior to the opening game. Courtesy of Yoko Suzuki.

野球王ベーブ・ルース氏と ヒゲノ天平

(*opposite*) Umpire John Quinn and players admire the souvenir pennants given to them prior to Game 1. John Quinn Collection.

(*below*) All Americans (*top row from left*) "Doc" Ebling, Earl Whitehill, Clint Brown, Eric McNair, Frank Hayes, Connie Mack, Babe Ruth, Bing Miller, Joe Cascarella, Lefty O'Doul, Lou Gehrig, and John Quinn; (*bottom row from left*) Earl Averill, Harold Warstler, Charlie Gehringer, Lefty Gomez, Jimmie Foxx, and Moe Berg. Courtesy of the *Yomiuri Shimbun*.

(*opposite top*) Kumeyasu Yajima bows to umpire John Quinn before entering the batter's box. John Quinn Collection.

(*opposite bottom*) Babe Ruth and Julia Ruth. Courtesy of Yoko Suzuki.

(*above*) Jimmie Foxx and Babe Ruth. Courtesy of Sotheby's, Inc. © 2007.

(*above*) Sotaro Suzuki, an unidentified All Nippon player, Lou Gehrig, Hisanori Karita, and Babe Ruth. Courtesy of Yoko Suzuki.

(*opposite top*) June O'Dea Gomez, Babe Ruth, and John Quinn enjoy sukiyaki. John Quinn Collection.

(*opposite bottom*) John Quinn enjoys a rickshaw ride. John Quinn Collection.

(*top*) Capt. Koji Muranaka.
Courtesy of *Mainichi Shimbun*.

(*bottom*) Lt. Asaichi Isobe.
Courtesy of *Mainichi Shimbun*.

Eiji Sawamura. Courtesy of Kobunsha Press.

The All Americans outside Nagoya Castle. Courtesy of Yoko Suzuki.

Visiting Nara. John Quinn Collection.

(*top*) Babe Ruth clowns with kids before a game. Courtesy of Yoko Suzuki.

(*bottom*) The All Americans survey the field at Kokura. John Quinn Collection.

(*above*) Babe Ruth plays while holding an umbrella in Kokura.
John Quinn Collection.

(*opposite top*) Victor Starffin. Author's collection.

(*opposite bottom*) Moe Berg holding his movie camera.
Courtesy of Special Collections of the Arthur W. Diamond
Law Library, Columbia University School of Law.

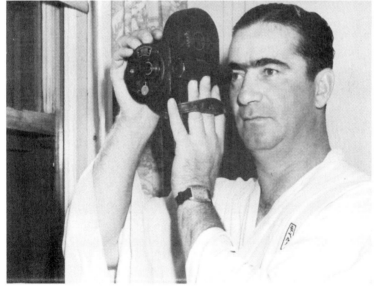

(*top*) Masao Date, All Nippon's top
pitcher. Author's collection.

(*bottom*) Osamu Mihara, star second
baseman for All Nippon.
Author's collection.

(*top*) Shigeo Mizuhara, star third baseman for All Nippon. Author's collection.

(*bottom*) Hisanori Karita, All Nippon's competitive shortstop. Author's collection.

(*left*) Toshiharu Inokawa, All Nippon's top hitter. Author's collection.

(*right*) Eiji Sawamura serving with the Thirty-Third Imperial Infantry Regiment. Courtesy of Kobunsha Press.

Ruth Team on the afternoon of November 11.[13] Six Americans and three Japanese played on each side, with the Ruth Team (Warstler, Hisanori Karita, Ruth, Foxx, Averill, Kumeyasu Yajima, Berg, pitcher Clint Brown, and Haruyasu Nakajima) batting first. Joe Cascarella took the mound for Miller's team (McNair, Isamu Fuma, Miller, Gehrig, Gehringer, Fujio Nagasawa, Jimmy Horio, Hayes, and Cascarella). Despite the intersquad teams, fans still watched a lopsided game, as Ruth's team crushed Cascarella with twenty-three hits and thirteen runs. The Bambino began the onslaught with a "tremendous wallop into the right field stands" in the first and to the fans' delight added a second homer in the sixth. After not hitting one out in the first three games, the Babe had hit five in the past three days. But he had to share the home run crown with Earl Averill, who also went deep against Cascarella. Foxx, who had seemed mystified by Japanese pitching, showed that he could still hit his fellow Major Leaguers, as he smashed three hits, including a homer and double. The Japanese also got into the act. All three starters on Ruth's team got hits, as did two of the three substitutes. Even the All Nippon members on Miller's team pulled their weight, as Fuma and Nagasawa picked up two of the team's six hits off underhanded hurler Clint Brown. Horio, however, went hitless again. He had played in all six games and led his team with fifteen at bats, but with one hit and a team-leading four strikeouts he was hitting just .067. The *Japan Times* did note that his fielding was outstanding, as he "pulled off one of the prettiest catches seen in weeks" when he ran down a line drive from Warstler in Saturday's game.[14]

Monday, November 12, was free, as would be Wednesday, the fourteenth. During these days the All Americans split up to shop, lounge around the hotel, or sightsee. Julia Ruth, either with her stepfather and mother or the handsome twenty-year-old catcher Frankie Hayes, visited Nikko—said by many to be the most beautiful historic site in Japan. They took an express train from Tokyo through the countryside northwest of the capital. Julia stared out the window as the train climbed through the mountains, noticing that nearly every plot of land was cultivated. Terraced rice paddies covered the hills. The crop had been harvested a month earlier, the long golden stalks cut down to a stubby grass. She spotted occasional farmers, wearing conical, wide-brimmed straw hats to shade their eyes. Some carried water buckets, one on each end of a long pole balanced across their shoulders. Their wives worked the fields beside them—not in kimonos, as they were reserved only for formal occasions and were beyond the means of many of these rural folk, but in heavy skirts with padded jackets and head scarves. Farmhouses dotted the hills. They were one-story wooden structures, containing just one or two rooms, and topped with steeply peaked thatched roofs. Their windows contained no glass but were open in warm weather and sealed with heavy sliding wood shutters when it turned cold. Julia saw no farm machinery—no tractors, threshers, harvesters, or items familiar to farmers of the American Midwest. The labor was done by hand with scythes and flails. She also saw no barns, oxen, horses, or cows. Few Japanese farmers had enough capital to own draft animals. Fields were plowed with wooden foot plows, the same tool that Japanese farmers had used for hundreds, if not thousands, of years. Milk was also not part of the Japanese diet. The average Japanese child in the 1930s had never tasted cows' milk, and it was not used in traditional baking.[15]

Three hours after leaving Tokyo, they arrived at Nikko, a complex of shrines and a temple that marked the burial place of the shogun Ieyasu Tokugawa. They began their tour with the magnificent Kegon Falls, where the Daiya River cascades more than three hundred feet into a misty pool. The long drop, twice the depth of Niagara Falls, causes the water to mist, creating an eerie yet beautiful scene. Its romantic beauty and depth made Kegon Falls a magnet for suicides. For safety the Japanese had installed an elevator so that tourists could view the falls from their base rather than their tempting heights.

From the falls Julia and her party motored past the sacred red-lacquered bridge that may be crossed only by the emperor or his emissaries and lunched at a nearby hotel before visiting the main shrine complex with its intricately carved and gilded buildings. Among the highlights was the stable containing a sacred horse, always saddled and ready in case Ieyasu's spirit wishes to ride forth from his resting place. Adorning the stable is a carving of the now famous three monkeys who helped popularize the Japanese saying "Speak no evil, hear no evil, and see no evil" in the West.

Moe Berg spent much of his free time visiting with Frank Matsumoto at Meiji University, where he addressed the student body. After thanking the institution for inviting him and sharing some stories about the All American players, Berg touched on the tour's important mission. "I believe that Emperor Meiji, for whom your great university was named, would have been happy to see foreign commerce and intercourse spread to the world of sports. . . . There is no greater leveler, no greater teacher of humility than competitive sports and I sincerely hope that our innocent junket through Japan will serve to bring the countries whom we represent unofficially closer together. There is no better place than the young heads of Meiji students to think out ways and means of keeping our two countries in unison, fast and binding."[16]

On Tuesday, November 13, the teams woke up early and traveled to Toyama—a small town on Japan's western coast, just under two hundred miles northwest of Tokyo. Temperatures dropped below freezing, and a light snow fell, frosting the infield. Just seventy-five thousand people lived in Toyama, but eighteen thousand of them came to the ballpark to watch one of the most popular players in Japan, former Keio star Shigeru Mizuhara, challenge the All Americans. Mizuhara could do it all. He was Japan's top defensive third baseman, one of the country's best hitters, and a star pitcher. He threw with an easy motion and sported a sneaking screwball and curve. *Yakyukai* called his play "glamorous," but his talent led to off-the-field trouble, as tabloids followed the young man's every move and spread unfounded rumors.

Mizuhara's pitching debut against the Major Leaguers did not last long. His troubles began with consecutive walks to Gehrig and Foxx to lead off the second inning. A double by Bing Miller, a rare hit from Moe Berg, a wild throw by Mizuhara's rival Osamu Mihara, a McNair walk, and a double by Gehringer plated five runs. With two on and one out, Ruth, the eighth batter in the inning, smashed a pitch on the outside corner over the right-field bleachers and into the lot beyond the stadium—his sixth home run in four days. Before the inning was over, the All Americans tacked on another to lead 9–0.

Daisuke Miyake, the All Nippon manager, had hoped to gain the advantage over left-handed starter Earl Whitehill by fielding an all right-handed lineup. The fiery Whitehill, however, was up for the challenge. In the opening game he had dominated the Tokyo Club with his fastball, but today he rarely reared back. Instead, he threw tantalizingly slow curves that broke sharply, baffling the Japanese batters. He would give up just three hits on the day, two of these slow rollers to the infield, and walk no one.

Miyake put Mizuhara back on the mound for the third inning. Whitehill led off and smacked Mizuhara's first pitch into the right-field stands for a home run. Surprisingly, Miyake allowed Mizuhara to remain in the game. The intense pitcher rewarded his manager by striking out McNair and retiring Gehringer and Ruth, but it would be his last inning. Now down 10–0, Miyake brought in the young Sawamura. Pitching with just two days of rest, he started wild, walking Gehrig and Averill, but strikeouts of Foxx and Whitehill limited the damage to just a run. Once the boy settled down he pitched well, shutting out the All Americans for three innings before giving up three runs on a Gehringer double and a Foxx home run in the eighth inning.

The game ended with an 14–0 All American victory, and the fans went home happy. The *Osaka Mainichi* summed it up best: "It is no longer a question of victory or defeat; the only concern of the baseball followers is how many home runs the renowned fence busters will make in the game. In that light the Toyama fans were not disappointed."[17]

There were no games for the next three days, but the All Americans had little free time, as they had to pose as diplomats. They attended a reception thrown by Ambassador Grew at the American Embassy. The ambassador invited two hundred for tea. The guest list included most of the city's prominent Americans, such as officers of the American Association, American Club, Columbia Society, and American Press Correspondents, as well as Japanese with cultural ties to the United States. These included officers of the America-Japan Society, dignitaries such as Marquis Okuma and the mayor of Tokyo, presidents of various Japanese sports associations, Matsutaro Shoriki, Sotaro Suzuki and a delegation from the *Yomiuri Shimbun*, and six friendly members of the Japanese press. Grew had also invited the entire All Nippon team, who, the ambassador pointedly noted in his diary, did not attend.

The party was a great success. Ruth, as always, dominated the room, telling stories to a scrum of admirers as he threw back cocktails and signed a continuous wave of baseballs. The Babe later told Grew that he signed four to five dozen balls each day in Japan, on top of other autograph requests. In a quieter corner Connie Mack held court with tales of bygone seasons and stars. The players remained at the reception until the last possible minute, enjoying a fine spread of American-style sandwiches, coffee, tea, hot chocolate, eight bottles of whiskey, and "several bowls of good strong punch."[18]

On the fourteenth at half past twelve the All Americans congregated in the Imperial Hotel's ballroom for a luncheon sponsored by the America-Japan Society. Japanese intellectuals founded the society in 1917 to maintain friendly relations amid growing hostility caused by the countries' conflicting interests in China. The group, which contained prominent Japanese and American businessmen, diplomats, and intellectuals, sponsored cultural and social events designed to foster a better understanding between the nations and maintain cross-cultural business relationships.

Ruth, Mack, Ambassador Grew, and the society's officers sat at the head table beneath large American and Japanese flags. The other players sat with the society's members at round tables. After lunch the society's president rose to speak. The seventy-one-year-old Iyesato Tokugawa was the adopted son and heir of Yoshinobu Tokugawa, the last shogun, and the ninth-generation direct descendant of Ieyasu Tokugawa, the shogun who united Japan in 1603. Chosen to succeed the abdicating shogun at the age of six, Iyesato had been educated in England and groomed to be a political leader and diplomat. In 1882 he was given the title "prince" and subsequently served as the president of the House of Peers (one of the two ruling bodies of Japan's parliament known as the Imperial Diet and similar to England's House of Lords) from 1901 to 1933. In 1921–22, Iyesato represented Japan at the Washington Naval Treaty and agreed to the infamous 5:5:3 ship ratio that limited the size of the Imperial Navy. His negotiations and his pro-Western attitudes so angered the right wing that Iyesato removed himself from politics and turned his attention to charitable causes, such as the Japanese Red Cross Society and the America-Japan Society.

Iyesato was also the president of the organizational committee for the 1940 Japan Olympics and a firm believer in the ability of sports to foster peaceful relations. Baseball, he proclaimed, was not only the American pastime but also the national game of Japan. "It is played everywhere in our country—in remotest villages and amid obscure lots in the humblest sections of our cities. . . . Many Japanese schoolboys do not know who is Premier but it is difficult to find a boy in Japan who does not know the names of Connie Mack and Babe Ruth." This mutual love of baseball made the United States and Japan "personal friends who must live together, work together, and best of all, play together. Between two great peoples who can really understand and enjoy baseball, there can be no national differences or diplomatic complications which cannot be solved in the same spirit of sportsmanship and fair play." Ruth and Mack spoke next, but each told tales of Major League ball rather than continue with the diplomatic bent. The following morning newspapers across the United States reprinted Tokugawa's words of peace and understanding in an Associated Press article.[19]

But not all Japanese shared Tokugawa's desire for harmony.

PART 3

"The Japanese are equal to the Americans in strength of spirit."

TOKIO TOMINAGA,
All Nippon Third Baseman,
January 1935

19

North of Tokyo on the Ryomo Plain, fifty thousand soldiers congregated on November 10 for the Grand Army Maneuvers. The emperor himself would observe and critique the war game. The Grand Army Maneuvers took place each year, but in 1934 the scale of the war game and its timing—just as the American-British-Japanese naval talks were failing—made a statement that was not lost on diplomats and newspaper correspondents. The battle scenario at least was not objectionable to the American and British foreign offices. Rather than training offensive tactics, the troops practiced repelling an invasion. The Western Army, commanded by the Young Officers' hero, Gen. Sadao Araki, was charged with fighting off the Eastern Army, which began the maneuvers near Japan's eastern coast. The games lasted three days and besides the fifty thousand troops involved one hundred airplanes, squads of tanks, armored cars, and nine thousand cavalry. Hirohito, mounted on his white horse Shirayuki, scrutinized the action on the front lines and inspected the generals' battle plans. The event ended with a grand review, as the troops marched past the emperor and hundreds of thousands of spectators on the morning of Tuesday, November 13.[1]

With so many units in close proximity the Grand Maneuvers allowed the Young Officers to meet. They must have discussed the current political situation, as soon after returning from the Ryomo Plain, twenty to thirty of the Young Officers who supported Mitsugi Nishida's plans for a Showa Restoration met at a Tokyo restaurant. Koji Muranaka addressed the group. The time was ripe for another coup attempt. He had been laying the groundwork and was ready to put his plan into action. On November 27 Japan's parliament, known as the Imperial Diet, would meet in a special session. Once the politicians had gathered, Muranaka, Asaichi Isobe, and Lt. Taro Kataoka would attack the Diet Building using sympathetic troops and cadets from the Military Academy. Enemies of the restoration would be slaughtered. Prime Minister Keisuke Okada, Home Minister Fumio Goto, imperial adviser Count Nobuaki Makino, and seven other leading politicians were also marked for assassination. The bloody assault on the diet would invariably lead to street battles with loyalist troops. Violence and chaos would erupt throughout Tokyo. At the height of the confusion high-ranking officers who shared their views could declare martial law. With the obstacles of the restoration removed, power would be returned to the emperor and Ikki Kita's reforms instituted. Join me and support the rightful restoration, Muranaka implored his comrades. The meeting lasted into the night as the Young Officers discussed the proposal.[2]

No mention was made of Babe Ruth and the ballplayers, but as the Imperial Hotel faced the emperor's palace and was just a few blocks from the Diet Building, Muranaka's plan put the Americans in the line of fire.

20

With the royal receptions and fan enthusiasm, the All Americans must have been surprised to learn that tickets remained for the game on Saturday, November 17, at Meiji Jingu Stadium. To lure additional fans, *Yomiuri* announced that the All Americans would hold a home run contest prior to the game. The event would decide who was the greatest home run hitter—Babe Ruth, Lou Gehrig, Jimmie Foxx, or Earl Averill. Furthermore, burly slugger Jimmie Foxx would play all nine positions—one for each inning—during the course of the game, and Connie Mack would manage the All Nippon team.

The added events did little to boost attendance, as just thirty-two thousand showed up for Saturday's game, the last contest scheduled in Tokyo. After batting and fielding practice, fans readied for the home run contest, some brandishing fishing nets to capture the flying balls. The rules were simple. Joe Cascarella would pitch two rounds to each batter, and prizes would be awarded to the player who hit the most and the longest home runs. Prior to the contest an announcement came over the loudspeakers instructing the fans not to catch the home runs so that the blasts could be measured accurately. Fans put away their nets and took off their baseball mitts, placing them on their heads for protection, as they were not allowed to touch the balls. Fittingly, the aging all-time home run king retained his crown. The Bambino blasted four over the outfield walls, including a 410-footer, to win both prizes. Averill finished second with three, Foxx third with two, and Gehrig, who had an off day, failed to hit one out.[1]

The contest merely warmed up the sluggers, as Ruth, Gehrig, and Foxx all went deep during the 15–6 rout of the All Nippon team. Much to everybody's surprise, All Nippon took an early lead by scoring three in the second inning. It was the first time they had scored the initial run during the tour. But tiny Shinji Hamazaki, the five-foot-one former star hurler from Keio University, could not contain the American lineup. Gehrig homered to lead off the third inning, and Foxx followed by hitting the longest home run in Meiji Jingu Stadium history.[2] The ball landed three-quarters up the high left-field bleachers, bounced once and careened out of the stadium into the empty lot below. The All Americans scored four more to take the lead and tacked on nine additional runs off poor Hamazaki, whom Miyake left on the mound to suffer for the entire game.

Although the final score suggested otherwise, the Major Leaguers did not take the game seriously. Not only did Foxx play each position as advertised, but the other players (except for catcher Frankie Hayes and pitchers Clint Brown and Joe Cascarella) also played a different position each inning. Portly Ruth even took a turn at shortstop. The Japanese reactions to this showboating are unknown. There are no known complaints from the players or fans, but two plays suggest that some players objected. In the bottom of the third, after giving up seven runs, Hamazaki threw inside to Clint Brown, striking him in the head with a fastball. Brown fell to the ground, rolling over three times in pain, and had to be removed from the game. Was it an accident or frustration? Two innings later, when Ruth took his turn at third base, the combative Hisanori Karita laid a slow-rolling bunt down the third base line. Huffing and puffing, the lumbering Babe rushed in, but by the time he reached the ball, the fleet-footed Karita had streaked safely to first. The crowd both cheered and broke into laughter. Karita's bunt was a smart baseball play, but was it also done to embarrass Ruth?[3]

On Sunday afternoon, November 18, Officer Hakamada patrolled his route in downtown Yokohama just outside the stadium. As always, the large events brought out the bad element—petty thieves, pickpockets, scalpers, a few scam artists, and thugs looking for trouble. Thousands of bicycles, unlocked, of course, lined the approaches to the stadium. Hakamada needed to ensure that they remained untouched. He strode along the back of the stadium toward the entrance. Perhaps Hakamada heard the crack of the bat, but he must have heard the tumult as a ball flew over the outfield wall, bounced, and landed at his feet. The policeman stooped and pocketed his souvenir, probably already thinking of the story he would tell when he returned to the station. Hakamada soon discovered that the mighty clout had been hit by none other than the Babe himself. A *Yomiuri* reporter jotted down his story and arranged for Ruth to sign the ball.[4]

Hakamada's souvenir was not the only ball to leave the park that day. For the second consecutive day Ruth hit two homers, and Gehrig, Foxx, and Averill each tallied one. One wonders if the tension from the previous game carried over. Perhaps the All Americans wanted to stress their superiority. On this day each player stayed at their natural positions, and the *Japan Times* noted, "There was no letting up by the visiting American professional ball players," as they piled up twenty-one runs on twenty-three hits. Foxx seemed to have finally recovered from the effects of the beaning, as he had now homered in four consecutive games and brought his average up to .297.

At long last the Japanese also began to hit. They had scored six on ten hits the day before, and against a tough Lefty Gomez they gathered another ten hits and four runs in Yokohama. Karita led the attack with three hits, including a double, but the highlight came with two outs in the ninth as fans filed out of the stadium. Toshiharu Inokawa smashed the first Japanese home run of the series into the left-field bleachers. Several of the All Nippon players now had respectable averages against the American pitchers. Karita and outfielder Mamoru Sugitaya were both just above .300, and Inokawa was hitting .273. Hits, however, still eluded Jimmy Horio. He had played in all eight of All Nippon's games and had twenty-two at bats but just one hit for a miserable .045 average.[5]

After the game the Americans congregated at the Yokohama Country and Athletic Club for dinner and dancing. The organization dated back to 1868, when a handful of homesick British merchants decided to create a cricket team. They soon added other athletic teams, and the organization gradually grew into a social club. The stress of international relations, etiquette, and being surrounded by a foreign language may have been getting to the All Americans, as during his brief speech umpire John Quinn emphatically thanked the club for organizing "the first all-foreign gathering that the team had experienced in their visit here." After speeches by the club's president, Mack, Ruth, and Quinn, staff removed the dining tables and cleared the floor for dancing, "which continued until a late hour."[6]

From the first game, it was obvious to the players and fans alike that differences existed between the American and Japanese brands of baseball. Although the rules were basically the same in the two countries, the men both played and approached the game differently. The much smaller Japanese were solid fielders and quick runners but weak hitters. Connie Mack noted that the emphasis on fielding started at a young age and was a fundamental difference between the two cultures. Japanese children, Mack observed, were first given a glove and ball, whereas American children learned how to swing a bat first. He reminded his hosts that even if you play great defense, if you do not hit and score runs, you cannot win.[7]

The Japanese defense, however, had flaws. Infielders rarely charged ground balls but sat back and waited for the ball to come to them. This not only allowed fast runners to beat out slow grounders but also led to an increase in errors. By charging a grounder an infielder can usually choose when to field the ball, thus increasing the likelihood of fielding it cleanly. Waiting for the ball forces an infielder to react rather than pick the optimum time to field. Thus, the infielder is more likely to have to field short hops and bad bounces. Japanese infielders, both waiting back and unaccustomed to the strength of Major League grounders, made twenty-three errors in the first nine games.

The Americans were generally impressed with the Japanese pitchers. They told reporters that Eiji Sawamura and Masao Date had the potential to play in the Majors. Lefty Gomez noted that they needed to learn how to conserve their energy. The Japanese pitchers warmed up for too long, walked unnecessary distances during games, and had unnecessary movements in their windups. Mineo Nakamura, a pitcher for Meiji University, recognized an important difference. Americans pitched from their waists, while Japanese relied on their arms. Relying on the larger, more powerful trunk muscles allowed the Major Leaguers to throw much faster and smoother and at the same time reduced the chance of arm injury.[8]

At the plate the Japanese and Americans differed greatly in style and ability. In general, the Japanese played the game as Americans did in the dead-ball era, emphasizing moving runners around the bases with place hitting. Most still hit off their front foot and had not mastered the hip-rotation technique that had enabled Ruth to change the way Americans played the game. They argued that their small size precluded hitting for power, but the Major Leaguers disagreed. It was not size but lack of technique and practice that held the Japanese back.

Both Mack and Ruth noticed that most Japanese batters crouched too much in their stances. The Babe explained to a *Yakyukai* reporter that bending their upper bodies so far forward caused the batters to tilt their necks and prevented them from keeping their heads and eyes level. Level eyes permit better spatial awareness, allowing a hitter to more accurately judge a pitch's velocity and trajectory—in baseball vernacular "to see the ball" better. He also noticed that after a pitch was thrown, the Japanese batters would straighten up, thus wasting time and adding excess movement in an upward direction rather than toward the ball. This would once again cause their heads to move and release force in a nonproductive direction.

The Americans uniformly commented that more than anything else the Japanese needed practice, and not just coached practices but more games. O'Doul told reporters, "It's not fair to make comparisons between the Japanese and American players. Even the best Japanese players have only several hundred games in their lifetimes." Gehrig agreed: "The key to hitting is timing. They have to play hundreds of games to get experience. I cannot make a comparison between Americans who play several hundred games per year and the Japanese who play tens of games." Ruth supposedly told a *Yakyukai* reporter that with the proper experience, Masao Date, Minoru Yamashita, and former Keio pitcher Saburo Miyatake had the ability to join the Majors, but considering the Babe's inability to remember names, and that Miyatake did not play against the All Americans, it is unlikely that he actually singled out these men.[9]

There were differences in baseball strategy. Stuart Bell noted, "The Japanese . . . do not realize the value of double plays . . . [when] there are men on first and second, the Japanese never try to make a double play if the ball is hit to the third baseman, who always goes to third for the force out of one runner." *Yakyukai* columnist Fujio Naoki wrote that the primary Japanese offensive strategy was a short hit, followed by a bunt, and another hit to drive in the runner. The Americans, on the other hand, relied on power. Although there was little doubt that the All Americans' most potent offensive weapon was the long ball, the box scores show that the All Nippons did not follow the strategy outlined by Naoki. The Japanese sacrificed only four times during the first nine games of the tour. Indeed, Ruth privately told Ambassador Joseph Grew that he was disappointed with the Japanese lack of team play and pointed to the few sacrifices as an example.[10]

The size of the American and Japanese strike zone also differed. The All Nippon players noted that American umpire John Quinn's strike zone was larger than the zone used in Japan. John Reardon, a National League umpire who had come to Japan with the 1931 Major League All Stars, explained that in the United States, if any part of the ball went over any part of the plate, it was a strike. In Japan the entire ball needed to cross the plate for the pitch to be called a strike.[11] With a small strike zone one would expect the Japanese batters to be more patient and selective at the plate, waiting for a good pitch to drive, but Stuart Bell noted that this was not the case. "Despite the fact they are small and difficult targets for pitchers, they will hit with two balls and no strikes, deriving no advantage at all from their statue."[12]

The differences between the All Nippons and All Americans went beyond skill, technique, strategy, and even practice. The teams approached the game differently, as the Japanese played their own style of the American pastime. Just as modern American baseball reflects its roots as a nineteenth-century urban game popularized during a time of industrialization, rapid economic growth, geographical expansion, and mass immigration, the Japanese game reflects its origins in the cultural turmoil of the early Meiji period.

Horace Wilson was twenty-eight when he arrived in Japan in 1871 to teach English at Ichiban Chugaku (renamed Kaisai Gakko in 1873). He had been born and raised in the small Maine town of Gorham, about sixty-five miles north of Boston. Unlike most Gorham boys, who received a basic education before learning to till the soil, Wilson attended Kents Hill, a Methodist seminary outside of Augusta, Maine. The school's headmaster, Dr. Henry O. Torsey, introduced baseball to the school in 1861, either just before or just after Wilson graduated. Soon after leaving school Wilson joined the Twelfth Maine Regiment and marched south to fight for the Union in Louisiana. If he had not already learned the game at Kents Hill, Wilson picked up the sport during his enlistment. Discharged in March 1866, Wilson returned to Gorham and taught school before leaving for San Francisco in 1870. There he worked as a clerk for another Union veteran until events across the globe would alter his life.

After the Meiji Restoration in 1868 the new government went on a crusade to modernize Japan. To achieve this goal quickly and efficiently, the Meiji government recruited more than three thousand foreign experts, or *oyatoi*, to create a modern infrastructure as well as political, educational, and financial institutions based on the most successful Western models. They recruited British engineers, Prussian diplomats and doctors, French soldiers, and American teachers. While in San Francisco Wilson signed a three-year commitment to teach English in Japan and left for Yokohama with his wife and young son.

His new school was an elite high school designed to draw the top students from the entire nation. Later, it would transform into Tokyo Imperial University—the alma mater of Matsutaro Shoriki. Like many Western teachers, Wilson found his pupils sickly and physically weak. In contrast to Western education that emphasized physical activity to hone the body and mind, most Japanese found exercise a distraction from intellectual pursuits. As a result, the notion of athletics as an end to themselves was alien to the Japanese. They had, for example, no native team sports. Legend relates that in 1872, Wilson decided to strengthen his students' bodies by teaching them his beloved game of baseball. Wilson, however, was not the only baseball player in Japan at the time. Albert Bates, who taught at Kaitakushi Tentative School (renamed Sapporo Agricultural College in 1873), also played and taught the game to his students, as did L. L. James in the southern city of Kumamoto. Although Wilson is credited with introducing the game, it is possible that Bates or James may have actually pulled out his bat and ball first. In any case by 1876 there were at least three baseball clubs (two foreign and one Japanese) in the Tokyo-Yokohama area.[13]

In November 1876 a correspondent, known only as "An Exile in the Far East," submitted five box scores along with a letter to the *New York Clipper*. He wrote:

> For some years we have been trying to get up a baseball club but without success, and it was not until just before the arrival of the United States flagship Tennessee that we were able to excite any interest in the game. However, I am happy to state that, after beating the navy, ball-fever seized on the largest part of the American community, and now we have in Yoko-hama a club with over forty members, and in Tokio, the capital, they have one with over thirty. . . . The first game was played in early summer before either of the clubs was formed, against the Japanese students of the Imperial College at Tokio [actually Wilson's school, Tokyo Kaisei Gakko]. . . . The Japanese take a great deal of interest in the game, and, as they are very quick and generally good throwers, they will make fair players with some instruction.

The box score, which shows the Foreigners as 34–11 victors, lists Wilson at left field. A fourth adult team was formed two years later when Hiroshi Hiraoka returned from studying railroad engineering in the United States, taught his coworkers the game, and formed the Shimbashi Athletic Club. Tokyo-area schools picked up the game, and students, clad in kimonos and wooden sandals called geta, could soon be seen playing on school grounds across the region. But the distinctive approach that would come to characterize Japanese baseball for more than a hundred years came from an unlikely source.

The First Higher School (Daiichi Koto Gakko), often called Ichiko, was created in 1886 to uphold traditions threatened by the country's rapid Westernization. Besides a strong academic education, students studied Shintoism, Zen, and the martial arts. Graduates routinely enrolled at Imperial University, the training ground for Japan's political and economic elite. During Ichiko's inaugural year the school surprised many traditionalists by creating a baseball team. Within a few seasons, however, Ichiko would develop a distinctively Japanese approach to the game.[14]

In the late 1880s and 1890s Japan struggled to establish its national identity. During the previous two decades it had transformed from a feudalistic medieval society into a modern country with radically new political, economic, educational, and even social institutions. Many Japanese feared that the country was losing its native culture and abandoning time-honored traditions and values in favor of shallow materialism and frivolous Western fads. These concerns led to the philosophy of *wakon yosai* (Japanese spirit, Western technology), the concept that Japan could import Western technology, institutions, and even ideas but would imbue them with Japanese spirit.

Exactly what Japanese spirit meant was nebulous. It meant different things to different Japanese, but to the Ichiko players and many others in the early 1890s, it meant the spirit of the samurai warrior. "Sports came from the West," a team member later explained. "In Ichiko baseball, we were playing sports but we were also putting the spirit of Japan into it. . . . *Yakyu* is a way to express the samurai spirit."[15]

Even though samurai had made up about 10 percent of Japan's population, by the late nineteenth century they had become the shared heritage of all Japanese. As the Meiji government searched for methods to unite the Japanese people, they consciously indoctrinated the conscript army with the values and ideals of the samurai—absolute loyalty, self-sacrifice, discipline, courtesy, and honor—that would after the publication of Inazo Nitobe's *Bushido: The Soul of Japan* in 1899 be known in both East and West as the Bushido code. These ideals spread throughout Japanese society and soon became seen as the essence of the Japanese national character, much like the cowboy is often used to personify the American national character.

Although the ballplayers believed they were following the ways of Japan's feudal warriors, the ideals they adopted actually had much later roots. The unification of Japan under the Tokugawa shoguns and the subsequent closing of the island's borders between 1635 and

1858 ended the need for a large warrior class trained in combat. As these idle warriors also posed a threat to the regime, the Tokugawa government developed rituals and ceremonies to divert the samurai's attention and resources. As time passed, many samurai became governors and bureaucrats in the new regime, becoming masters of the brush rather than sword. As their daily lives began to resemble those of merchants and other commoners, the samurai developed a lifestyle to set them apart culturally and maintain ties to their warrior heritage. Many turned to Confucian philosophy to develop a code of moral behavior that separated them from other social classes. This code emphasized spirituality, discipline, self-control, fealty, and honor, virtues that would help maintain the samurai's leadership roles in a peaceful society. These virtues became projected back onto the classical samurai, thus creating a romanticized and idealized version of the warrior, much like late-medieval European concepts of chivalry were projected onto early-medieval warriors, such as King Arthur and Sir Lancelot.[16]

With the interrelated idealization of the classical warrior and the removal of most samurai from actual warfare, approaches to martial arts changed. The practical mastery of technique for survival was replaced by a Zen-influenced approach, later known as *dô* (the way), that emphasized perfection of form as an avenue to moral enlightenment. The concentration, self-reflection, discipline, and dedication that led to perfect form would also lead to spiritual strength.[17] With the development of the concept of *dô* came an emphasis on etiquette, technique, and the "correct" way to accomplish nearly every task. Manuals appeared on the tea ceremony, flower arranging, and even the proper way to commit seppuku, which had developed from a rare battlefield suicide to a common ritual of honor during the peaceful Tokugawa period.

The practice of *dô* increased throughout the nineteenth century, culminating with Jigoro Kano's transformation of the martial art of *jujutsu* (the technique of pliancy) to *judô* (the way of pliancy) in the early 1880s. Kano argued that *judô* was more than a fighting technique; it was a way of life. "The principle of a way (*dô*) is that it is applicable to other aspects of a person's life. The true meaning of *judô* is the study and practice of mind and body. It is, at the same time, the model for daily life and work."[18]

With a victory of Kano's *judô* club over rival *jujutsu* clubs at the Tokyo Metropolitan Police Force's tournament in 1886, *judô* and Kano's philosophies spread throughout Japan. The students at Ichiko were particularly impressed. They formed a *judô* team, and Kano became the school's headmaster in 1893. With the popularity of Kano's philosophies and the prevailing belief that all true Japanese embodied the spirit of the samurai, it is not surprising that Ichiko ballplayers created an approach to the game called *Seishin Yakyu* (Spirit Baseball) that emphasized unquestioning loyalty to the coach-manager and team as well as long hours of grueling practice to improve both players' skills and mental endurance. Proponents of *Seishin Yakyu* argued that a strong spirit could overcome physical shortcomings and lead to victory on the field. Thus, practices were designed to not only hone skills but also develop the spirit. Ichiko batters took one thousand swings during practice, while pitchers hurled hundreds of balls each day. Difficult workouts were known as "Bloody Urine Practice," as players would pass blood later in the evening. Despite the challenges, players were forbidden to speak of the pain but could only proclaim, "It itches!"

In 1896 the Ichiko team felt ready for the ultimate test. They challenged the American squad from the Yokohama Country Club, the same organization that hosted the All Americans for dinner and dancing. Although just an amateur team made up of businessmen stationed in Japan, the Americans deemed the schoolboys unworthy of their time and dismissed the challenge. Eventually, when they acquiesced, the young Japanese crushed the Americans in three straight games, despite the country club's reinforcing its squad in the third game with ringers from the USS *Yorktown* and *Detroit*. The Japanese had mastered the American pastime.

With Ichiko's victories interest in baseball flourished. By the first decade of the twentieth century it had become the most popular sport in Japan. Although few teams mimicked Ichiko's extreme approach, many adopted their fundamentals of discipline and intense practice to hone the spirit as well as improve technique.

In 1904 both Waseda and Keio university teams defeated Ichiko, ushering in a new era of Japanese baseball. Both universities were run on Western models with the mission of strengthening ties between East and West. Waseda's manager, Iso Abe, had attended the Hartford Theological Seminary in Connecticut and was a Christian, fluent in English, and a committed socialist. He eschewed Ichiko's samurai approach to baseball and instituted more relaxed training methods, emphasizing egalitarianism and fair play. Despite Waseda's success on the diamond, not all of his players agreed with Abe's philosophy. Team captain Shin Hashido, upon returning from Waseda's 1905 baseball tour of the United States, concluded that to compete with Americans, Japanese needed to adapt their "3,000-year old martial arts" that combined "physical and spiritual strength" to baseball.[19]

Five years later, in 1910, the University of Chicago baseball squad came to Japan and easily defeated Waseda in six straight games, including a 20–0 blowout.[20] Frustrated by the one-sided contests, second baseman Suishu Tobita assumed responsibility for the losses and quit the team—vowing to avenge the humiliating defeats. After graduation Tobita became a sportswriter before returning to Waseda as their manager in 1919.

Tobita had been raised in a conservative samurai household that cherished traditional Japanese values and opposed the Meiji Restoration and opening the country to the West. Although Tobita had attended liberal Waseda and played the American pastime over his father's protests, as a manager he returned to his family's values and instituted an approach to baseball modeled after Ichiko's Spirit Baseball.

By explicitly forging ties between baseball, Zen Buddhism, and Bushido (at this point a widely used term in both Japan and the West), Tobita's brand of baseball surpassed even Ichiko's rigor. He called his practices *shi no renshu* (death training) and worked his players past their limits of endurance to improve their spirit. Players would field ground balls "until they were half dead, motionless, and froth was coming out of their mouths." He explained in one of his many tracts on baseball theory:

A manager has to love his players, but on the practice field he must treat them as cruelly as possible, even though he may be crying about it inside. That is the key to winning baseball. If the players do not try so hard as to vomit blood in practice, then they cannot hope to win games. . . . The purpose of training is not health but the forging of the soul. To hit like a shooting star, to catch a ball beyond one's capabilities . . . such beautiful plays are not the result of technique but . . . are made possible by a strong spiritual power.[21]

Following this rigid approach that Tobita would call *yakyudô* (the way of baseball), Waseda became Japan's best team, winning nine of thirteen championships during Tobita's reign. In 1920 the University of Chicago club returned to Japan. The two teams met five times, each winning twice, with one game ending in a tie. Tobita must have been pleased, but his revenge for the 1910 drubbing was insatiated. Five years later Chicago came again. This time Tobita was ready for them. Chicago opened the tour by beating Waseda 2–0, but Tobita's team played the Americans to 0–0 and 1–1 ties, before winning 1–0 in the trip's eighth game. Chicago played several more games against the other Tokyo universities before facing Waseda in the tour's final contest. Waseda crushed the Americans 10–4 and took the series two games to one (along with two ties). Deeming his revenge on Chicago complete, Tobita stepped down as manager and returned to sports-writing.

Tobita's views had a dramatic impact on Japanese baseball for decades and even linger in a watered-down form today. Waseda's success and Tobita's works on baseball theory caused many high school and collegiate coaches across the country to adopt aspects of *yakyudô*. As Japanese nationalism increased during the 1920s and early 1930s, Tobita's reliance on Japanese traditions and *wakon yosai* appealed to many. Soon samurai baseball, or *yakyudô*, became the pervasive approach in Japan and offered hope to the All Nippon team. Infielder Tokio Tominaga told *Yakyukai* readers, "Many fans think that the small Japanese can never compete with the larger Americans, but I disagree. The Japanese are equal to the Americans in strength of spirit."[22]

21

The Imperial Japanese Army Academy stood on Ichigaya Heights, a hill about a mile northeast of Meiji Jingu Stadium. Visitors checked in with guards at the gatehouse before proceeding up a broad, steep, winding road to the main hall—an imposing three-story Western-style building capped with a cupola that would look at home on any New England college campus. Subsidiary buildings and barracks surrounded the hall.

The academy could hold several thousand cadets. Class size varied greatly from more than 1,000 in 1907 to just 276 the following year. Cadets were drawn from military preparatory schools or by special examination from a civil school. Conditions at the academy were harsh. The cadets lived in shabby barracks constructed in the 1870s with little to no heat. Food was scarce and of poor quality. With the poor diet, the average cadet in his early twenties put on just three pounds and grew only a half inch during his three-year stay.[1]

Equally harsh was the daily routine. Reveille came at 5:30 a.m. The cadets spent their mornings at private study and lectures and their afternoons at physical training, often bare-chested, regardless of the weather. Training included gymnastics, kendo, fencing, judo, riding, and drill. Western sports were forbidden. The cadets' evenings were filled with private study. Roll call came at 9:30 p.m. and lights out at 10:00. Cadets were also responsible for cleaning their uniforms, gear, and the buildings. According to the Inspector-General's Rules and Regulations, the instruction should focus on "fostering a spirit of loyalty and patriotism." Free exchange of ideas, original thinking, and even discussion were discouraged and often forbidden. A British observer noted that science was "distorted and its disfigured shape used to substantiate the moral training . . . that [the Japanese are] morally superior to all others," while history "after very considerable doctoring is used to cultivate only pride of country and national confidence."[2] This curriculum fostered a close-minded nationalism and bigotry that would lead its graduates to commit brutal and criminal acts on enemy populations and ultimately bring Japan down a path to national disaster.

In 1934 Koji Muranaka not only taught classes at the academy but also, like his mentor, Mitsugi Nishida, led private study sessions that focused on Japan's current socioeconomic situation and Ikki Kita's solutions. Descendants of the samurai no longer dominated Japan's officer corps; the cadets came from all economic and geographical backgrounds. Many were born in rural areas, like the northern Tohoku district, where the Great Depression had hit particularly hard. They had witnessed widespread ruin and famine and seen their sisters and friends sold into prostitution to save their families from starvation. With their indoctrination of emperor worship and their skewed education, these cadets were fertile ground for Kita's radical ideas and Muranaka's plans. The young captain soon had a core of followers willing to sacrifice their lives to restore the emperor to full power.

22

On the mound for All Nippon, the young pitcher felt confident, as if his opponents were the fellow high schoolers he had shut out just a few months before. On November 20, 1934, the one o'clock sun came directly over Kusanagi Stadium's right-field bleachers, blinding the batters. He knew this. It had enabled him to retire the leadoff batter on a pop fly and strike out Charlie Gehringer. The batters saw his silhouette windup, then a white ball explode in on them, just a few feet away. It was nearly unhittable. Fanning Gehringer thrilled the boy. Known as the "Mechanical Man" for his reserve and precise play, the batter's swing revealed no flaws to the pitcher. When facing him the boy imagined them as samurai dueling to the death with glittering swords. It was a spiritual battle, to see who could outlast the other—will the other to submit. He felt that Gehringer was the only American player who showed the spirit of a samurai.[1]

The third batter strode to the plate. He was old (more than twice the pitcher's seventeen years), and he was heavy (outweighing him by a hundred pounds), with a sizable paunch. His broad face usually bore a smile, accentuating his puffy cheeks and broad nose. His twinkling eyes and infectious good humor forced smiles even from opponents. Instinctively, the pitcher looked at his face—a mistake.

There was no friendly smile. The Sultan of Swat glared back like an *oni*—those large red demons that guard temple gates. The boy's heart fluttered, his composure lost. Babe Ruth dug in.

Eiji Sawamura breathed deeply, steadying himself. This was, after all, why he had left high school early and forfeited a chance to attend Keio University—an opportunity to face Babe Ruth. He had read Sotaro Suzuki's profiles of the Major League stars in *Yomiuri Shimbun*.

He admired these great ballplayers, but as he read the desire to top their feats, or even beat them face-to-face, grew.

Sawamura wound up, turning his body toward third base before hurtling the ball toward the plate. The blinded Ruth lunged forward, his hips and great chest twisting until they nearly faced the wrong direction. The fastball pounded in catcher Jiro Kuji's mitt. Strike one.

It was now his third time facing the powerful American lineup. Although they had hit him hard in the previous two games, he had learned from his mistakes. Fanning Ruth and Gehrig in his first outing on November 10 helped Sawamura grasp that even the greatest had weaknesses. Ruth, for example, had difficulty with knee-high inside curves. As Sawamura told a writer for *Yakyukai*, "I was scared but I realized that the big leaguers were not gods." Recalling how he had struck out Ruth before, Sawamura wound up and fired another fastball.

The Babe readied for the second pitch. Damn if he could see a thing. That sun was right behind that kid, he thought. Crafty little son of a bitch, too. He had a nice hummer—not so fast that he could throw it by you, but fast enough to keep you honest so that you couldn't just sit back and wait for the curve. And that was a Major League curve, that was. It broke from twelve to six. Been burned on that pitch before back in Toyama.

Sawamura's fastball burst through the glare. The Bambino flailed his thirty-six-inch, forty-four-ounce Louisville Slugger at the ball. But it was too late. The ball smacked into Kuji's glove. Strike two.

The sellout crowd at Shizuoka's Kusanagi Stadium roared. Earlier that morning the All Americans had left Tokyo by express train for the modest-size city of 136,000. Mount Fuji dominated Shizuoka's northeastern skyline. As the train steamed close to the mountain's base, Ruth and the others rushed to the right windows, pointing and shouting "Fujiyama! Fujiyama!" each time its snowcap came into view. Although often called "Fujiyama" by Westerners, Japanese refer to the sacred dormant volcano as "Fuji-san."

Kusanagi Stadium was small, even by Japanese standards. Only eight thousand fans could press into the grandstands that ringed the field. The outfield contained about ten rows of bleachers, and young trees poked their branches over the low walls. In the infield the ballpark was more substantial, containing twenty to thirty rows of bleachers with a press box, and even a covered section. The fans, primarily men, wore light wool overcoats with fedoras or wool driving caps in the pleasant forty-eight-degree afternoon. Once home they would remove their Western garb, bathe, and don a kimono. Here and there, however, a man dressed in the traditional manner could be seen in the stands. The fans cheered and shouted on every play, making them louder than an average American crowd. But to the Americans a familiar sound was missing from the din. There were no vendors advertising their wares. No "Hot dogs! Get your hot dogs here!" No "Popcorn!" or "Cracker Jack!" or even the heavenly sound of "Beer! Ice cold beer here!" Eating in the stands was not a Japanese tradition. In fact, eating while walking or sometimes even standing was considered rude. Those who wanted to eat would purchase a small *bento* (boxed lunch) from an outside vendor or a stand just inside the stadium's entrance and quietly eat fish or octopus with rice, or maybe fried noodles, with their chopsticks.

With Ruth in the hole, Sawamura knew just what to do. Like any good warrior, he attacked his adversary's weakness. As he readied himself the boy pursed his lips, twisting them in a peculiar fashion. He then reared back and fired.

Ruth brought his bat back, raising his rear elbow to shoulder height before taking a short stride with his front foot and snapping his hips forward. The bat followed along a level plane through the strike zone. Just before contact, the ball dropped. Fooled by the curve, Ruth's momentum carried him forward, his body twisting around as his bat clouted only air.

As Ruth walked back to the dugout, a surge of confidence and hope swelled through Sawamura and the crowd. Maybe today would be the day. The Japanese had improved with each game. Both their fielding and their pitching were shaper, even if their hitting was still weak. Maybe today their fighting spirit would be strong enough to defeat the Americans.

Three quick outs later, Sawamura was back on the mound. Earl Whitehill had taken care of All Nippon in the second by striking out the side. Lou Gehrig strode to the plate. Minutes later he walked back to the dugout shaking his head. Between the sun and that fastball, the Iron Horse had barely seen the three pitches shoot past him. The Beast, Jimmie Foxx, came next. He also returned to the dugout, another strikeout victim.

The crowd roared. Many in the stands and dugouts shook their heads in disbelief. Earlier that summer New York Giants pitcher Carl Hubbell had made the headlines on both sides of the Pacific by striking out Ruth, Gehrig, Foxx, Al Simmons, and Joe Cronin in succession during the 1934 All-Star Game. Sawamura stood on the verge of equaling the feat, having fanned Gehringer, Ruth, Gehrig, and Foxx in a row. Now came Earl Averill. Even with the sun, he would make a tough out. Over the past two Major League seasons, Averill had struck out in only 5 percent of his plate appearances. The Babe, by comparison, struck out 15 percent of the time. A few pitches later Averill got wood on the ball and grounded out to second, ending Sawamura's strikeout streak, but keeping alive his no-hitter.

It was Sawamura's day. With one out in the top of the third, the young hurler hit an easy grounder to Foxx at third and watched it trickle through the burly third baseman's legs. An out later Sawamura reached second, as Kumeyasu Yajima singled to break up Whitehill's no-hitter. Cocky Karita came to bat with a chance to give Japan the lead but could manage only a slow roller to short to end the inning.

In the bottom half Bing Miller, another difficult man to strike out, flied to right field before Sawamura threw the ball by both Frankie Hayes and Whitehill to raise his strikeout total to six. Three up, three down. Whitehill equaled the feat by putting down the Japanese in order in the fourth.

The second time through the batting order would be more difficult for Sawamura. Although the sun still glared in the hitters' eyes, the Americans had seen his pitches and would be ready. They knew to attack the first hittable pitch. Rabbit McNair led off the bottom of the fourth, rocketing the first pitch into the hole between short and third. Karita scooted to his right, reached across his body, backhanding the ball at the last instant, turned, and threw a strike to Minoru Yamashita at first base. One down. No-hitter saved.

Gehringer came to the plate. Again, they would duel. Sawamura would later tell reporters that he could feel the Mechanical Man's fighting spirit reaching toward him, choking his breath. But it ended with a slow roller to second. Eleven straight outs.

And then the no-hitter was over. Ruth lined a clean single into center field. With Ruth on first, Sawamura focused on Gehrig.

Eiji felt his spirit soar, urging him to challenge the Americans, enabling him to ignore the burning sensation in his elbow. Yet, like any strong samurai, he could control his adrenaline. His fighting spirit had always been strong, even when his body lagged.

He had been born in Ujiyamada, once called the Divine City, but now known as Ise City. Not far from Eiji's birthplace stands the Grand Ise Shrine, the most sacred Shinto site in Japan, that supposedly houses the mirror of Amaterasu Omikami, the Sun Goddess and direct ancestor of the emperors. Eiji had been a thin, sickly child, and doctors urged his parents to give him more exercise. Baseball was the natural choice.

His father, Kenji, had been a ballplayer as the game became Japan's national sport in the early years of the twentieth century. After school Kenji was supposed to push a vegetable chart through town as his uncle peddled the produce, but the boy would run off to abandoned lots or fallow fields to play ball. His uncle scolded him, but when Kenji made the school team, the uncle would watch from behind the fence, secretly cheering for his nephew. A dozen years later Kenji taught his sickly son how to throw and catch.

Eiji grew stronger but collapsed from exhaustion after pitching his first game in elementary school. Bedridden with fever, he wept, clutching his uniform, afraid that he would never pitch again. As soon as the fever broke he returned to the diamond, determined to work harder. In the sixth grade Eiji led Meirin Elementary to the prefectural championship and pitched a no-hitter in the first game of the national championship tournament in Kyoto. An error by his first baseman, however, led to the game's only run and knocked Meirin from the tournament.

At eleven years old Eiji enrolled at Kyoto Commercial Middle School, a six-year institution that took the student from elementary school to college. The school had been founded just a year earlier and had a poor baseball team, but Principal Konan Tsujimoto declared that he would "construct a baseball team that can conquer Koshien" (the annual tournament to decide the national champion). Despite the team's lack of talent, Sawamura spent his first two years as an infielder, as older boys were allowed to pitch. In his third year, about the time he turned fourteen, Eiji was given his first start after the regular pitcher became injured.

Sawamura's old coach from Meirin Elementary watched as Eiji won the game against much older boys. After the game the coach drew his former player aside. "Your pitches aren't especially fast, but they rise up naturally and are difficult to hit. If you gained some velocity, it would really be something." These words, which would have been forgotten by most boys, became the competitive Sawamura's goal. He would become the hardest thrower in Japan. He practiced at every opportunity, begging teammates and friends to play catch. His catcher, Senmangoku Yamaguchi, would show off his battered, swollen fingers as proof of his battery mate's prowess. Eiji watched the aces of rival teams. He studied their techniques, copied their strengths, noted their weaknesses, and vowed to beat them. He took the games personally, viewing opposing teams as enemies to be conquered. Prior to an important game against the rival Heian Middle School, Sawamura wrote the names of their best hitters on his glove to remind himself of the upcoming challenge.

By his fifth year at Kyoto Commercial Sawamura had become one of Japan's top pitchers, and the school reached the spring National Middle School Baseball Tournament at Koshien. Sawamura won his first two games before losing 2–1 in the third round to the powerful Akashi Middle School team. His senior year (1934), Kyoto Commercial once again made the spring championship tournament and once again lost to Akashi. Sawamura had one more chance to lead Kyoto Commercial to a national championship and fulfill Principal Tsujimoto's goal. Since 1915 *Asahi Shimbun* had sponsored a summer middle school tournament at Koshien Stadium. Considered more prestigious than the spring tournament, Kyoto Commercial had previously failed to qualify for the summer games. In the qualifying games Sawamura pitched brilliantly. Against Ichioka Middle School, he struck out the first eighteen batters and added seven more during the next three innings. But weak-hitting Kyoto Commercial could not score. Eiji battled through thirteen scoreless innings, allowing only two hits and striking out thirty-one, before the game ended in a tie.

Soon only their archrival, Heian Middle School, blocked Kyoto Commercial's path to Koshien. Kyoto would have to play them twice, once in a league match and probably again in the final of the regional Keishin tournament. Having already qualified for the regional tournament, Kyoto Commercial's manager, Takenosuke Takasu, decided to rest Sawamura and start the backup pitcher in the first game against Heian. The decision angered fans of both teams. Kyoto supporters, many of whom had bet on their team, were incensed that Sawamura was not pitching, while Heian fans felt insulted that Kyoto did not use their best starter. Immediately after the final out of the 3–1 Heian win, both groups rushed the Kyoto dugout, searching for Takasu and Sawamura. Police surrounded the Kyoto boys and escorted them safely to their hotel.

As expected the two teams met in the regional final, and this time Sawamura took the mound. Knowing that it would be his last game against the hated rival, Eiji bore down and hurled one of his finest—a one-hitter with nineteen strikeouts. By the end of the 7–0 Kyoto Commercial romp the Heian fans lost control. Their yells echoed across the stadium. "Break Sawamura's right arm!" "Beat him to death!" As Sawamura recorded the last out, police moved onto the diamond, forming a wall around the Kyoto team. Officials handed the championship pennant to Sawamura. Looking at the pennant in his hands, the police, and the tumultuous crowd, Eiji trembled with both fear and joy. There was one last task. As the captain of the winning team Eiji had to lower the flag in center field to mark the end of the tournament. Eiji dashed toward the flagpole. A legion of police followed, their wooden swords clattering in their belts as they ran beside him, as the crowd began to spill onto the field. His task done, he was escorted to safety.

The Koshien tournament lasted just two days for Kyoto Commercial. Sawamura surrendered only four hits in their first-round game, but an error by the shortstop, a misplayed soft liner, and poor hitting led to a 3–1 loss, elimination, and an end to their dreams. That was just two months ago. It felt like a lifetime to young Eiji. So much had happened since then, and now he was containing the best hitters in the world. He reared back, fired, and Lou Gehrig grounded out to second base. Three outs. Still no runs.

Both sides went down in order in the fifth, and Whitehill retired the Japanese in the top of the sixth, giving up another single to Yajima but no runs. In the bottom of the sixth, Sawamura ran into his only jam. A walk to Whitehill and a single to McNair, followed by a Gehringer fly out, brought Ruth to the plate with runners on first and second and two outs. The Babe was ready for Sawamura this time. He had a plan. Sawamura threw his fastball with a two-finger rather than four-finger grip, giving it extra movement and causing it to sail away from left handed batters. His curve ball had a sharp break but was more predictable and, of course, slower. In the dugout Ruth had been instructing the All Americans to let the fastballs go by and sit on the curve. He had probably done just that when he had singled in his last at bat.

On second base Whitehill was most likely seething. He was, after all, the man who threatened to punch his own shortstop for making an error in a tight game. He had pitched six innings of two-hit, shutout ball, striking out seven, and his teammates could not score off that kid. It wasn't like he was Cy Young, and they had lit him up before when he pitched in Tokyo.

The newspapers do not tell us why he did it. Perhaps the ball scooted away from catcher Jiro Kuji, or maybe he decided to take matters into his own hands, but with two outs and the Sultan of Swat at the plate, the hotheaded Whitehill decided to swipe third base. He did not make it. Third out. Score 0–0.

The base-running blunder may have irked Whitehill, as he walked Isamu Fuma to lead off the seventh. Slugger Minoru Yamashita bunted Fuma into scoring position, but the next batter, star Shigeru Mizuhara, could manage only a weak fly ball to right field. Fuma remained at second but advanced to third moments later as Whitehill balked. Whitehill next walked veteran catcher Jiro Kuji. The potential winning run was now at third with two outs and weak-hitting third baseman Saburo Shintomi up. So far Shintomi had gained just one hit in fourteen at bats against the Major Leaguers. Miyake, the Japanese manager, had better hitters on the bench, including Toshiharu

Inokawa, who was hitting .333 with the only Japanese homer, and Mamoru Sugitaya, who had picked up seven hits in his twenty-four at bats, but Miyake allowed Shintomi to bat. Moments later the third baseman grounded back to the pitcher's mound for the third out.

The game still locked at zero, Ruth led off the bottom of the seventh. He still planned to wait for a curve and drive it, but Sawamura surprised him with a rare change-up. Way out in front, the Bambino topped the ball weakly to Sawamura for the first out. Gehrig may have stopped talking to Ruth, but he knew good advice when he heard it. He too would wait on the curve ball. He let a pitch go by for a ball before getting it. As the pitch came in he dropped his hands, pointing the head of the bat toward the stands behind home plate, took a giant step forward with his front foot, and pivoted his entire body at the ball. With a bang the ball rocketed off the bat, hurtling toward the right-field wall. At Meiji Jingu Stadium it would have lined straight into Kumeyasu Yajima's glove, but here in Shizuoka Yajima could only look up as the ball landed just beyond the low concrete right-field wall.[2] It was now 1–0 All Americans. The score would stand, as the Japanese failed to drive in the tying run, despite getting a runner to second with one out in the bottom of the eighth and having a runner at first with one out in the ninth.

That night at the Daitokan Hotel in Shizuoka, Connie Mack invited Sotaro Suzuki to his room. The regal manager closed the door, and they sat down for what Suzuki realized would be a serious discussion. Mack had not been at the ballpark. He had elected to visit a resort with the wives and nonplayers, but Ruth had provided a report on Sawamura's remarkable outing. Mack asked Suzuki, would the young pitcher be interested in coming to the United States to play professionally? The Athletics' manager knew of the plans to start a pro league in Japan, but nonetheless it would be an opportunity for Sawamura to play at the highest level. Sotaro promised to ask Sawamura. The answer, however, was predictable. Despite his competitive spirit and drive to beat the Major Leaguers, Sawamura would remain in Japan and honor his decision to play in the new league. "I'm interested, but also afraid to go" was the young pitcher's official response. Mack smiled and did not press for a more definitive answer.

By the next morning, as readers unfurled their newspapers and read the headlines, Sawamura would be a national hero. Although the Japanese had not won, they showed that they were capable of conquering their opponents. A writer for the *Yomiuri* concluded that the game demonstrated the "possibility of a Japan-America World Series." The game would become a symbol of Japan's struggles against the West, just as Ichiko's victory against the Yokohama Country Club had forty years earlier. Many Japanese felt that with enough fighting spirit and practice, their countrymen could surpass the Major Leaguers, just as they believed their military would surpass the Western powers. As years passed the importance of the game grew, and Sawamura's stature increased as he became a symbol of Imperial Japan.

23

Capt. Koji Muranaka's plans to save Japan were almost ready. The special session of parliament would convene in seven days. Knowing that previous coup attempts had been betrayed from the inside, Muranaka had kept his group of assassins small. Only two fellow officers, Lts. Asaichi Isobe and Taro Kataoka, and a half-dozen academy cadets would help him initiate the Showa Restoration by eliminating the offending politicians during the special session.

But Muranaka had not scrutinized his followers closely enough.

Capt. Masanobu Tsuji commanded the Imperial Japanese Army Academy. Thirty-four years old, thin with a shaved head, an arrogant high forehead, a small mustache, and small eyes hiding behind round rimmed glasses, Tsuji was both ingenious and unstable. His future war record would bear both out. He would be responsible for the brilliant plan to capture Singapore and would be cited for bravery, but would be argumentative, insubordinate, and extraordinarily brutal. He ordered the massacre of five thousand civilians in Singapore and numerous executions during the Bataan Death March. In 1944 while in command in Burma, Tsuji reportedly held a banquet for his officers where he served the liver of a captured Allied pilot. He supposedly declared, "The more we consume, the more we shall be inspired by a hostile spirit towards the enemy," and chastised the men who would not eat it as cowards.[1]

Although Tsuji would rant about the immorality and slovenliness of fellow officers, claiming that they had forgotten their duty to the emperor, he was no friend to Muranaka or his fellow restorationists. After the failed coup in October 1931, the Imperial Army had split into two distinctive cliques. The Kodo-ha, or Imperial Way, consisting of Mitsugi Nishida's Young Officers, still pushed for the Showa

Restoration and the complete reform of Japanese society through the principles of Ikki Kita, while the Tosei-ha, or Control Faction, made up of the more established officers who had formed the nucleus of the Cherry Society, had abandoned the ideal of societal reform. These ideological differences were now directing internal army politics, appointments, and even military strategy. Tsuji supported the Control Faction and recently discovered a chance to ingratiate himself with the leaders of the Tosei.

Muranaka had made little secret of his political views. He was widely recognized as one of the Imperial Way's spokesmen and had even met with the rival Control leaders, including Tsuji, to discuss reuniting the factions in November 1933. Catching wind of Muranaka's talk of a coup, Tsuji instructed a cadet named Sato to infiltrate the group. Once Muranaka's plans were revealed, Tsuji contacted a fellow member of the Control Faction within the War Ministry, who called the Kempeitai, Japan's brutal military police.[2]

On November 20, the same day Eiji Sawamura pitched his masterpiece, the Kempeitai arrived at the Imperial Japanese Army Academy. They probably came at dawn—they often did, both to inspire terror and to catch their prey unawares. Wearing the standard khaki cavalry uniform with high, shiny black leather boots and the infamous white armbands with the two red kanji for "Law Soldier" on their left arms, they marched up the hill to the academy's barracks. Probably rousing Muranaka and his conspirators from their beds, they made their arrests and led the group away to the Kempeitai's dreaded headquarters.

News of the arrests and conspiracy would remain hidden until the Tokyo War Crimes Tribunal in 1946. Only a handful of men knew that bloodshed, revolt, and maybe even civil war had nearly disrupted the All American baseball tour.

24

Sawamura's pitching masterpiece gave All Nippon confidence as the two teams embarked on an eight-day, six-game junket of southern Japan. Their one-thousand-mile journey included stops in Nagoya, Osaka, Kokura, and Kyoto.

There was little to do on the long train rides. To the amusement of the Japanese sportswriters, the Americans passed the time playing cards and drinking. The private cars contained well-stocked bars, and the Babe took full advantage of the whiskey and Japanese beer, which he declared the best he had ever tasted. It was Earl Averill, however, who astounded his hosts with the amount that he could, and did, drink. But not all the travelers were thrilled with the refreshments. Julia Ruth recalled that while there was plenty of alcohol, their hosts had neglected other beverages. Not a beer drinker, Julia remembers being parched, wishing for a glass of water, as the train whizzed by terraced rice paddies, mountains, and villages.[1] Moe Berg most likely followed his usual routine of carrying a suitcase full of newspapers to read on the train. Current issues of his usual papers from the United States, Britain, and France were hard to find in Tokyo, but the *Japan Times*, *Japan Advertiser*, *Mainichi Daily News*, and *Japan Chronicle* would have kept him abreast of the local and international news.

The team arrived in Nagoya, Japan's fourth-largest city with 989,000 inhabitants, on November 21. Known as a friendly, easy city in contrast to the bustling and businesslike atmosphere of Tokyo or the gruff, gritty life in industrial Osaka, Nagoya was the center of Japanese textiles, lacquerware, and porcelain production. The regional accent was, according to a popular travel guide published earlier in the year, "the best language in which to make love." The author added, "No mortal man can resist a beautiful woman whispering in the dulcet accents of Nagoya. The secret of this tongue consists in its endless flow of incomprehensible cadence; it goes on winding and twisting like an eel, ungraspable and interminable, in which you can make neither head nor tail of a single sentence, and in which 'yeses' and 'noes' are so intermixed amid a maze of honorifics that you cannot tell whether the speaker is paying you compliments or gibing you."[2]

No game was scheduled, so they spent the day sightseeing. The party wandered down the city's narrow, crowded streets, turned a corner, and stopped in wonder. Ahead rose Nagoya Castle with its breathtaking wedding-cake-shaped, 184-foot, five-story keep. At its apex stood two golden dolphins, each reportedly worth more than a million yen. They had been the finishing touches in 1612, talismans to ward off fire. They would do their job for 333 years, until American bombers would destroy the castle along with the city in May 1945. The group toured the castle and grounds and stopped before the southwest tower for a group photograph. Afterward, they visited one of the city's porcelain factories. Struck by the beauty of the wares, most of the women ordered table settings and arranged for them to be shipped directly to their homes in the States. The tourists also signed stacks of unfired plates with a brush and slip. The pottery immediately went into the kiln and would later be delivered to the players as souvenirs.[3]

It was back to baseball the following afternoon (Thursday, November 22), as the teams clashed at Narumi Ballpark in Nagoya. Joe Cascarella, who had been pounded for twenty-three hits and thirteen runs in the intrasquad game eleven days before, took the mound for the Americans. Inspired by Sawamura's performance and the near victory in Shizuoka, the Japanese attacked Cascarella early. Kumeyasu Yajima began the game with a triple down the right-field foul line and scored moments later as Hisanori Karita singled up the middle. Hot-hitting catcher Toshiharu Inokawa then singled for the third consecutive hit. With runners at first and second and no outs, Miyake ordered his cleanup hitter, Minoru Yamashita, to sacrifice. Yamashita dutifully laid down the bunt to advance the runners, and Karita scored on the next play as Isamu Fuma grounded out to second. Star second baseman Shigeru Mizuhara, who was hitless in four games, struck out to end the inning, but for only the second time in eleven games, the Japanese led.

The lead lasted for just five batters, as the Japanese committed two errors in the bottom half of the inning. Three singles later the All Americans led 3–2. At that point Masao Date, the former Waseda pitcher who had pitched well in the 5–1 loss in All Nippon's first game, settled down and shut out the mighty All Americans for the next six innings. The Japanese batters, meanwhile, were hitting Cascarella hard. Fourteen hits, including a triple by Date, two RBI hits by Fuma, and an RBI single by Karita put All Nippon ahead 5–3 entering the bottom of the eighth. On the bench Ruth, who was managing the All Americans, was noticeably agitated. His large face scrunched in a frown, "he directed every move with growing signs of unrest," reported the *Osaka Mainichi*.[4]

Earl Averill led off the eighth for the Americans. Although he had already hammered six home runs in the series, the Earl of Snohomish patiently worked out a walk. On the mound Date was visibly tired. Many waited in anticipation for Miyake to take the ball from Date and bring in Sawamura to finish the game, but the manager remained in the dugout. Date next walked Bing Miller and surrendered a weak single to catcher Frank Hayes that drove in Averill. It was now 5–4 with runners on first and second and nobody out. Miyake remained in the dugout, and Date remained on the mound. A sacrifice bunt and sacrifice fly scored Miller to tie the game. With two outs Charlie Gehringer drove the ball into right field to knock in the go-ahead run and ended up at third after Yajima bobbled the ball. At last an exhausted Date induced Ruth to ground to second for the third out. The Japanese lead was gone. They now trailed 6–5.

With Cascarella spent, Whitehill tired from his complete game in Shizuoka, and games scheduled for each of the next four days, Ruth brought in Jimmie Foxx to pitch the ninth. After Yamashita popped up Fuma tripled into the right-center alley, his fourth hit of the day, to put the tying run just ninety feet away with one out. Osamu Mihara, the infamous Nosey from the 1931 tour, was due up next. Mihara had just one hit and five strikeouts in fourteen at bats against the Americans, so Miyake decided to bring in the five-foot-one pitcher, Shinji Hamazaki, to pinch-hit. Hamazaki was not inept with the bat. When not pitching for Keio University, he played the outfield and had hit .308 during the 1927 Big Six season. But still it seems a strange choice. The All Americans brought the infield in to defend against the squeeze and also to prevent Fuma from scoring on a ground ball. Hamazaki swung away and struck out. Mamoru Sugitaya, the solid outfielder with seven hits against the Major Leaguers, popped out to second to end the game.

Afterward, both Lou Gehrig and the *Japan Times* criticized Miyake's managerial decisions. Each felt that the Japanese might have won the game had Miyake brought in Sawamura in the eighth inning or tried a squeeze play to score Fuma in the ninth. Gehrig told Sotaro Suzuki that either of these moves would have made things tough strategically and psychologically for the American team.[5]

After the game on Thursday evening the All Americans' trainer, Edward "Doc" Ebling, told Sotaro Suzuki, "No more tough games after this. Tomorrow, Gomez is starting. Even if Sawamura pitches after that, there won't be any problem." What could he mean?, Suzuki wondered, but Doc would not elaborate. Later that night the players attended a fireworks display. Before the show started Suzuki sat down next to Lefty and June Gomez and asked what Ebling meant. Gomez smiled and replied, "You'll see . . ."[6]

With Gomez on the mound the following day, the All Americans won easily, 6–2. The Major Leaguers took a 4–0 lead into the sixth when Gomez walked the pitcher Takeda and allowed a double to Sugitaya, a single to Mihara, and a triple to Fuma. All Nippon scored twice, but it would have been more if Gehringer had not turned an unusual double play. With nobody out and Sugitaya on third and Mihara on first, Karita hit a sharp grounder to third. Foxx fielded it, looked Sugitaya back to the bag, and threw to second to force Mihara. As Foxx threw Sugitaya dashed home, but Gehringer fired a strike from second base to nip him at the plate. The Americans added two more runs in the seventh to pull away, and Gomez shut down the Japanese bats to win in just an hour and a half. By dusk the players had checked out of the hotel and were on the limited express to Osaka.[7]

With its proximity to the medieval capital at Kyoto, Osaka had long been Japan's commercial center and a rival city to Tokyo. In the 1930 census it was the largest city in Japan with a population of 2.5 million (compared to Tokyo's 2.1 million) and produced nearly a trillion yen worth of industrial goods annually. As befitting a commercial and industrial center, the city's culture focused on money, and its inhabitants were known for their directness and gruff demeanors.

On the western outskirts of the city stood Koshien Stadium—the pride of Japanese baseball. Opened in 1924, two years before Meiji Jingu Stadium, it was the largest stadium in Asia, having recently been expanded to hold seventy thousand. A mighty metal overhang supported by massive iron girders sheltered steep infield stands from the elements and cast the upper seats in dark shadow. The playing field was huge: 360 feet down the lines, 394 feet to straight-away center, and 420 feet in the alleys. Yankee Stadium at the time, by comparison, was about 300 feet down the lines, 350 feet in the right-field alley, 402 feet in the left-field alley, and a distant 487 to center. The Americans complained that the field was too large. Mack told reporters that Koshien's size limited home runs and made the games "boring and no fun," while Ruth cursed, "Whoever built this ballpark is an idiot!"[8]

The All Americans woke up early at the Koshien Hotel on Saturday, November 24, and were brought to Matsuzakaya department store, one of Osaka's largest, at ten. After shaking hands and smiling for pictures, they were presented with souvenir silk scarves and fed lunch before rushing off to the ballpark.

At least fifty thousand fans packed Koshien Stadium to watch the All Americans. Osakans have a reputation as boisterous people, and the fans did their city justice, shouting and cheering throughout the game. Miyake decided to start Masao Date, who had pitched so well for seven innings two days earlier. Date was up for the challenge and dominated the Americans for the first three innings. But in the fourth an error by second baseman Osamu Mihara put Foxx on first and rattled Date. The Japanese ace then walked Averill and gave up consecutive hits to Bing Miller, Frankie Hayes, pitcher Earl Whitehill, and Rabbit McNair. By the time little Shinji Hamazaki came on in relief, Date had surrendered four and the game was essentially over. Hamazaki fared no better. He limited the damage in the fourth to just another run, but gave up two more in the fifth and another four in the sixth before leaving the game. On the other side, White- hill pitched masterfully, shutting out the Japanese in all but one in- ning. The only hiccup came in the sixth when Mihara singled up the middle, Karita walked, and Isamu Fuma came through again with another RBI triple. Fuma would later score on an Inokawa ground- out. At the end of nine the All Americans finished with fifteen to All Nippon's three. Despite twelve American and seven Japanese hits, there were no home runs.[9] Even Ruth had not come close, hitting two singles before a Kenichi Aoshiba pitch hit him on the ankle in the seventh and he had to be helped off the field. Doc Ebling went straight to work in the dugout, massaging the swollen joint, and Ruth told reporters that he expected to play the following day.

The *Japan Weekly Chronicle* called Sunday's game "a dull sort of af- fair." It was another split-squad match with Ruth's men (Warstler, Karita, Ruth, Foxx, Averill, Nidegawa, Nakajima, Berg, and Aoshiba pitching) taking on Miller's men (Mihara, Horio, Gehringer, Geh- rig, McNair, Miller, Yajima, Hayes, and Brown on the mound). To attract fans the All Americans held a rematch of the home run con- test between Ruth, Gehrig, Averill, and Foxx. This time Foxx won with a 396-foot shot, but the contest failed to attract a large crowd. Only thirty thousand showed up, and there were "sizable gaps" in the stands. The *Chronicle* speculated that "fans had little stomach for an exhibition game."[10]

As the fourth game in as many days, the players looked tired. They played mechanically, just going through the motions. Ruth's ankle had recovered enough for him to play, but he fared poorly at the plate, gaining a single in three at bats and flying out with bases loaded in the sixth. Once again the All Americans failed to hit a home run—the last one had been Gehrig's game winner off Sawamura in Shizuoka. But to nearly everybody's surprise nineteen-year-old Usa- buro Shintomi, who had joined the All Nippons straight from Kokura Technical School and was playing third base for Miller's team, whis- tled a line drive into the left-field stands off Aoshiba. It was only the second Japanese home run of the series. To add spice to the listless game, the local promoters convinced Lefty Gomez to pitch the ninth inning for both teams. He set both sides down easily.

For Stuart Bell the trip back to the hotel was more memorable than the game. Bell decided to try a local taxi. He had no trouble with communicating his destination; it was the driver's skill that caused concern. "My chauffeur ran a bicyclist, who was doing nothing more out of the way than delivering a case of beer, into the side of a truck, scraped the hide off a horse, and finally ran by a school building, thus bringing a Japanese policeman along side. The policeman took no notice of me, thank heavens, but subjected the driver to long questioning. The driver happened to be dumber than most Japanese drivers and thus got out of the difficulty by being entirely speech struck."[11]

After dinner, the players boarded a southbound sleeper train to Shimonoseki, a city at the southwestern tip of the main Japanese island of Honshu. It was pouring when the teams arrived at 7:40 the next morning and had been raining all night. Most of the players expected the game to be canceled, but they were scheduled to play in Kyoto the next day, leaving no opportunity for a makeup game. Ruth, therefore, agreed to play in the rain.

The players checked into the Sanyo Hotel, ate, and changed into their uniforms. Dressed to play, they boarded a ferry to cross the famed Straits of Shimonoseki (more properly known as the Kanmon Straits). This two-thirds-of-a-mile stretch of water separating Honshu from the southern island of Kyushu has been a strategic military site for more than a thousand years and the site of several significant naval battles. By 1934 Japan had fortified the straits and declared the area a strategic zone. No photographs or drawings of the area were permitted, but that did not stop Moe Berg. Out came his movie camera, and moments later he had recorded the famous body of water.

At the docks on the other side cars met the players and brought them to the Itozu Grounds in the town of Kokura, hometown to All Nippon's newest home run hitter, Usaburo Shintomi. Though the rain had mostly stopped, the condition of the field was laughable. Ankle-deep mud covered the dirt infield, and pondlike puddles dotted the outfield. Normally, the game would have been called at this point, but between twenty and thirty thousand fans had squeezed into the tiny stadium and were waiting to watch the great American stars. They had begun to arrive early in the morning, and the seats were filled hours before game time, despite the driving rain. The outfield contained no bleachers, just a grassy slope where spectators huddled together. The rains had flooded the area, and eleven thousand squatted or knelt with water up to their hips. Among the dedicated wet fans sat a man with an ancient samurai sword. He had walked eighty miles to attend the game and announced that he would present the sword as a token of friendship to the first American to hit a home run. Another fan carried a large doll made in the likeness of the Babe.[12]

The game itself was a joke. Ruth, Gehrig, Averill, and Rabbit McNair played in rubber boots, and Ruth borrowed an umbrella from a fan, huddling under it while playing first base. The score remained at zero for the first three innings before the Americans started to hit. Three came across in the fourth, and Averill won the sword by hitting a long fly into the soggy fans sitting beyond right field.

An inning later Osamu Mihara, playing second base, readied himself for the next pitch. His soaking wool uniform seemed to weigh a hundred pounds. Cold rain hit the back of his neck and trickled down his back beneath his jersey, sending shivers down his spine. Their pitcher, Shinji Hamazaki, was in a tight spot—bases loaded and Babe Ruth at the plate with a 3-0 count. Mihara shifted his feet, trying to find a better footing. His cleat escaped the mud with a loud sucking sound, only to sink back in the mire moments later. Hamazaki would have to put this next pitch down the middle of the plate or walk in a run.

Ruth stepped out of the batter's box, looked up at the stands, and gestured to the outfield fence. The fans cheered. Mihara and his teammates looked at each other. No, thought Mihara, that's too much. But, of course, he had done it before. Every fan knew of the Babe's "called shot" in the 1932 World Series. Ruth stepped to the plate and dug in with his big rubber boots. The crowd laughed and began chanting, "Home run! Home run!" Hamazaki's pitch came right down the middle, belt high, and the Sultan of Swat connected with a mighty swing. The ball rose in a majestic arc and sailed over the right-field seating area and into the mist beyond. Mihara watched it bounce off the roof of a nearby building, shattering its clay tiles.

Initially stunned by the blast, the wet and happy fans erupted with a "tremendous ovation" for the Bambino.[13]

The All Americans ended with eleven hits and eight runs, but the *Osaka Mainichi* noted that "they can hit almost at will" and would have hit many more "had they cared to run out every hit." On the mound Cascarella dominated the Japanese hitters with "baffling hooks and drops," as he scattered seven hits and gave up a single run for the victory.[14]

Immediately after the final out the drenched players hurried back to the ferry and to their hotel in Shimonoseki to change. Several hours later they were back on the train headed north to Kyoto.

PART 4

"There will be no war between
the United States and Japan."

CONNIE MACK, January 1935

25

Eiji Sawamura's near victory on the twentieth had brought Kyoto fans to a near frenzy as the game on the twenty-eighth approached. Many were convinced that the local boy, whom they had watched pitch Kyoto Commercial School to the championship just months before, could handle the All Americans in front of his hometown supporters. Promoters sold more than thirty thousand tickets within days of the event being announced and sent out invitations to local celebrities, including Prince Taka Kuni, a member of the imperial family and the chief priest of Ise Shrine. Game day would be full of special events. Prior to the game the All Americans would conduct a demonstration on fielding, and local businessman Tanejiro Yasuda promised one hundred yen to every player who hit a home run.[1]

The rain that swamped Kokura's field continued to fall throughout the night, and by the time the train pulled into Kyoto at 9:25 a.m., the promoters had postponed the afternoon game until the following day, November 28. Once the team checked into the Kyoto Hotel, representatives from the local office of the *Yomiuri Shimbun* came to see Ruth. After exchanging pleasantries the newspaper officials handed the Babe three thousand yen to cover the players' entertainment expenses during the off day. Equivalent to about nine hundred dollars, it was a generous amount in Japan—more than four times the average annual salary of a skilled laborer such as a carpenter or blacksmith. Kyoto was famous for its high-class geisha houses, and perhaps the *Yomiuri* representatives had this form of entertainment in mind when they presented such a gift. Ruth thanked the gentlemen, pocketed the cash, and went about his business.[2]

The players had the day free to visit the ancient capital. In 794 Emperor Kammu, wanting to escape the strong Buddhist presence at the capital of Nara, moved the imperial court three hundred miles to the northeast and built the city of Kyoto. Despite numerous attacks during Japan's many civil wars and being nearly destroyed during the Ōnin War of 1467–77, Kyoto remained the country's capital and center of culture for the next 1,074 years. In 1934 the city contained more than a thousand temples and shrines, including some of the oldest and most spectacular temples in Japan. Highlights included Kiyomizu, a Buddhist temple established in 798, with the current buildings dating to 1633. Built on a cliff with magnificent views of the city, a wooden platform in front of the main temple hangs over a forty-foot precipice, supported by a robust wooden scaffold. Folklore stated that if a person jumped from the temple and survived the fall, his wish would come true. Of the 234 known attempts of the feat, only 34 people had their dreams dashed on the rocks below.

A new player joined the All Nippon squad that evening. He was impossible to miss, standing six foot three with blond hair, blue eyes, and speaking Japanese like a native. The Americans must have wondered how Victor Starffin ended up on the Japanese team, but even their wildest conjectures could not rival the true story.

Victor was born in Nizhny Tagil, an industrial city and mining center in the Ural Mountains of Russia, in 1916. His father, Konstantin Starffin, had graduated from the Russian Military Academy and was an officer in the czar's Imperial Guards when the Russian Revolution began in 1917. As Konstantin fought against the communists, Victor and his mother, Evdokia, fled east. On the run for more than a year, they finally rendezvoused with Konstantin in Yeniseisk, a small town in eastern Siberia. But even there they were not safe. The communists now controlled the entire country and were hunting down czarist sympathizers. The Starffins decided to flee to Harbin in China. Disguising themselves as local farmers, they traveled southeast. The Red Army, however, was on the lookout for refugees. At one point, finding themselves cornered, Konstantin led Evdokia and five-year-old Victor to a wagon packed with corpses. They hid among the decaying bodies until the danger passed.

At last the Starffins arrived in Harbin in 1921. They had been "on the run" for three years. Harbin, however, was no safe haven. The city was swollen with refugees, jobs were scarce, and poverty and even starvation were commonplace. The situation worsened in 1924 when the Soviet and Chinese governments concluded a treaty giving the Red Army control over Russians in Harbin. Once again the Starffins fled, this time to Japan.

To prevent Russian expatriates from settling in one place, the Japanese government allocated a certain number of refugees to specific areas. The Starffins, along with twenty other families, were assigned to the city of Asahikawa in Hokkaido. Nine-year-old Victor soon made friends with the local children, who taught him a new game—baseball.

Victor began attending Nissho Elementary (which contained the equivalent of American grades 1–8) and joined the baseball team. He excelled and as a fourth grader began pitching for the varsity squad. His fastball was nearly unhittable, and Nissho soon became the city's best baseball team. By the time Victor reached the sixth grade he routinely struck out seventeen to eighteen opponents per game and began playing on adult amateur teams.

The Starffins adapted well to Asahikawa. Konstantin began selling textiles and used the profits to open a café that featured Russian-style breads. In the summer of 1932 Konstantin hired twenty-eight-year-old Maria Nikolaevna Stokanova as a waitress and "poster girl." Rumors soon flourished of an affair between the beautiful waitress and her employer. In October 1932 Maria met another Russian refugee named Dmitri Fyodorovitch Korsatokov. The two developed a relationship and planned to marry, and Maria moved into Korsatokov's apartment on January 13, 1933. Within a week of the move, she quit her job at the café.[3]

At 8:30 p.m. on January 23 Konstantin went to the apartment. Korsatokov was away on business, but Maria was home. The two began arguing. The topic has never been adequately explained. Some believed that Konstantin was jealous of Maria's relationship with Korsatokov. Konstantin would tell the police that it was a political discussion, but few believed that. The equally unconvincing official explanation was that they argued over Maria's treatment at the café. The argument escalated and turned physical. Konstantin drew a jack-knife. Pushing her down and straddling her, he stabbed her in the chest. Then he ran.

At 9:10 Konstantin entered the Asahikawa police station and confessed his crime. Officers hurried to the apartment and brought Maria to the hospital, but she died at 11:30. Over the next few days police interrogated Konstantin before officially charging him with murder. He remained incarcerated until sentenced in June to eight years. With Konstantin in jail and disgraced, Evdokia was forced to sell the café. The family was now destitute. Evdokia tried selling cosmetics, but it did not bring in much money. Luckily, Victor's success on the mound enabled them to make ends meet.

Victor was now enrolled at Asahikawa Middle School, which had high academic standards but a poor baseball team. The school hoped that Starffin could lead them to the celebrated Koshien tournament. The idea seemed plausible, as soon after joining Victor led Asahikawa to the quarterfinal of the Hokkaido baseball championship, where they lost 2–1 to Hakodate Middle School. After Konstantin's arrest Victor's teammates chipped in to pay his tuition, and his coach, Shinazo Yotsudo, provided an allowance for the family. Victor responded by pitching his team into the Hokkaido championship game in each of the next two seasons. In 1933 Victor hurled a no-hitter in the first round of the tournament, but Asahikawa lost in the final. The story repeated itself in 1934, as poor fielding allowed Sapporo Commercial to overcome Asahikawa in the championship. The year 1935 would be Victor's last at Asahikawa and his final chance to go to Koshien. After graduation he planned to attend Waseda University.

Victor's success naturally drew the attention of Tadao Ichioka. The more Ichioka heard about Starffin, the more he wanted him for the future professional baseball league. The problem was how to convince the young man to join the All Nippon team and give up a chance to pitch at Koshien and forgo a Waseda education. Ichioka first turned to his old Waseda teammate Jiro Kuji, who was the most famous player in Hokkaido and would catch for the All Nippon team. He asked Kuji to pressure the young man to join, as it is socially difficult in Japan to refuse an explicit request of an elder member of the same organization.[4]

Although he felt that he could not ignore Ichioka's request, Kuji had strong reservations. As a Hokkaido native Kuji also wanted Starffin to lead his school to a championship at Koshien. Choosing a passive-aggressive route, Kuji decided not to confront Starffin but instead to ask the boy's coach, Shinazo Shinobe. Shinobe, however, refused to help and backed Victor's decision to remain in school.

Despite Starffin's refusal to join, on October 5, 1934, the *Yomiuri Shimbun* announced that Victor would be a member of the All Nippon team. Shinobe was livid and assured local fans and newspapers that Victor would remain with his high school team and then go to college. Yet *Yomiuri* continued to feature Starffin as one of its players. On October 8 the paper proclaimed, "Victor Starffin is the monster of middle school baseball."[5] *Yomiuri*'s lofty claims backfired. After the All Americans began defeating the Japanese, readers wrote to the paper, demanding to see the "monster of middle school baseball" stop the Major League bats. Embarrassed, Ichioka searched for another method of procuring Starffin.

Ichioka contacted his old friend Tsutomu Mori, a former member of the Waseda University judo club who had formed a right-wing group called the Juo Club. Using his connections within Japan's ultranationalistic organizations, Mori contacted Mitsuru Toyama, head of the Dark Ocean Society and underworld leader. Toyama penned a letter to Evdokia Starffin promising financial support if Victor would forgo his amateur career and join All Nippon. Mori entrusted the letter to his henchman Motoo Akimoto and on November 15 sent him north to bring Victor to Tokyo. Word of Akimoto's impending visit leaked out, and the local newspaper ran an article on the sixteenth proclaiming, "Mr. Akimoto has come to Asahikawa to take Victor to the professional baseball team." Fans, now concerned for Victor's welfare as well as his amateur career, hid the Starffins.

Not being able to locate either Victor or his mother, Akimoto drew on Toyama's political connections and had the local police find Victor. But before Akimoto could visit Starffin, Victor's teammates and fans formed a bodyguard to keep the gangster away. Akimoto, however, had one more trick.

Refugees who committed a crime in Japan were often returned to their place of origin. As a former White Russian army officer, sending Konstantin back to the Soviet Union was equivalent to a death sentence. Akimoto used his influence with the Special Higher Police (Tokubetsu Kôtô Keisatsu), a unit created to monitor and control politic dissent, to prepare Konstantin for deportation. Faced with Akimoto's extortion, Victor finally gave in. Working through middlemen, Akimoto promised a large signing bonus, a twenty-yen monthly salary, and a guarantee that *Yomiuri* would provide the Starffin family with a stipend should Victor become unable to pitch. A further surprise awaited the Starffins. Konstantin's prison sentence was inexplicitly reduced by two years, and he was transferred from the regular cells to the more comfortable prison hospital.

Fearing a possible riot when the agreement was announced, Victor and Evdokia packed a small suitcase and left their apartment at 2:00 a.m. on November 25. They met Akimoto at his *ryokan* and left town on the 3:10 a.m. train. When they arrived in Tokyo on the twenty-sixth at 1:30 p.m., Shoriki met the train. The *Yomiuri* president brought the Starffins to meet Toyama and then sent Victor on the 10:55 p.m. train to Kyoto to join his new teammates.

In Kyoto the rain had stopped, and the morning of November 28 was clear but cold. Yet a storm of a different sort began. Somehow word of the All Americans' entertainment stipend leaked out. Many Japanese were outraged. Rival newspapers declared that if *Yomiuri*'s profits were so high that they could afford to waste three thousand yen, they should be donating more to the starving farmers in northern Japan and not giving it to foreign ballplayers. The All Americans would not learn of the controversy until after the game, when dumb luck would intervene.[6]

The game began on time at 2:00 p.m. As expected Eiji Sawamura took the mound for All Nippon amid "thunderous applause" by the thirty thousand fans.[7] Alas, the young hurler could not repeat his stellar performance. The All Americans jumped to a 2–0 lead in the bottom of the first, adding five more in the third and another three in the fourth. Sawamura was wild, walking seven and throwing a wild pitch. At Shizuoka the Americans had been fooled by his curve and the late movement on his two-seam fastball, but in Kyoto the Major Leaguers refrained from chasing the curve ball, letting most break harmlessly out of the strike zone. When they did swing, the All Americans hit Sawamura's pitches hard. On top of the seven walks Sawamura surrendered eight hits before Miyake removed him with one out in the bottom of the fourth. It was almost as if the Americans knew what type of pitch was coming.

Kenichi Aoshiba, also from the Kyoto area, finished the game for All Nippon. He did only slightly better, giving up seven runs in four and two-thirds innings, including a one-hundred-yen winning home run to Bing Miller. Once again the Japanese defense did little to help their pitchers. They booted the ball six times during the game. At the end of nine the Americans had cruised to a 14–1 victory.[8]

After the game, the players returned to the Kyoto Hotel to change and eat before catching the train to Tokyo. Mack, the older men, and most of the women would stay in Kyoto and visit the ancient city of Nara. To the annoyance of some of the players, Claire Ruth and Violet Whitehill accompanied the team—perhaps to keep an eye on their husbands. Rabbit Warstler wrote in his diary, "Mrs. Ruth and Mrs. Whitehill just *had* to go along."[9]

That evening, Sotaro Suzuki stopped by Ruth's room to explain that he had lost some photographs the Babe had asked him to keep safe. Hearing the news, the Babe began to erupt when Lefty Gomez diverted Ruth's attention.[10]

"Suzuki, remember what you asked me at the fireworks?" Both Ruth and Sotaro turned to look at Gomez. "Babe told us to study Sawamura's habits," Gomez continued, "and we figured that he twists his lips when he throws the hook, and twists them a lot when he tries to put extra break on it. That's why even a pitcher like me got a hit off of him today."

The Babe smiled before adding, "That's big league baseball . . ."

Later in the evening Suzuki was in his hotel room when Sawamura knocked on the door. He came in smiling and seemed in high spirits despite the loss. They talked for a few moments, with Suzuki probably revealing how Sawamura was tipping his pitches. Suzuki's roommate, Lefty O'Doul, entered and, joining the conversation, told Sawamura, "All the American players like you. We all think you're a great pitcher. But in a game, things are different. In serious baseball, we can't make allowances. We couldn't go easy on you just because you're the hometown kid."

Just before the team left town, Connie Mack was told of the controversy surrounding the entertainment stipend. Mack had never seen or heard about the money. He questioned Ruth, who produced the wad of cash. The Babe had misinterpreted the gesture and thought the money was meant exclusively for his use. Luckily, he had not spent it. He now gave it to Mack, who eased the tension by donating the sum to the City of Kyoto to help rebuild the damage caused by the typhoon in September. The gesture not only extradited the *Yomiuri Shimbun* from an embarrassing position but also furthered the All Americans' reputation as goodwill ambassadors.[11]

On the train back to Tokyo, Moe Berg was planning. He had been reading the local newspapers as usual when a small notice in the Monday, November 26, *Japan Advertiser* caught his attention. Mrs. Cecil Burton Lyon, Ambassador Joseph Grew's daughter, had just given birth to a daughter at St. Luke's Hospital in Tokyo. An outlandish idea had popped into his head. Tomorrow, he would attempt it.[12]

26

The next morning, Thursday, November 29, was Thanksgiving in the United States. The game that day would be played in Omiya, about fifteen miles north of Tokyo, as Meiji Jingu Stadium was hosting the first true American football game on Japanese soil. Earlier in 1934 Waseda, Meiji, and Rikkyo universities organized football clubs manned primarily by American nisei students. To showcase the newly imported sport, league organizers held a traditional Thanksgiving Day football classic featuring an all-star squad from the universities against members of the Yokohama Country Club. Although larger than their Japanese opponents, few of the country club's squad had played organized football prior to the Thanksgiving match. Ambassador Grew and Prince Chichibu, the younger brother of the emperor, watched as the younger, fitter, faster, and better-trained Japanese collegians pummeled the foreigners 26–0. The Japanese victory helped popularize the sport, and just three years later twenty-five thousand watched college all-star teams from eastern and western Japan clash. The sport's popularity, however, died with the start of World War II, as the trappings of American culture first fell out of favor and then were banned by the military government.

As the All Americans gathered in the lobby of the Imperial Hotel for the short trip to Omiya, Moe Berg was missing. Later reports suggest that nobody noticed his absence and the players left without him. Once his teammates departed Berg dressed in a black kimono, combed his black hair in a Japanese style, and put on geta (traditional wooden sandals). It was just above freezing outside, so he probably slipped on an Inverness overcoat, concealed his 16mm movie camera beneath it, and quietly left the hotel. He headed southeast through Ginza. Berg knew the neighborhood well. In 1932 he had enjoyed strolling through the upscale shopping district, which he nicknamed Ginzberg, and had returned often during this trip. He probably took the most direct route to the bay down Harumi Dori (Harumi Avenue). Close to his destination he passed the Kabuki-za, a dramatic four-story theater built in the style of seventeenth-century Japanese castles. Every day the theater held a Kabuki performance that would last most of the day. Spectators came and went throughout the performances, eating *bento* (boxed lunches) and snacks and drinking beer and sake as they watched.

Despite the disguise Berg must have been conspicuous. He was a solid six foot one and 185 pounds, with broad shoulders and a large, square head and jaw. In 1934 the average Japanese twenty-year-old man stood just five foot two and a half, while his father averaged five foot one, a foot shorter than Berg.[1] His heavy build was also uncommon, as most Japanese men weighed between 120 and 130 pounds. At some point in his walk through Ginza, Berg stopped and, speaking Japanese, purchased a bouquet of flowers.

Harumi Dori ended at the Tsukiji Honganji temple, a bizarre-looking structure designed after an ancient Indian temple that had just been completed several months earlier. Beyond the temple the Sumida River entered Tokyo Bay. The smell of fish was unmistakable. Just out of sight was the newly constructed Tsukiji fish market. More than a thousand stalls sold about a thousand tons of fish daily. Nearly four hundred types of fish could be purchased, including large chunks of whale. Luckily, the morning's cold air suppressed the stench.

Berg turned north, parallel to the river. A few hundred yards ahead stood the new 5.7-acre campus of St. Luke's International Hospital. Founded in 1902 as an eight-room hospital by American missionary Dr. Rudolph Bolling Teusler, St. Luke's had become the most modern hospital in Japan. The original structure went through several renovations before being destroyed in the Great Kanto Earthquake of 1923. The new complex, just completed in 1933 under Teusler's direction, consisted of a seven-story concrete main building, topped with a tower, a shorter wing, and outbuildings. In a city rightly terrified of earthquakes, few buildings rose higher than four stories, and none came close to the height of St. Luke's tower. Teusler's tower drew the ire of at least one Japanese newspaper, which claimed that it was actually a "spy turret."[2] One wonders if Moe Berg knew of this allegation.

Berg strode up to St. Luke's entrance and announced that he was there to visit the ambassador's daughter, Elsie Lyon. Told that she was in a room on the fifth floor, he entered the elevator and pressed five. By the time the elevator arrived, he was alone. He tossed the flowers into the garbage just outside the elevator and, before the door closed, jumped back in and pushed seven.

In the center of the seventh-floor piazza within an enclosed dining area stood a narrow metal staircase spiraling up a dizzying 160 feet. Before ascending Berg probably removed his geta. The wooden clogs with their uneven soles would have been unstable on the winding, narrow metal stairs and would have boomed like a gong with each step, announcing his presence. Berg climbed. At first the only support was an open guardrail, but after he reached the roof of the dining area, the walls of the stone tower closed in around him. Open windows, covered with decorative metal grills, provided light, but as the day was overcast the winding staircase remained in shadow. As he neared the top a cold wind rushed through the open windows. The view at the top was magnificent. St. Luke's had commanding views of downtown and Tokyo Bay. Berg pulled out his Bell & Howell movie camera and took panoramic footage.[3] He panned the skyline, holding the camera still on a group of factories to the west and again on the waterfront. To cap off the footage he focused on Mount Fuji, just visible on the southwestern horizon.

After the game his teammates found Berg relaxing in the Imperial Hotel. He told those who asked that he had felt ill and, according to later interviews of his teammates, "discouraged any extensive probing of the matter."[4] Moe Berg wisely kept his adventure to himself. As an avid newspaper reader, Berg was undoubtedly aware of the Japanese spy paranoia and its harassment of foreign tourists with cameras.

In a confidential memo written on December 26, 1934, Ambassador Grew reported to Secretary of State Cordell Hull, "During recent months there have been renewed manifestations of spy hysteria in Japan. . . . Whereas the tendency to suspect foreigners . . . of nefarious prying into military secrets seems to be ingrained in the Japanese race and had always existed to an exaggerated degree, it is believed that recent spy scares . . . are largely the result of . . . the military to foster public apprehension."[5]

In the months prior to the tour, nationalistic newspapers titillated their readers with rumors of espionage. On March 16, 1934, the *Kobe Yushin Nippo* ran an article under the headline "Spies Are Displaying Activity under False Flag. Mysterious Actions of Aliens of Japanese Race Spying Our Military Secrets. They Are Extending Their Evil Hands to the Flowers of Our Army and Navy." The article warned readers to be wary of the Japanese Americans visiting Japan. "Some of them serve as spies in Japan for the . . . [American] government, and most of the rest fascinate people of the opposite sex with their accomplishments in dancing and dressing and fluent conversation and corrupt public morals, thus making themselves a nuisance to the Japanese government." The police, the paper noted, were "maintaining a strict watch over these thorns."[6]

Even ballplayers did not escape suspicion. During their 1932 visit Lefty O'Doul, Ted Lyons, and reporter Joe Cohen took a walk along Tokyo's waterfront on the morning of October 26. According to the *New York Times*, Cohen "was busy snapping the more picturesque scenes of the harbor when a policeman intervened and arrested him." The three were taken to a station house, where O'Doul identified himself and his friends. "When he told the policeman he was the great Lefty of the National League, everyone was apologetic. Permission to take all the pictures they wanted was given."[7]

Faced with numerous complaints of police harassing tourists, in November 1934 the Tourist Industry Bureau of the Railway Ministry insisted that a special government committee be formed "to consider better treatment of foreigners visiting the country." But only a month later, when the tour was over, the chiefs of the Foreign Affairs sections of the Metropolitan Police Board (Tokyo), Kanagawa, Hyogo, and Nagasaki prefectures met "to take positive measures in dealing with foreign spies as well as the entry of questionable foreigners."[8]

Moe Berg would tell no one about his climb up St. Luke's tower until the late 1950s. In 1958 he met Cecil and Elise Lyon, as well as their daughter, Alice, at a party in Paris. Berg entertained the family with the story of his exploit and their role in the affair.[9] But even then he did not explain why he had risked imprisonment to take those pictures. As we will see, it was not until after Berg's death that possible explanations emerged.

By staying in Tokyo Berg missed an opportunity to beef up his paltry .111 batting average. The ballpark at Omiya was small, holding just eight thousand spectators, with short outfield fences. Miyake started Kaichi Takeda for All Nippon, and the All Americans wasted little time crashing home run after home run. By the end of the first they were up 10–0. The Major Leaguers added one each in the third, fourth, and fifth innings, to build a 13–1 lead. Up by such a large margin, All American pitcher Earl Whitehill lost his focus and gave up four in the sixth, as Jimmy Horio finally came through with a three-run homer. After Takeda surrendered twenty hits and thirteen runs, Miyake brought in little Shinji Hamazaki. Hamazaki fared no better, giving up eight runs in the bottom of the sixth and two in the seventh. In the bottom of the eighth, with the score 23–5, Miyake allowed Victor Starffin to pitch. For all the misery Ichioka and Shoriki had put Starffin through, this would be his only inning in the entire series. The young Russian was wild at first, walking Lou Gehrig and later Earl Averill, but both his fastball and his curve were working well, and he struck out Jimmie Foxx between the two walks and induced Bing Miller to ground into a double play to end the inning. In all, the All Americans hit ten home runs—three by Gehringer, two by Ruth and pitcher Earl Whitehill, and one each by Foxx, Gehrig, and Hayes. Jimmy Horio finally had a reason to smile. Not only did he hit the three-run homer, but he also picked up a pair of singles. Yet even with the three hits, his batting average was still a miserable .216, not likely to lead to a Major League contract.

The All Americans returned to the Imperial Hotel for dinner. To their disappointment there was no American-style Thanksgiving feast. They ate off the menu as usual, or went to the American club for sukiyaki—Ruth's favorite Japanese food. Violet Whitehill complained that "the only thing we got to eat was fish."[10] They were having a wonderful time in Japan. It was the trip of a lifetime. But missing Thanksgiving made many homesick. It was time to return home.

27

The players had Friday, November 30, off. Some, like Harold Warstler, slept in. Warstler awoke around ten, ate breakfast, and headed over to the Kodak store. There, he met Eric McNair and Lefty Gomez and viewed their pictures. Perhaps inspired by his teammates' shots, Warstler spent the afternoon wandering the back streets of Tokyo, taking photographs. The players were on their own for dinner. Foxx, Warstler, and Bing Miller went to one of the few places in town that served American fare. After the meal the three took some pictures that would have made Moe Berg proud. A Japanese acquaintance—Warstler was not sure of his name but thought that he was with the mayoral office—invited the ballplayers to see a new Japanese cargo plane. The small group drove out to a nearby airfield where they were proudly shown one of the largest planes they had ever seen. The impressed Americans pulled out their cameras and snapped both still and movie footage for their albums.[1]

The All Americans woke up early on December 1, ready to play their last game on Japanese soil. They met in the lobby of the Imperial Hotel at nine for a brief meeting. Ruth got up from one of the hotel's deep armchairs and addressed the team. "This will be the last game in Japan so we are going to have Suzuki as today's manager."[2]

Sotaro Suzuki swallowed hard, thanked Ruth for the honor, and promised to do his best. He could feel the butterflies start in his stomach. "What if I lose?" he thought. Sawamura would pitch for All Nippon, and Suzuki knew that the boy was determined to end the games with a win. The Americans were also tired and homesick. They would not be at their best. The responsibility was almost too much to bear.

The team boarded a bus to travel sixty miles north to the small city of Utsunomiya for the game. Partway through the trip, umpire John Quinn stumbled down the aisle to Suzuki's seat. He handed Suzuki a heavy bag. "This is a present from all of us to you," he laughed. Sotaro opened it to find it full of coins. He smiled. Throughout the tour Suzuki had been in charge of the baggage. He was always scrounging for fifty-sen coins to tip the porters, and it had become a running joke. The bag contained nearly four hundred yen, a generous joke present.

At Utsunomiya they checked into the Seiyokan Hotel to lunch and change into their uniforms before heading to the ballpark. The day was clear but bitter cold, and the groundskeeper had set up charcoal stoves in the dugouts to help the players keep warm. Just before the start of the game, jovial fans passed several bottles of sake to the dugout, and the ballplayers, who had adapted well to Japanese drinking customs, heated the liquor over the burner and drank. Walking into the dugout, Suzuki noticed the bottle and ordered his players to stop. Before Suzuki could even finish the sentence, Earl Averill grabbed the bottle and emptied it in a single gulp. Smiling, the outfielder then ran out to his position in center field.

Clint Brown took the mound for the All Americans and immediately ran into trouble. After retiring Mihara to start the game, he walked Kumeyasu Yajima. Jimmy Horio, now batting third after his home run in Omiya, pounded a deep fly ball to center field. Averill staggered back and positioned himself under the ball, but with his impaired reflexes the ball glanced off his mitt, and Horio slid safely into second. With runners on second and third, Brown retired Minoru Yamashita, but consecutive singles by Usaburo Shintomi, Tokio Tominaga, and Hisashi Asakura gave the Japanese a 3–0 lead.

The butterflies in Suzuki's stomach felt like dive-bombers. Sawamura took the mound with a lead. The kid looked confident out there. Maybe he should not have told the young hurler how he was tipping his pitches. His generosity might cost him the game and make him the laughingstock of Japanese baseball.

But Suzuki had little to fear. Perhaps worried about tipping his pitches, Sawamura could not find the plate. He began by walking Warstler, then Gehringer, and then Ruth. With bases loaded and nobody out, Gehrig came to the plate. Sawamura had already given up 6 home runs during the tour, including the game winner to Gehrig on November 20. Four balls later the Iron Horse trotted down to first, forcing in Warstler for the first American run. The tipsy Averill struck out, but Sawamura then walked Foxx, scoring Gehringer. The inning ended as Bing Miller grounded into a double play.

Brown settled down in the top of the second and kept the score at 3–2. But Sawamura's control problems continued in the bottom half of the inning. He walked both Hayes and McNair before Gehringer took a 2-2 pitch deep for a 3-run homer. With a 5–3 lead and Sawamura not pitching well, Suzuki relaxed a little. The All American assault continued over the next two innings. By the time Kenichi Aoshiba replaced Sawamura to start the fifth, the young pitcher had surrendered 9 runs and walked an eye-popping 9 batters. Meanwhile, Brown scattered 7 hits to give Suzuki a comfortable 14–5 victory.

After the game, the hosts presented awards for the statistical leaders during the 18-game series. For leading the teams with a .408 batting average and 13 home runs, Babe Ruth received two large bronze vases. The Babe also finished first with 27 runs scored and 33 RBIs. Averill finished second in nearly every category with a .378 average, 8 homers, and 29 RBIs. Almost every American hit well, as the team combined for a .326 average (224 hits in 687 at bats), with 47 home runs and 193 runs scored. Just three of the position players hit under .275. Utility man Rabbit Warstler hit .267, and rookie Frankie Hayes hit a miserable .226 with 10 strikeouts, but honors for the lowest American average went to Moe Berg, who hit just .111 in his 18 at bats.

The Major League pitchers had dominated the Japanese. Discarding the November 11 split-squad game where Americans pitched for both teams, the pitchers had surrendered just 37 earned runs in 17 games for a 2.18 ERA and held All Nippon hitters to a paltry .210 batting average. Although the Japanese considered Lefty Gomez the top pitcher with his 5–0 record, 1.47 ERA, and 34 strikeouts, Earl Whitehill actually pitched better, going 6–0 with a 1.41 ERA and 11 fewer walks than Gomez. Even Jimmie Foxx performed admirably on the mound, posting a 1.50 ERA with 5 strikeouts in 6 innings.

Despite the overall poor performance by the Japanese hitters, a handful hit Major League pitching well. The catcher Toshiharu Inokawa led the team with a .348 average and a homer in 23 at bats. Kumeyasu Yajima and Isamu Fuma both finished just under .300 (.295 and .294, respectively), and Hisanori Karita, the outspoken shortstop, hit a respectable .276 with only 1 strikeout in a team-high 58 at bats. Another standout at the plate was pitcher Masao Date, who after going 2 for 8 against the Major Leaguers in 1931 added 4 hits in 9 at bats, including a double and triple, against the All Americans. Most of the stars of the Tokyo Big Six University League, however, fared poorly. Minoru Yamashita, the slugger from Keio, hit just .158, Shigeru Mizuhara, another Keio star, hit an embarrassing .095, while his Waseda rival, Osamu Mihara, came in at .158.

American Jimmy Horio finished at .195 with 6 strikeouts in 41 at bats but did hit a home run. His gamble to impress the All Americans and gain a Major League contract had failed. He lamented, "I wish I could have performed better. I regret that I wasn't in good condition during the series, probably because I wasn't accustomed to the Japanese circumstances. For the first two days in Japan, I was physically fit, and my arm was fine. After that, I got sick, and I was no good at all on the field. Otherwise, I am confident that on the field I could have fielded and thrown as well as Averill did." He added, "I was very happy to have played the American stars as a member of the all-Nippon. In the States, even PCL [Pacific Coast League] players have few opportunities to play those great stars. So I consider this a once-in-a-lifetime chance. I was glad that the Japanese players were so nice to me. So were the American players. O'Doul, Whitehill and others were kindly and gave me advice."[3]

The Japanese player who drew the most attention was Eiji Sawamura. Later in Manila Mack told the local press that Sawamura "is a good big league prospect. He could break into the big leagues in another two or three years, provided they don't kill him off."[4] Mack had no way of knowing the irony of his statement. Despite the young hurler's promise, his stats from the tour were unimpressive. In 28 and ⅔ innings Sawamura posted a 7.85 ERA with 25 walks and 25 strikeouts. Kenichi Aoshiba actually finished with a slightly lower 7.83 ERA with 5 more innings pitched. Sawamura's batting average against, however, was a respectable .277, by far the best on All Nippon's staff.

Once the awards were presented, the All Americans changed at the hotel and took a train back to Tokyo. As the acting manager, Sotaro Suzuki announced that he was fining Averill one hundred yen for drinking in the dugout. The inebriated center fielder had not only missed Horio's fly ball but also went a disappointing 1 for 4 with 2 strikeouts. Ruth praised Suzuki's decision, and Averill promptly paid.

They arrived late at the Imperial Hotel. It was nearly eight o'clock, and they had reservations on the express train to Kobe in an hour and a half. No time for dinner. Warstler grabbed sandwiches and ate in his room while he finished packing. Like most of the players, Warstler and his wife, Grace, had left their bulky luggage and bags of souvenirs at the Imperial during their southern road trip. He now had to gather these together and get them on the express train. An army of porters swarmed to the second floor to haul the players' luggage to the waiting cars.

Thousands waited for the players at Tokyo Station. Fans waved American and Japanese flags and shouted "Goodbye! Goodbye!" as officials escorted the players to the platform. Matsutaro Shoriki, Tadao Ichioka, other *Yomiuri* officials, and the entire All Nippon team were waiting by the train. The players exchanged good-byes as the fans screamed "Banzai!" and "Goodbye!" Ruth yelled back "Sayonara! Sayonara! Banzai Nippon!" as he sniffled back tears. The other Americans joined in: "Goodbye! Sayonara! See you again!" Tears slid down tough Earl Averill's face.[5]

At last it was time to board. Porters tried to load more than a hundred bags, suitcases, and trunks as the players supervised. It looked like a scene from the *Three Stooges*, with "Ruth stomping around looking for his 16 [*sic*] pieces of baggage . . . Frank O'Doul chanting 'Who's got my bag' over and over . . . Lou Gehrig running madly through the train looking for the box which was resting peacefully behind [a] seat."[6]

The cheering continued as the train prepared to depart. Ruth addressed the fans for the last time: "I don't know how to show my appreciation. If I get a chance, I will come back!" As the train pulled away, thousands screamed a final, "Banzai Babe Ruth!"[7]

The train arrived in Kobe at 9:30 the next morning, Sunday, December 2. The players met their wives, Connie Mack, and the rest of the party at the Oriental Hotel for breakfast and spent the rest of the day preparing for their departure. Harold and Grace Warstler did some last-minute shopping, picking up an extra suitcase and more film. The team boarded the *Empress of Canada* at 6:00 p.m., checked their luggage, and dined. The great ocean liner pulled away from its mooring at 1:00 a.m.

The trip to Japan was over, but three more games remained.

28

The *Empress of Canada* sailed around the southern tip of Japan and then due west to Shanghai. On December 4 Warstler noted in his diary, "The water has turned yellow." They had entered the Yellow Sea—a body of water between eastern China and Korea tinted yellow by sands washed from the Gobi Desert. The *Empress* docked at the Jardue and Mathenson Wharf in Shanghai at nine in the morning on December 5. More than one player groaned as they prepared to disembark. It was a frigid day with a cold mist, and few wanted to play the scheduled game against a local amateur team.

As the players came ashore they were met by representatives of the Shanghai Amateur Baseball Club and swarms of rickshaw drivers. The All Americans split up, each spending the morning sightseeing or shopping. Known as the Paris of the East, as well as the Whore of Asia, Shanghai was a divided city, a city of contrasts. It was a center of education, culture, enlightenment, liberal ideas, and wealth. It was also the home to extreme poverty, opium warlords and their gangs, casinos, cabarets, and brothels. Stuart Bell, who had arrived a few days earlier, found the atmosphere of Shanghai a relief after Tokyo. "It doesn't make any difference who or what you are in Shanghai, you are welcome," he told his readers. "The Chinese smiles were spontaneous and not automatic as smiles were in Japan." And "what nightclubs!" Bell sampled several and ended his night with ham and eggs at three, noting, "Can you imagine ham and eggs at three in the morning? Of course you can unless you have been to Japan where there is no three in the morning and where gendarmes with short swords on their belts would arrest you if you sought such food at three in the morning."[1]

Prior to 1842 Shanghai was a small fishing village, as the Chinese government restricted foreign merchants to the coastal cities of Hong Kong, Guangzhou, and Macao. With their victory in the 1842 Opium War, the British forced the Chinese to grant them a settlement in Shanghai. The town grew quickly and became divided into three sections, the International Settlement and the French Concession, both of which were outside of Chinese jurisdiction, and the Chinese section. With the political and intellectual freedoms practiced in the West, the International and French sections became centers of learning and a safe haven for dissidents. By 1930 the foreign sections of Shanghai contained nearly ninety thousand Europeans and Americans and the highest standard of living in Asia.

The Japanese also settled in Shanghai, primarily in the Hongkew District, where they built factories and businesses. The area soon became known as Little Tokyo, and by 1930 Japanese made up 80 percent of the city's foreign population. With the Japanese invasion of Manchuria in 1931, tension between the Japanese and Chinese residents mounted. It came to a head on January 18, 1932, when a group of Chinese beat five Japanese Buddhist monks and torched a Japanese-owned factory. During the ensuing riots a policeman was killed and another seriously injured. Seizing on the disturbances to extend their control in China, the Japanese military brought thirty ships, forty airplanes, and nearly seven thousand troops to the region. Meanwhile, Chinese nationalist forces arrived on the outskirts of Shanghai.

Ten days later, the Japanese attacked—targeting not only the Chinese troops but also civilian sections of the city with carrier-based aircraft. After the bombardment Japanese troops invaded the city, clashing with resisting civilians and nationalist troops in brutal house-to-house fighting. The conflict continued for more than three months, eventually involving one hundred thousand Japanese troops. On May 5 the two sides reached a cease-fire, with the Japanese in control of the burned-out Chinese section and much of the surrounding area. Under the terms of the cease-fire, the Japanese continued to administer the Chinese section.

Shanghai was an eye-opener for many of the All Americans. They had just spent a wonderful month in Japan where they had been treated like gods. Their hosts had always been polite, even warm, and many of the ballplayers formed close friendships with a few of the Japanese. But in Shanghai they saw another side of Japan. It was their first true encounter with the Japanese military, and some seemed surprised, even appalled, by the tyranny of Japanese rule. During his tour of the city Warstler noted the bombed-out buildings and the dirty, overcrowded conditions of the Chinese section, while he noted that the Japanese ruled their section "with an iron hand."[2]

Baseball had come to Shanghai ten years before Horace Wilson introduced it to Japan. A Shanghai Baseball Club existed in 1863, probably founded several years earlier by the 378 Americans living in the city. The group, however, remained small and was of little consequence to the subsequent development of the sport. The popularity of baseball in Shanghai, and China, spread once St. John Missionary College created a team in 1895 and imported two Chinese Hawaiians to coach the squad. Other colleges and the Shanghai YMCA soon formed teams, and in 1905 St. John and the YMCA met on the diamond in the first all-Chinese baseball game in the Middle Kingdom. With St. John at the forefront, Shanghai became the center of Chinese baseball.

After arriving in Shanghai most of the All Americans lunched with the local baseball club, but Earl and Violet Whitehill and Doc Ebling accepted an invitation from a local fan and St. John student-player. Bao-Jun Li was a twenty-eight-year-old baseball fanatic. As a student Li had fallen in love with the sport and played catcher for the St. John's team. His passion for the sport continued after graduation, and he was thrilled to meet Whitehill. Li took his guests for a tour of the city and then to the restaurant Sun Ya for lunch. Whitehill brought along two small souvenir bats and two balls signed by the All American team as thank-you gifts. Li protected the souvenirs through fifteen years of strife as World War II and then the Chinese civil war raged through Shanghai. In the 1950s he used the miniature bats and one of the autographed balls to teach his children how to play the American game. The other ball he kept safe. During the Cultural Revolution, Red Guard units ransacked his home, looking for evidence of Western contamination. They destroyed pictures of Li and the Whitehills, and Li was sentenced to four years of rehabilitation by digging rice fields. The remaining ball, however, had been carefully hidden and was waiting for Li when he returned. When Chinese-American relations thawed and baseball was once again played in the Middle Kingdom, Li became a translator for the Shanghai Sports Institute. In 1989 Li entrusted the ball to a visiting American coach and asked him to bring it to the National Hall of Fame in Cooperstown, where it is now enshrined.[3]

After lunch the All Americans reunited at the local stadium for the afternoon game. A stiff north wind blew across the field, chilling the players to the bone. They complained bitterly that the weather was better for football or even ice hockey than baseball, but with fifteen hundred fans waiting in the stands, they donned sweaters and winter gloves and took the field for practice. The Babe told reporters, "I'm wearing four shirts and red underwear but still I'm frozen. It's too cold for an old man." From the stands Li gaped as Ruth and Gehrig hit home run after home run during batting practice. Years later he remembered "Ruth's long, slow mortar shots, Gehrig's liners moving at bullet speed."[4]

The game itself began as a dull affair. Hampered by the cold, bulky jackets, woolen shirts, and winter gloves, the batters swung half-heartedly, as Joe Cascarella and the local Lefty Morris held their opponents scoreless for the first three innings. After giving up two runs in the fourth, Morris began to tire in the fifth as his defense fell apart. The locals made error after error as the All Americans pounded out eleven runs without a home run.[5] Morris left the game, but his relief did no better as the Major Leaguers tacked on nine more. By the end of the 22–1 rout the All Americans "were just loafing around to quicken the end and help the Shanghai players score a run to prevent a whitewash."[6] By seven the All Americans were back aboard the ship, and the *Empress of Canada* steamed south toward Hong Kong.

Around noon on December 7 they steamed into magnificent Victoria Harbor. The bay was filled with ships—British warships, ocean liners, cargo vessels, and hundreds of colorful junks. Victoria Peak towered over the tall, stately buildings of the city's Central section. The players disembarked at noon on the Kowloon side and took a 12:00 ferry to the island of Hong Kong. They spent the day touring the city and shopping before returning to the *Empress* and weighing anchor for Manila at 10:00 p.m.

The *Empress of Canada* arrived behind schedule off Manila at 5:30 a.m. on Sunday, December 9. More than twenty-five launches, blowing their horns in welcome, rushed to meet the ship. On the dock stood the mayor of Manila, the commander of the American garrison, other dignitaries, and the color guard of the Thirty-First Infantry, along with a squad of riflemen readying for a seventeen-gun salute. But the elaborate welcoming was not for the Sultan of Swat and his cohorts. On board were four U.S. senators on a fact-finding mission to the Philippines that would affect the territory's economic ties with the mainland.[7]

The ballplayers would not be met by the dignitaries on the dock. They had an 8:30 a.m. game scheduled at Rizal Memorial Baseball Stadium and would be hard-pressed to get there in time for adequate practice. They grabbed a quick breakfast, changed into their uniforms, and boarded a launch before the *Empress* docked. The boat sped to shore, where the players boarded buses to take them to the stadium.

Fifteen thousand sat waiting for the All Americans to arrive. Most had purchased their tickets days or weeks before, but some had stood in long predawn lines to buy a spot on the specially erected bleachers. Promoters had built a special press box right on the field, upgraded the sound system, and arranged for the games to be broadcast on the radio. Everything was ready for the greatest team to ever play on Philippine soil.

Other Major League teams had come to Manila before. They had played baseball in the Philippines since May 1898 when conquering U.S. sailors and marines clashed on the diamond. Four years later regimental and naval teams formed the Manila Baseball League. Games between the occupying forces became a popular attraction for native Filipinos, and it was not long before the locals began playing themselves. A six-team school league was organized in 1905–6, and adult amateur teams followed. American observers noted that "the Filipinos play [baseball] eagerly and expertly," and in 1915 the Philippines captured their first of five baseball gold medals at the Far Eastern Olympic Games, beating Japan each time.[8] The strong teams made Manila a usual stop for teams traveling through Asia. The Reach All Americans had stopped on their way back from Japan in 1908–9, as had the New York Giants and Chicago White Sox in 1913; the Herb Hunters All Stars, featuring Waite Hoyt and Casey Stengel, in 1922; and numerous collegiate teams from both the United States and Japan. But the All Americans with Babe Ruth would be the highlight of Filipino baseball. Newspapers had tracked the team's progress across Asia and whipped local sports fans into a frenzy. Columnists wondered if Ruth or one of his teammates would be the first to hit a ball out of Rizal Memorial Baseball Stadium.

The stadium was large for its time—350 feet down the left-field line and 337 feet to right—and was less than a year old. Some locals speculated that even the All Americans would fail to clear its walls. Batting practice began about half past eight. The All Americans had previously entertained the crowd with a splendid display of shadow ball, including a behind-the-back flip from shortstop Rabbit McNair to Warstler at second. The Babe hit first. He dug in, and seconds later the ball flew over the right-field wall, hitting the wall of the adjacent tennis pavilion and bouncing back onto the ball field. So much for the unconquerable walls. The next pitch came in, and Ruth pounded even farther—off the scaffolding in the unfinished tennis pavilion, at least 400 feet from home plate. The Babe deposited the third pitch in the same spot. Three pitches, three mammoth home runs. The crowd roared with delight.

Governor Frank Murphy threw out the first pitch at 8:59 a.m.—a high and tight fastball that brushed back leadoff hitter Rabbit McNair. Used to politicians bouncing the ball to the plate, McNair looked shocked, and the crowd cheered as their governor took an honorary seat on the All Americans' bench.

The morning game was against the Manila Bay Leaguers, an all-star team drawn from the local league. The All Americans would face a more challenging opponent, the Philippine Olympic All Stars, after lunch. It did not take long for the All Americans to take control. McNair led off with a double down the left-field line, which rattled the Bay League pitcher, Alexander Nelson. Nelson then walked Gehringer, Ruth, and Gehrig in succession before being removed from the game. Reliever Charlie Erdman held the big leaguers to just one more run until the third, when Frankie Hayes knocked in a pair with a triple. The All Americans added another in the fourth and fifth, before Gehrig delivered the coup de grâce with a three-run homer—the first official one in the stadium—in the sixth. Ruth went deep in the seventh—just missing the tennis pavilion—en route to an easy 13–1 win.

Rizal Memorial Baseball Stadium had a capacity of eighteen thousand, yet, somehow, more than twenty-five thousand squeezed their way into the ballpark for the 3:30 p.m. game. Those who could not fit through the gates perched in nearby trees and utility poles or on the roof of the tennis pavilion. Unlike the Japanese who crowded the ballparks to watch Ruth and the All Americans hit home runs, the Manila fans came to watch their team win.

The Philippines' national team had captured the gold at the Far Eastern Olympic Games in May. The squad contained the country's top players and was noted for its defense. The *Tribune* (Manila) called its infield "a veritable stone wall" and noted that "the outfield is composed of the greatest and fastest trio of fly chasers in the Far East." Indeed, one local expert even declared, "The visiting players do not outclass the locals by a very wide margin in the outfield and battery positions." He concluded that the pitching staffs were about even and that the Olympics were stronger than the All Americans at catcher and left field.[9]

The All Americans got off to another fast start, as McNair doubled again to open the game and Gehringer moved him to third with a long fly ball. Ruth came to the plate to face Armando Oncinian. Oncinian tried a series of curves and change-ups, causing Ruth to pull three mighty blasts foul before swinging through the third strike. A pop-out by Lou Gehrig ended the inning. Lefty Gomez took the mound for the All Americans and had little trouble, shutting out the opposition for the first four innings. Meanwhile, led by Averill and Gehringer home runs, the All Americans took a 4–0 lead. But then three unanswered Filipino runs made it 4–3 going into the seventh inning. Hopeful fans cheered for an upset.

But it was not to be. Singles by Gehringer and Gehrig in front of a 375-foot blast by Earl Averill put the game out of reach. Gomez regained his focus and shut down the Olympics for the final three innings to win 7–3. Later Mack would praise the Olympics as the best players they faced on the tour, and Ruth would add, "I think this team right here [referring to the Olympic nine] could kick any they have in Japan right now."[10]

That evening Governor Murphy threw a gala event at his residence. The society-page editor of the *Manila Daily Bulletin* noted, "Thousands of guests . . . called at the palace from nine-thirty until after midnight. Elegant Filipino costumes and striking European gowns of the latest mode . . . added an unusually colorful and glamorous touch. Multicolored electric lights sparkled like jewels from the trees and hedges surrounding the palace. The mansion itself . . . was a blaze of light. . . . [It] was a scene of magnificent gaiety until long past midnight."[11]

The All Americans and Olympics met for a second game on Monday at 2:30 p.m. To make the game more competitive Clint Brown would pitch for the Filipinos (catcher Frank Hayes would also play for the Olympics), while Joe Bautista of the Olympics would pitch for the Major Leaguers. The twenty thousand fans voiced their displeasure as soon as the lineups were announced. Even if a loss was likely, they wanted to watch the local boys strive against the Major Leaguers. With Brown pitching, a win by the Olympics would be meaningless.

According to the *Tribune*, "The moment Brown took the slab, several hundred fans in the left and center bleachers began their chorus of boos." By the second half of the first inning thousands had joined in. Soon "the attitude of the crowd . . . grew menacing and police rushed to the field." A fan climbed over the wall into center field and beckoned others to rush the diamond. None followed, and policed chased the invader back into the screaming crowd. At the start of the second inning, "the din became so loud the officials could no longer ignore the fans' wishes."[12]

From the first base coaching box, Ruth called to umpire John Quinn for time. He then motioned for Olympic manager Captain Del Villar to join them on the field for a conference. A few minutes later the Filipino battery joined their teammates on the field. The fans had won. The game would continue with each team's roster intact.

Perhaps the fans were mistaken. The game was a blowout. Led by a Gehrig homer the All Americans pounded out thirteen hits and nine runs. Meanwhile, Brown and Joe Cascarella gave up just four hits and no runs through the first eight innings. With two quick outs in the ninth, it looked as if the Filipinos would be shut out. The All Americans had tried hard to avoid shutting out their hosts in Shanghai, and one wonders if they did the same again in this game. Cascarella gave up a walk, a single, and another walk to load the bases. At third Ramon Echem inched down the line. As Cascarella went into his windup, Echem dashed down the line, beating the pitch by inches, and sliding safely under Hayes's tag. With the embarrassing shutout avoided, Cascarella induced Johnny Santa Rosa to pop weakly to second to end the game.

The *Empress of Canada* would leave port early that evening. Most of the players hurried to the dock to begin their journey home. Others, however, had decided to take a more leisurely route back to the States. The Gehrigs left for Europe a few hours later on the *President Polk*. The Ruths, Gomezes, Warstlers, Hilleriches, and Doc Ebling stayed in Manila for a few days before heading for Indonesia—the first stop on an around-the-world voyage.

As the players left Manila, workmen leaned ladders against the outfield walls at Rizal Memorial Baseball Stadium and painted six large white balls. Next to each ball they painted a name and a date— Babe Ruth, December 9, 1934; Charlie Gehringer, December 9, 1934; Lou Gehrig, December 9, 1934; Lou Gehrig, December 10, 1934; and Earl Averill, December 10, 1934, twice. It began a tradition to paint a ball marking the location of every home run hit out of the stadium.

29

The *Empress of Canada* put into its berth at Yokohama on December 20, eighteen days after the All Americans left for Shanghai and seven weeks after the team had first arrived in Japan. There were no cheering crowds this time. No welcoming committee. Most of the players stayed on board during the brief stop. But two disembarked. Moe Berg would stay briefly in Japan before continuing to Korea, where he would begin a trip across Asia, Europe, and finally the Atlantic. Lefty O'Doul and his wife, Abigail, would spend a few weeks in Tokyo. O'Doul and Sotaro Suzuki had work to do. It was time to create the Japanese professional baseball league.

The Japanese had long regarded professional baseball with suspicion. Baseball, they argued, should be played with a pure heart for spiritual growth, not for money. Influenced by the idealized image of the samurai and Meiji-era Bushido code, Japanese at the turn of the century believed that players should model themselves after these mythical ancient warriors and focus on their tasks rather than worldly concerns. The ideal ball games were played at Koshien, where high schoolers fought on the diamond solely for their schools' honor. At one point fans considered the Tokyo Big Six University League to also contain the proper spirit, but by the early 1930s critics argued that the star players were professionals in all but name—responsible for little except playing ball and receiving benefits and endorsements for their success on the field. The corruption of the Tokyo Big Six University League became a selling point for professional baseball. Once Japan had pro ball, then there could be a stricter boundary between amateur and professional behavior.

Babe Ruth and the All Americans had paved the way for pro ball in Japan. The Americans' on- and off-the-field behavior, as well as their skills, helped Japanese fans overcome their aversion to profession-als. As Sotaro Suzuki told the *Sporting News* in March 1935, "Practi-cally every kid in Japan now wants to emulate Babe Ruth."[1]

Relying on the residual enthusiasm for the tour to quell most of the criticism, *Yomiuri* announced in December that it had formed a professional baseball club called the Dai Nippon Tokyo Yakyu Club (Greater Japan Tokyo Baseball Club). To distance the team from the newspaper company, Matsutaro Shoriki was not named an officer. Instead, Marquis Nobutsune Okuma, who had thrown out the first pitch of the 1934 tour, served as the club's first president. Tadao Ichioka would serve as general manager, and All Nippon manager Daisuke Miyake would be the club's field manager. Lefty O'Doul joined the organization as an official adviser. Sotaro Suzuki, who had done so much to make the club possible but had never played collegiate baseball and thus was not part of Japan's baseball net-work, was not given an official title. He would continue to write for the newspaper and help the team make travel arrangements in the United States.

The club announced that the primary purpose of the organiza-tion was to start a professional circuit that played a "faster brand of baseball" than the Tokyo Big Six University League. Appealing to widespread nationalist sentiment, the club added, "The second goal is to compete eventually with the United States for the real baseball championship of the world and not leave the World Series exclusively to the pennant winners of the American and National Leagues."[2]

The team consisted of the younger players from the All Nippon roster. Eiji Sawamura, Victor Starffin, and Kenichi Aoshiba were the core of the staff. The more experienced Masao Date, the most effective pitcher in both the 1931 and '34 tours, did not join, nor did little Shinji Hamazaki. Position players included former college stars Shigeru Mizuhara, Osamu Mihara, Hisanori Karita, Kumeyasu Yajima, and Isamu Fuma. Surprisingly, All Nippon's leading hit-ter, catcher Toshiharu Inokawa, was not on the roster. The power-hitting first baseman, Minoru "Babe" Yamashita, who had hit just .158 against the All Americans, also was not included. Initially, thirty-seven-year-old catcher Jiro Kuji joined, but he soon decided to return to his beloved Hokkaido. He would continue to play amateur ball until a tragic day in 1939. Kuji was batting during an intercity tournament when the catcher attempted to catch a base runner napping off second base. Kuji failed to get out of the way, and the throw hit him in the back of the head with a sickening thud. He died two days later from internal bleeding.

The Dai Nippon Tokyo Yakyu Club's roster contained another surprise. Having not impressed the All Americans enough to gain a Major League contract, Jimmy Horio was unemployed. As a member of the amateur All Nippon team, he also had not earned a paycheck for several months. No doubt influenced by Ichioka's earlier promise to pay him retroactively once professional baseball was established, Horio decided to join the Japanese club for the time being. He would not have to stay in Japan long. With no other Japanese professional teams to play against, the Dai Nippon Tokyo Yakyu Club would head to the United States in mid-February 1935. O'Doul and Suzuki were in the process of arranging a 109-game, four-month tour that would take the team to thirteen states, four Canadian provinces, and the territory of Hawaii. On January 14, 1935, O'Doul left Tokyo for San Francisco, where he would make the final arrangements. As he steamed across the Pacific, O'Doul received an urgent radio message that would make his task easier. Charlie Graham, his good friend and owner of the San Francisco Seals of the Pacific Coast League, had just purchased his contract from the New York Giants. His Major League career was now over, but Graham offered O'Doul his dream job—the opportunity to become the player-manager of his hometown team. O'Doul radioed back his acceptance, eager to start his new career as manager of the San Francisco Seals.

As O'Doul finished up in Tokyo, his All American teammates began to trickle home. Connie Mack, John Quinn, and the other passengers on the *Empress of Canada* docked in Vancouver on January 2. The Gehrigs, Ruths, Gomezes, Warstlers, and those who had continued their sightseeing tours arrived home before spring training. Each returned home gushing with admiration for Japan. In interview after interview they described their reception and the fans' enthusiasm for the game. Many on both sides of the Pacific declared the tour a diplomatic coup. Connie Mack summed up the consensus that the trip did "more for the better understanding between Japanese and Americans than all the diplomatic exchanges ever accomplished."[3]

Grandiose claims of baseball's social importance had been around the game even longer than Mack. By the 1880s proponents endowed baseball with almost supernatural abilities. It could indoctrinate immigrants with the values of democracy, "civilize savages," and even initiate harmony and world peace. Some of these claims were partially true.

In keeping with the times the earliest international baseball tours espoused the loftiest goals. As A. G. Spalding embarked on his 1888 World Baseball Tour with the Chicago White Sox and their All American opponents, he claimed that baseball was a civilizing force that would help bring progress to backward peoples. Anthropologists of the day argued that societies could be plotted on a linear hierarchy from savagery to civilization based on a checklist of cultural traits. For some social theorists organized sports were among the traits of civilization. For others sports merely taught the values needed in civilized society. Many Americans saw baseball as the most complex, nuanced, and challenging game in existence. For example, Francis Richer of the *Sporting Life* concluded that "baseball [reflects] the qualities that make the American male the most highly-organized, civilized being on earth."[4] It followed that societies capable of adopting baseball were on their way to higher civilization. Headlines like G. W. Axelson's 1914 *Harper's Weekly* article "Enlightening the World with Baseball" were common.

Despite the blatant racism that many Americans felt toward the "little yellow men from the land of Mikado," esteem toward Japanese rose as they became proficient at America's pastime. Axelson's 1914 article, for example, praised the Japanese for their skill, effort, and sportsmanship. Even some Japanese seemed to tie proficiency at baseball with the adoption of Western civilization. Writing for the May 1919 issue of *Everybody's,* Kinnosuke Adachi concluded that Japan's baseball frenzy placed the nation "pretty far in the right direction on the highway of civilization!"[5]

Although the belief in baseball's civilizing powers remained alive, by the 1920s a more modest goal for international baseball emerged—

mutual respect and friendship. On November 1, 1934, the day before the All Americans arrived in Japan, an editorial in the *Sporting News* summed up this philosophy:

The eagerness with which this instruction is absorbed by the Oriental players is proof enough of their desire to learn and if the occasional jaunts from this country did nothing else but satisfy that yearning, they would be well worth the enterprise. But these barnstorming journeys across the Pacific Ocean accomplish more than that. . . . There must be international respect, friendship and understanding. The American must learn that the Oriental isn't much different from himself beneath the skin and the Oriental must be made to realize that the American is not a hobgoblin. When the two meet on the diamond, they have something in common. They come to realize that sportsmanship is the same in any language. . . . International competition in sports and the exchange of ideas for its improvement and the interpretation of its rules will not bring the millennium of peace by itself, but the mutual respect thus engendered is certain to furnish the basis on which all nations can meet to discuss their problems without ill feeling. Therefore, as Americans are making the Orientals baseball-conscious, they are in consequence making themselves better understood. We hope that someday the Orient will have developed so far in the game that it can send to this country a team able to meet the best in the United States on equal terms and prove to the Americans that the so-called "yellow peril" wears the same clothes, plays the same game and entertains the same thoughts. In other words, that we are all brothers.[6]

Initially, the 1934 trip seemed to accomplish these goals.[7] Articles in the *New York Times*, *Washington Post*, *Time*, and, thanks to the Associated Press, small newspapers across the country proclaimed the tour as a diplomatic coup. Billy Dooly's conclusions published in the *Philadelphia Record* were typical. "Plainly, the ball players' tour of Japan accomplished more toward engendering regard and respect for America than any notes our politicians might send across the cable.

There was not one untoward incident throughout the trip. Kids and grown-ups heaped attention, gifts, acclaim and stood patiently for hours waiting to see the Yankee ball players arrive, leave or appear on the streets." The *Sporting News* added, "We believe that the recent trip to the Orient of baseball's finest has served to delay, if not prevent, any possible conflict. We like to believe that countries having such a common interest in a great sport world rather fight it out on the diamond than on the battle field."[8]

The players returned home with warm feelings for both Japan and the Japanese. "It was a wonderful trip in every respect," John Quinn told the *Philadelphia Inquirer*. Although the language barrier discouraged close friendships between most of the opposing players, English-speaking Japanese such as Sotaro Suzuki and Frank Matsumoto formed lifelong friendships with Lefty O'Doul and Moe Berg. The players also left with a favorable impression of Japanese society. Closely escorted, they saw Japan at its best—beautiful and interesting tourist destinations; opulent hotels, restaurants, and department stores; and throngs of delirious baseball fans. The players' itinerary had been carefully arranged. They saw nothing of Japan's rural poverty, having passed through the Tohoku region on the train at night, and had little inkling of the social and military unrest. Decades later Julia Ruth Stevens recalls seeing little poverty and only an occasional soldier during the entire trip. Moe Berg, writing about his 1932 trip, claimed, "There are no Japanese loafers—everybody seems to work—have not seen one beggar yet." The Japan Tourism Bureau and the Ministry of Foreign Affairs had been using tourism as a diplomatic tool for years. Their goal was to present Japan as a modern, forward-thinking country and natural leader of Asia, thus supporting their country's expansion across the continent. As one tourism expert wrote, "Those of us who are involved in international tourism do not only wish to correct and improve foreign understanding of Japan, but desire to raise the overall level of awareness abroad concerning Japan's proper actions during this holy war [in China]."[9]

The intense Stateside media coverage of the '34 tour allowed millions of fans in the United States to view the Japanese through the All American players' eyes. Newspapers, magazines, newsreels, and radio reports depicted thousands of Japanese waving the Star-

Spangled Banner and cheering wildly for Babe Ruth and other American heroes. Americans heard the ballplayers' glowing descriptions of Japan and its friendly inhabitants. The *Chicago Tribune* summarized, "Reports from Japan by radio and cable reveal the Japanese people in an animated state of great good will toward the United States. At least it would be assumed that a party of traveling [players] could not be received with so much popular delight without their country sharing some of the general affection."[10] With newspaper headlines also screaming Japan's hard-line stance at the naval talks, the All Americans' reports from Japan were the most favorable press the Japanese had received for some time.

Of course, some of the news coverage contained elements of the time's racial bigotry. A number of articles spoke highly of Japanese baseball and the game's role in the peace process, but undermined the message of mutual respect by using racial slurs and stereotypes or accompanying the articles with racist cartoons. Terms such as *little brown men*, *slant-eyed fans*, and *Japs* were sprinkled throughout the media coverage. Stuart Bell's columns in the *Cleveland Press* were often accompanied by cartoons drawn by James Lavery. Lavery routinely confused Japanese and Chinese imagery and drew Asians in the style now known as "yellowface" that emphasizes racial differences and marks Asians as alien and inferior through demeaning caricatures.[11] Lavery's Japanese had squinty, overly slanted eyes and buckteeth; dressed as Chinese peasants; and spoke in pidgin English. These negative images, however, were in the minority.

Many of the news stories focused on the Babe's extraordinary success as a diplomat. "Ruth, an Idol and Diplomat, Wins Japan as He Won U.S.," announced the *Washington Post*. "Babe, the Ambassador: Ruth Makes Japan Go American," proclaimed the *Sporting News*. It continued, "The stars and stripes have not been much in evidence in Japan within recent years, because of various diplomatic and political aspects, but Babe Ruth, by one visit to Nippon has changed all of that, for the Ginza—Tokyo's Broadway—broke out with a rash of Red, White, and Blue when the Bambino and his American League Stars came to town." Bob Considine of the *Washington Herald* told readers, "The cries of 'Banzai Babe,' which are booming over the island have drowned out the propaganda mummers against U.S. imperialism."[12]

Perhaps the most enthusiastic supporter of the tour's diplomatic success was Connie Mack. Mack was so taken with the fans' enthusiasm and his new friends that he assured anyone who would listen that Japan would never begin a war with the United States. Soon after the *Empress of Canada* docked in Vancouver, Mack told reporters, "When we landed in Japan the American residents seemed pretty blue. The parley on the naval treaty was on, with America blocking Japan's demand for parity. There was strong anti-American feeling throughout Japan over this country's stand. Things didn't look good at all and then Babe Ruth smacked a home run, and all the ill feeling and underground war sentiment vanished just like that!" A month later at the Twelfth Annual New York Baseball Writers' Association meeting, Mack told the assembly that "there would be no war between the United States and Japan, pointing out that war talk died out after his All-Star team reached Nippon. Connie urged Major Leaguers to join together in promoting these good-will tours every three or four years." Umpire John Quinn agreed, writing in the *Spalding Official Base Ball Guide, 1935,* "On the day the tourists arrived there was war talk, but that disappeared after they had been in the empire twenty-four hours." Many Americans wanted to believe Mack and Quinn. With the isolationist movement dominating foreign policy and national sentiment, Americans eagerly seized on signs of peace, turning a blind eye to Japan's increasingly aggressive military. *Time*, however, offered a more realistic summary of the tour's importance: "It would be naïve to suppose that Japanese baseball frenzy for baseball's Babe will sway public opinion, but last week it did ease tension."[13]

Ambassador Grew summed up the success in a letter to Major League Baseball commissioner Landis:

> So far as I can judge, their visit to Japan has been an unqualified success. . . . I told Babe Ruth that while he was here there were two American Ambassadors to Japan, he and I. Certainly he and Connie Mack and the rest of the team did an immense amount of good towards the development of Japanese-American friendship and they all acquitted themselves in the finest way which made me very proud of them. I should like to tell you

of the splendid impression they made here and of their material contribution to the development of good feeling between Japan and the United States, at least among certain sections of the people.[14]

Unfortunately, it was the other portion of the Japanese population that would be the problem.

PART 5

"To hell with Babe Ruth!"

UNKNOWN JAPANESE SOLDIERS,
March 1944

30

Katsusuke Nagasaki's breath billowed as he left the War Gods Society's dojo. The morning of February 22, 1935, was chilly. But that was good—part of the plan. Nobody would look twice at his bulky overcoat. A regal-looking 1931 Chrysler Imperial idled outside. The luxury car with its long chassis and wide running boards could sit all five of them comfortably. Nagasaki sat down next to Sukeyasu Atsuta and Inspector Suzuki, a dojo member with fanatical nationalistic tendencies who was also an officer of the Special Police, and fellow War Gods Society member Raisuke Kudo. Behind the wheel a thug named Nagamon began to drive through Tokyo's narrow, crooked streets.[1]

Nagasaki's neighbors in working-class Okachimachi rose early. Men and women dressed in padded traditional jackets called *hanten* were sweeping the sidewalks before their small wooden houses and discount shops. Others were hauling display tables stacked with ceramic teapots and dishes, small kitchen appliances, or crispy rice crackers called *sembei* out from their cluttered one-room shops to the narrow sidewalks. Above the street women leaned out of second-story windows, beating their colorful futons with wooden paddles to cleanse them of musty night smells before airing them out on the windowsills.

As the Chrysler reached the wealthier Ginza neighborhood, the streets became wider and cleaner. Delivery men glided by on heavy black bicycles piled with crates of beer and sake bottles for the area's many bars, fresh fish from the still-under-construction Tsukiji market, and bundles of wrapped cloth for the dress shops. Occasionally, an aging black truck lumbered down the larger streets. As the depression had deepened, trucks and gasoline became too expensive for all but the most prosperous businesses. Besides, the Imperial Army had requisitioned most of the fuel for the several hundred thousand troops deployed in Manchuria as well as the standing armies in the colonies of Korea and Formosa.

Soon the three-story concrete *Yomiuri* newspaper building loomed ahead. The sidewalks became crowded as men in suits and fedoras rushed to work at the newspaper and the nearby offices. In a three-piece brown suit and dark tie peeking out from beneath his overcoat, Nagasaki would blend into the crowd.

Since the initial meeting between Atsuta and Yasuichi Marunaka of the *Tokyo Nichi Nichi* newspaper in November, the two had met several more times. Marunaka had presented Atsuta with two gifts of three thousand yen (about nine hundred dollars) along with three pictures of Shoriki, his car's license plate number, the addresses and floor plans of his home in Tokyo and his country house in Zushi, and the time he usually came to his office. At the last meeting Marunaka had indicated that Atsuta should not delay any longer.

Atsuta, Nagasaki, and Kudo had met the day before at a restaurant called Kuroume to work out the details of the attack. They would strike as Shoriki entered the office building to start the workweek. After the attack Nagasaki would surrender himself to Inspector Suzuki, who would be conveniently nearby, and make a statement. Under no circumstances would Nagasaki reveal the true plan. He would instead claim that he was acting alone out of patriotic outrage and had planned only to wound the newspaper owner, not kill him. Suzuki would ensure that Nagasaki would be treated well.

Just before 8:00 a.m., Nagasaki slid a short samurai sword into a makeshift string harness on his back, adjusted his overcoat to cover the weapon, and stepped out of the Chrysler Imperial. He walked down the street toward the *Yomiuri* building, watching for Shoriki's limousine. The newspaper owner was known for his punctuality. Nagasaki should not have long to wait.

Minutes passed without any sign of Shoriki. Nagasaki knew that he could not loiter long without somebody becoming suspicious. It was too cold for casual strollers. He walked by the street's wooden shops and warehouses, looked down at the canal by the edge of the road. Nobody seemed to notice him. At the end of the street his conspirators remained in the Imperial to ensure that Nagasaki accomplished his task. Time went by. No Shoriki. Unbeknownst to the War Gods, Shoriki had an early-morning visitor at his Tokyo home, preventing him from maintaining his usual schedule.

Finally, at 8:40 a.m. a black sedan cruised down the street. Nagasaki approached the newspaper building and halted in front of a bulletin board to the right of the entrance. He appeared to study the announcements as a short, balding man with black-framed, Coke-bottle-thick glasses emerged from the car. The man did not seem imposing, but Nagasaki knew that Matsutaro Shoriki should not be underestimated. Like Nagasaki, the newspaper's owner was a judo master. As Shoriki said good morning to the doorman and began to climb the stairs into the building, Nagasaki strode forward. It was his only chance. He drew his short samurai sword from beneath his coat, and the gleaming blade flashed through the air, striking Shoriki's head.

Shoriki stumbled forward as he felt a sharp pain. Looking behind him, he saw a man stuff a sword beneath his overcoat and flee. He reached for his head and found a gaping wound. Shoriki pressed his hand against it as blood squirted through his fingers. The doorman and an office boy rushed to help. Supported by his employees, Shoriki climbed the stairs to the infirmary, kicked off his shoes, and stepped into the slippers waiting by the door before keeling over unconscious. His overcoat and jacket were soaked with blood. The staff doctor cut the garments off his body to assess the damage. A two-inch-deep gash ran six inches from the back of Shoriki's head to his neck. His pulse was faint.

Down the street, the Chrysler Imperial rumbled away.

Later that day, Nagasaki walked into a local police station and gave a detailed confession, presumably to Inspector Suzuki. The primary reason for the assassination: Shoriki had defiled the memory of Emperor Meiji by allowing Babe Ruth and his team to play in the stadium named in the ruler's honor.

Nagasaki's trial was short. Appearing before the Tenth Division of the Tokyo Regional Court in June 1935, he admitted to the crime but claimed that his action was motivated by a pure spirit and love of country. Furthermore, he argued that he had not meant to kill, or even severely wound, Shoriki, just maim him. Shoriki had survived. A blood transfusion and his exceptional strong constitution had saved his life. After fifty days in the hospital and a convalescence at a hot spring, Shoriki returned to work. The judge, perhaps recalling the "pure spirit" of the forty-seven *ronin*, sentenced Nagasaki to just three years for assault.

Although Nagasaki insisted that he had acted alone, the authorities had a file on the "newspaper thug" and knew of his connections to the War Gods Society. Atsuta and eleven other group members were detained for questioning soon after the attack. Eventually, all but Nagasaki were released due to lack of evidence, but in June 1935 *Tokyo Nichi Nichi*'s role in the incident began to emerge.

Not content with the six thousand yen already paid by Yasuichi Marunaka, the ever-greedy Atsuta had gone to *Nichi Nichi* headquarters to extort more. He had informed the newspaper's director of Marunaka's plan to assassinate Shoriki and promised to expose the newspaper if he was not paid an additional three thousand yen. The director complied, but during Nagasaki's trial hints of Atsuta's actions emerged. An investigation began, but before authorities could interview Marunaka, he disappeared. Lacking proof of *Nichi Nichi*'s involvement, police dropped the larger investigation but arrested and tried Atsuta for extortion. He was sentenced to a six-month prison term. In January 1936 Marunaka's body was found in a cave near Atami, a resort town southwest of Tokyo. The official cause of death was suicide. Supposedly, the stress and embarrassment of jeopardizing his company's reputation caused him to take his own life, but doubts over the agency of his death remain.

Newspapers around the world covered the attack on Shoriki. "Assassin Stabs Nippon Sponsor of Ruth's Tour," blared the *San Francisco Bee*; "Babe's Patriot," quipped *Time*; while the *New York Times* headline proclaimed "'Patriot' Stabs Noted Publisher in Tokyo for Sponsoring Babe Ruth's Tour in Japan." Unaware of *Nichi Nichi*'s role, the articles concluded that the attack was another example of Japan's unfettered nationalism. *Time* explained, "In the eyes of Japanese jingoes [Shoriki's] conduct has long merited death. . . . last year he even went to the extreme of bringing Babe Ruth to Japan just as her jingoes were successfully working up public opinion to believe that the U.S. is the 'White Menace.'"[2] Reporters asked Ruth and Connie Mack for comments. Both expressed their concern for Shoriki, reiterated their friendship for the Japanese people, and viewed the incident as an anomaly carried out by "some crank." Unfortunately, it was the goodwill exhibited during the tour that was the anomaly.

31

Jimmy Horio was just wiping the sleep from his eyes when they came. Eighty-one dive-bombers and twenty-seven torpedo bombers rounded Diamond Head, sped past Horio's home in Kaimuki, and hit the base at Pearl Harbor. They were the second wave. The first had attacked at 7:48 a.m., catching the base by surprise. The destruction was devastating—2,386 American servicemen dead, 1,139 wounded, and eighteen ships, including five battleships, sunk or run aground. The war that Connie Mack swore would never happen had begun.

From his backyard Jimmy watched the black smoke rising to the west. He stared in disbelief and sadness. He could not understand why Japan would start a war it could not possibly win. His thoughts probably turned to his father and brother, who were still living in Hiroshima. What would become of them?

So much had happened since he had played for the Japanese against Babe Ruth in 1934. After the attack on Shoriki, the Dai Nippon Tokyo Yakyu Club came to the United States as planned in the spring of 1935. They stayed for 118 days, playing 109 games during a 13,770-mile trek across thirteen states and four Canadian provinces. It did not take long for Lefty O'Doul to insist that the team change its name. Dai Nippon Tokyo Yakyu Club was too cumbersome, especially for Americans. Instead, he suggested "Tokyo Giants." Sotaro Suzuki, acting as the traveling secretary, agreed, and the nickname of Japan's most famous club was created.

The Giants did well against collegiate and amateur teams, winning 72 and losing just 14. They fared less well against the Pacific Coast League AA teams, losing 17 of the 23 contests. But at times they shone. On March 13 Eiji Sawamura shut out the Yankees AA farm club, the Oakland Oaks, 2–0 while holding them to just four hits. Sawamura, in particular, impressed the Americans. An unscrupulous scout from either the Pittsburgh Pirates or the St. Louis Cardinals even resorted to subterfuge, hoping to sign the young pitcher. Before a June 11 game in Milwaukee, Sawamura was chasing down a loose ball near the grandstands when a man pushed a paper over the railing and asked for his autograph. Eiji dutifully signed, returned to practice, and later pitched six innings of shutout ball. After the game the same man approached Sotaro Suzuki, waved a baseball contract signed by Sawamura, and demanded that the pitcher accompany him. Aghast, Suzuki called over Eiji, who explained how he mistakenly signed the contract. When Suzuki refused the scout's request, the man complained that he would report the breach of contract to baseball commissioner Landis. "It is no problem," Suzuki replied. "The Tokyo Giants are not in organized baseball." Nevertheless, Sotaro slipped the man some money in exchange for the invalid contract.[1]

Horio played well during the trip, hitting .275 with forty stolen bases and scoring seventy-eight runs. His play finally led to a high-caliber professional contract with the Sacramento Solons of the Pacific Coast League. Although technically a double-A Minor League outfit, during the 1930s the caliber of play in the PCL was nearly equal to the Major Leagues. With no Major League teams west of the Mississippi, PCL rosters were stocked with big league–caliber players who wished to stay on the West Coast. To entice talented men to stay, PCL teams often paid better than Major League franchises. Horio would play against Joe and Vince DiMaggio, Bobby Doerr, and even Lefty O'Doul. At long last Jimmy was playing to his potential. He was hitting .291 in late July 1935 when he received devastating news.

His wife, Yoshiko, had been involved in an automobile accident in April. She had been thrown from the car, but her injuries seemed minor and she was soon released from the hospital. Discomfort in her abdomen, however, persisted and soon grew worse. The doctor had missed her more serious internal injuries, and she developed peritonitis—an inflammation of the membrane that lines the abdominal cavity. On July 29 Yoshiko was rushed to a hospital in Los Angeles. Jimmy immediately left the Solons to join his wife. Yoshiko lost consciousness on August 2 and, after an unsuccessful blood transfusion, died two days later. In mid-August Horio returned to the Solons but went into a prolonged batting slump, finishing the season at just .250.[2]

Over the winter of 1935–36, Matsutaro Shoriki and his advisers created the Nippon Professional Baseball League. The initial league consisted of seven teams, four owned by newspaper publishers and three by private railroads. League play would consist of a series of tournaments beginning in April. To prepare for the inaugural season, the Tokyo Giants would take a second trip to the United States to sharpen their skills against Minor League and top amateur teams. Just after the Giants left Japan the military once again attempted to overthrow the Japanese government.

After their arrests on November 20, 1934, for the plot to attack parliament and murder opposing politicians, Capt. Koji Marunaka and Lt. Asaichi Isobe had spent several months in jail before being released and placed on reserve duty. In July 1935 the two published *Opinions Regarding the Cleaning of the Army*, a pamphlet revealing the infighting between the Imperial Way and Control factions within the army and detailing the abortive Cherry Society coup attempts of March and October 1931. For this, but not the plot of November 1934, Marunaka and Isobe were court-martialed and dismissed from the army. Now civilians, they spent even more time at the Jikishin Dojo, planning the Showa Restoration.

On February 26, 1936, the time had come. As snow blanketed Tokyo about two dozen Young Officers led fifteen hundred soldiers into the city streets, seizing strategic areas. Meanwhile, groups of officers attacked the residences of government officials, killing the keeper of the Privy Seal and the inspector general of military training, while seriously wounding a member of the Privy Council and the minister of finance. Prime Minister Keisuke Okada narrowly escaped when the Young Officers mistakenly assassinated his brother-in-law instead.

After the initial attacks, the Young Officers presented their manifesto to the army minister and emperor. "Recently, evil and selfish people have encroached upon the authority of the Emperor, caused utmost misery to the people, and brought humiliation by foreign powers upon our country. These rascals . . . usurped the Emperor's right of supreme command. . . . Our duty, as the servants of His Imperial Majesty, called upon us to remove the evil advisors who overshadowed his Throne. If we refrained from doing this, our country would have been doomed. Therefore, we . . . have risen to smash the traitors and save Japan."[3]

Much of the army was sympathetic to the Young Officers' ideals. Had the emperor agreed to take control of the government, the coup would have been a success and the Showa Restoration accomplished. Unfortunately for Marunaka and his fellow Young Officers, they never stopped to think how Hirohito might react to having his life-long advisers slaughtered. Upon reading the manifesto, the emperor ordered the rebellion crushed and the officers brought to justice.

The rebels held their positions for three days as loyal troops moved to oppose them. The expected fighting, however, never came. On the morning of February 29, the Young Officers and their troops received a direct order from the emperor to disperse. Reluctantly, they returned to their barracks without firing another shot. Marunaka, Isobe, the other Young Officers, as well as Ikki Kita and Mitsugi Nishida, who had not participated in the revolt, were arrested, tried, and shot. The failed coup and subsequent executions ended the Imperial Way faction, leaving the Control Faction in charge of the army. Unfettered with calls for domestic reform, the army could now focus on foreign expansion.

Jimmy Horio did not return to the Solons in the spring of 1936. He tried out for the Seattle Indians of the Pacific Coast League but failed to make the team. With few options left he returned to Japan, looking for a job in the new professional league. He ended up with the Hankyu team, based in Osaka. Horio was not the only American to join the fledgling league—six Japanese Americans, two Caucasians, and one African American also played. Once again Horio failed to play to his potential, as he hit just .179 in 123 at bats, but he was invited back for the following season.

True league play began in 1937 with separate spring and fall seasons. Not surprisingly, the Tokyo Giants with their star pitchers Eiji Sawamura and Victor Starffin and many of the 1934 All Nippon players captured the league's first pennant and would win seven of the league's first nine championships. Sawamura continued as the league's marquee player, leading the league in wins, ERA, and strikeouts; pitching a no-hitter; and capturing the first Most Valuable

Player award. But Sawamura's dominance, like a Japanese cherry blossom, would be fleeting.

On July 7, 1937, as Sawamura was pitching a one-run game against the Dai Tokyo, a skirmish between Japanese and Chinese troops at the Marco Polo Bridge, about ten miles southwest of Beijing, touched off the Second Sino-Japanese War. The excessively brutal conflict would last eight years and kill or wound at least 20 million Chinese and 1 to 1.8 million Japanese. With the Imperial Army's "Rape of Nanking" in December 1937 through early 1938, attacks on Western nationals in China, and the Nazi-Soviet pact in 1939, Japan found itself isolated. American-Japanese tension increased sharply, making it unpleasant for the American ballplayers to remain in Japan. Bucky Harris McGailliard, the most successful American in the Japanese league, winner of the 1937 fall season MVP award, and the last non-nisei to remain, left after the 1938 season. A number of the nisei, including Jimmy Horio, remained in Japan despite the possibility of being drafted by the Imperial Army, which considered all ethnic Japanese eligible for military duty. Now playing for Hanshin, Horio stayed through the first part of the 1941 season, never becoming a star and rarely hitting above .250. In June 1941 Jimmy realized that his window for leaving Japan was narrowing. He resigned from the Hanshin club and relocated with his second wife, Eileen, and their son, James, to Hawaii.

And now, only six months later, he stood in his backyard in a daze, watching the oily black smoke rise to the west. Unlike the 120,000 Japanese Americans on the West Coast of the mainland who would be forced into concentration camps, most of Hawaii's nisei population would remain free. Worried about being labeled a Japanese sympathizer, Horio would burn his Japanese-language library as well as the portrait of the emperor that hung in his home. After the attack Jimmy began working at the Pearl Harbor shipyard, painting boats. Eventually, he would earn enough to purchase a gasoline station in Honolulu. In 1943 his father died of natural causes in Hiroshima. Two years later, an American nuclear bomb obliterated his family home along with his brother, Kiyoto. Jimmy never had a chance to visit his father's grave or the remaining family in Japan. He developed bone cancer and died in 1949 at the age of forty-two.

32

Moe Berg heard the news over the radio at 2:30 p.m. While others across the United States gathered with loved ones for comfort, Berg sought solitude. At 4:30 he sat in front of a pad of lined paper and wrote to collect his thoughts and channel his emotions. He scrawled:

> During two trips to Japanese countries we thought the people as a whole were kindly, hospitable, cheerful and kindly disposed toward Americans. But beneath this, or rather aside from this, was a strata of Japanese . . . , nationalistic, the Ku Klux etc., which every nation has. . . . The hope of the world is in anticipation, a decent internationalism, a charitable regard for others, live and let live—an aristocracy of the intellect, i.e. of people who think and not live by the sword—there is room for all—there must be a league of nations—an international police force.

At 5:00 p.m. he wrote in katakana, the Japanese alphabet for foreign words, "I don't like to appear to be a soothsayer but I predicted in the year 1933 that there would be a war between two philosophies, fascist and democratic."[1] Fifteen minutes later Berg added, "A state of war has just been declared with the United States." Then, at 5:30, "A feeling of relief comes with this announcement. . . . It is now here and all the pseudo patriots will have to shut up. The blind will now see that the so-called internationalists were merely foreseeing. . . . I feel sorry for the Japanese, as well as Italians and Germans who see as we do; [my old friend Frank Takizo] Matsumoto must be having a bad time today."[2]

Berg came back from the 1934 tour still infatuated with Japan. He continued to practice Japanese, told stories about the country in the bullpen to bored relief pitchers and wide-eyed rookies, and wore his kimono around the house. But he had not returned. As Mack and many of the All Americans steamed homeward on the *Empress of Canada* in December 1934, the Major League Baseball owners gathered for their annual winter meeting. Worried about injuries to their star players, they voted to discontinue all postseason international tours. Coming off the diplomatic success of the tour to Japan, the *Sporting News* editors were outraged, calling the decision shortsighted and puerile, but the owners prevailed. There would be no more Major League visits to the Far East for seventeen years.

Berg, however, stayed in touch with his Japanese friends. He exchanged greeting cards with Sotaro Suzuki and letters with his traveling buddy Frank Matsumoto. In 1937 he had helped Matsumoto enroll at Harvard Business School. Despite his upbringing in the United States and his friendships with Berg and American ballplayers, Matsumoto became an outspoken supporter of Japan's expansionist policies. During his two years at Harvard, he made sixty-three public appearances, including seven open debates, to argue Japan's case for invading China. Afterward, he returned to his professorship at Meiji University and served on the Japanese Olympic Committee. In 1943 Matsumoto published in English *The American Ventures in East Asia*, a 111-page book outlining Japan's grievances with the United States and justifying Japan's offensives against China and America.

The attack on Pearl Harbor pushed Berg into action. He retired from baseball on January 5, 1942, and joined the Office of Inter-American Affairs, a bureau in charge of political and economic intelligence in South America. Before Berg left on a six-month tour of South America, the U.S. government asked him to address the Japanese by shortwave radio.

On February 24, 1942, he told Japanese listeners, in their own language:

> I speak to you as a friend of the Japanese people, as one who has studied the origins of your language, your history, your civilization, your progress, your adaptability, your culture, and I

have found much to admire. . . . It may seem presumptuous of me to speak to you, the Japanese people, while we are at war with you, but may I recall that I was greeted by thousands of you on two other and happier occasions. . . .

I am able to talk to you somewhat in your own language, because I studied it in order to know you better. I lived among you, and traveled with intimate Japanese friends, to see your historic sites and appreciate your cultural history. I have admired the exquisite delicacy of your art, the woodprints of Hokusai, Toyokuni and Hiroshige. I stood on the bridge, sacred to you, in Kyoto, where Ushiwakamaru fought his famous battles. I journeyed to and admired the temples of Nikko and the falls of Kegon no Taki. . . . Just ten years ago I watched, with thousands of you, the return of your Emperor from military maneuvers on his way across the Nijubashi. And my head too was lowered in reverence.

Even in those days, when an excess of nationalism seized upon many of you, still there were innumerable delightful contacts possible. You loved us enough to copy our national game— baseball. We appreciated it when thousands of you gave our All American baseball team a great reception in 1934, waving American flags. I ask you, what sound basis is there for enmity between two peoples who enjoy the same national sport?

This war is no great surprise to me. Exactly ten years ago I could see that war was imminent unless you, the Japanese people, could rise up and break the power of the warlords. . . . I know your glorious history, about your samurai, the Cult of Bushido, your love of the Confucian classics. I was impressed by your hospitality and customs—all these things I still admire. But you betrayed your friends—you made a sneak attack on Pearl Harbor while your Ambassadors Nomura and Kurusu were carrying out diplomatic conversations with us; you have lost face and are committing national seppuku.

We assumed you were civilized even in battle—we thought we saw that when we taught you our national game and watched you play it. We thought that you played and would fight according to rules. But you have outraged us and every other nation in the world with the exception of two—two that are tainted with blood, Germany and Italy. They welcome you as friends. But your temporary victories will bring you only misery.

You cannot win this war. We and the twenty other republics of America are unified—we are united. Your leaders have betrayed you. They have misinterpreted democratic freedom and debate for weakness. The Matsuokas, your Jingoist army and navy officers, and your Axis partners, Hitler and Mussolini, have misjudged us, have misled you. . . . Believe me when I tell you that you cannot win this war. I am speaking to you as a friend of the Japanese people, and tell you to take the reins now. Your warlords are not telling the truth. The people of the United States and the people of Japan can be friends as they were in the past. It is up to you![3]

The speech was pure Moe Berg—formal and pompous with references to literature and history, but also optimistic, or perhaps naive, that reconciliation was still possible. The broadcast had little to no effect on Japanese morale.

Berg might have remained optimistic that the mutual love for baseball could somehow reunite the countries, but the *Sporting News* had given up on the Japanese. Unwilling to admit that baseball might not have the power to spread democracy, international brotherhood, and peace, its writers concluded that Japan had never truly understood or internalized the game. "After looking at the 70 years of Japanese baseball in retrospect, this treacherous Asiatic land was never really converted to baseball. . . . They may have acquired a little skill at the game, but the soul of our National Game never touched them. No nation which has had as intimate contact with baseball as the Japanese, could have committed the vicious, infamous dead of the early morning of December 7, 1941, if the spirit of the game ever had penetrated their yellow hides."[4]

Two weeks later in the column "Rambling Round the Circuit with Pitcher Snorter Casey," the *Sporting News* elaborated through the thoughts of the fictional Casey, "I always feel that if a guy can play baseball, he is a real sportsman. I get the idea that before a human being can take part in the give and take, they accept them decisions the way the umpire gives them on the ball field, he has to have something of the American way of living in him. But Pearl Harbor takes all that out of my mind." "It is the first failure of baseball."[5]

Players who had traveled to Japan and had previously expounded the virtues of baseball diplomacy now claimed to have seen the seeds of Japanese deceit. Tom Oliver, a member of the 1931 touring team, claimed in 1944, "While the Japs treated us nicely on that tour, there was just something about it that led many of us to believe that secretly these people would much sooner have jeered us than cheer as they did." Fred Hoffman, who went to Japan a decade earlier, told readers in 1943, "We were never able to teach them the sportsmanlike customs connected with the game. Their so-called sportsmanship was only a sham—a transparent mask to anyone who has seen them play the game."[6]

In his 1942 New Year's editorial, J. G. Taylor Spink argued that Japan did not even deserve to play baseball. He suggested that Major League Baseball make a New Year's resolution to "withdraw from Japan the gift of baseball," as the treacherous Japanese were unworthy to "share the benefits and the God-given qualities of the great game with us." There was now no doubt that the diplomatic goals of the 1934 All American tour had failed.[7]

Soon after Berg addressed the Japanese, he contacted the FBI and offered to show the films he took in Japan, including the shots taken from St. Luke's tower. The FBI found the films intriguing and suggested that he show them to members of the Office of Strategic Services, the newly formed intelligence agency that would transform into the CIA after the war. A week later Berg screened them for a wider audience. He wrote his mother, "I'm going to show my moving pictures to all the intelligence officers of all our armed forces—that means officers of the Army, Navy, Marines etc. who put together all information and give it to the fliers who bomb Tokyo or Berlin. . . . I'll tell you what they say. . . . I have pictures nobody else in the world has." A couple of weeks later, Berg wrote his sister Ethel, "The movies were received triumphantly. They wondered how I got them."[8]

Berg returned from South America in February 1943 and in August joined the OSS. He went through the OSS training camp in the Cato-ctin Mountains of Maryland where he learned the standard skills of the trade—how to pick locks, survive in the wilderness, self-defense, the art of surveillance, how to use codes, and how to kill quietly and gouge a man's eyes out with a knife.[9] Berg had various small assignments until he was shipped to Italy in May 1944 to discover the whereabouts of German physicist Werner Heisenberg and assess the progress of the Nazis' atomic bomb program. In early December the OSS learned that Heisenberg would lecture in Zurich on December 15. They sent Berg with instructions to ascertain if the Germans were close to completing an atomic weapon and if they were to assassinate Heisenberg. The former catcher attended the lecture and even questioned the enemy physicist after the event before concluding that the German atomic program was in its infancy. He let Heisenberg live. Berg's espionage career ended with the war. The OSS disbanded in 1945 with its core transforming into the CIA two years later. To Berg's great disappointment he was not asked to join the new agency.

Little was known about Berg's life as a spy until just after his death in 1972. Berg was notoriously secretive about his clandestine operations, fearing, even decades later, that the information might be useful in the wrong ears. His obituaries, for example, note that he had worked for the OSS as a secret agent but provide little detail. In 1974 Berg's first biographers, Louis Kaufman, Barbara Fitzgerald, and Tom Sewell, would retell Berg's exploits, including his daring climb up St. Luke's tower. The book, which lacks notes and relies on secondhand sources and interviews with suspect characters such as the notorious prankster Lefty Gomez, is responsible for many of the myths and exaggerations about Berg's life. The authors state, for example, that Berg conversed with Emperor Hirohito at a reception for the players at the Imperial Palace, that the 1934 tour was one of Berg's first missions as a spy, and that his films were used to plan the Doolittle raid.[10] Newspaper columnists picked up the story, often simplifying the tales and exaggerating details until Berg's exploits became even more fantastic. Despite Nicholas Dawidoff's thoroughly researched 1994 biography that refutes many of these myths, a good story, even if untrue, dies hard. Nearly twenty years after Dawidoff's book, Internet sites, sports memorabilia auction catalogs, and newspaper articles still claim that Berg spied on the Japanese. One ambitious auctioneer even had Berg speaking the rare dialect of court Japanese. He claimed that "President Roosevelt [sent] an American baseball team to Japan not for 'goodwill' but to allow Moe Berg to photograph the skyline of Tokyo—and to speak to Emperor Hirohito privately, in Court Japanese, which the Emperor's guards did not understand."[11]

Most of these myths are easily refuted. Berg, for example, never met the emperor of Japan. Hirohito had no interest in baseball and would not attend a professional game until June 25, 1959, when Shigeo Nagashima would win the famous game with a sayonara home run. The All Americans, therefore, were not invited to the Imperial Palace. Hirohito did occasionally meet foreign dignitaries, but these were usually diplomats, not common ballplayers. Even if Berg and Hirohito had met, they would have spoken English. Berg's Japanese was not fluent enough to conduct a serious conversation, and he certainly did not speak court Japanese.

Likewise, Kaufman and his coauthors conclude, "Research indicates that Moe Berg had spied for the American government during his baseball-playing years." But the evidence for Berg being a sanctioned spy in 1934 is slim to none. To begin with, there is no primary evidence that Moe Berg was working for the U.S. government in 1934. In researching his Berg biography, *The Catcher Was a Spy*, Nicholas Dawidoff combed the declassified records of the period and found no mention of Berg. Subsequent analysis of the *Confidential U.S. Diplomatic Post Records*, recently declassified OSS papers, and the personal papers of Ambassador Joseph Grew also contain no evidence that Berg was a spy at the time. The only mention of Berg in Grew's papers is a diary entry for November 2, 1934, stating, "The Clive girl, who came over on the ship with them [the All Americans] is enthusiastic about Mo [*sic*] Berg who, she says, speaks French, Italian and some other languages and is really a cultured gentleman."[12] The comment and misspelling of *Moe* suggest that Grew had no knowledge of Berg prior to Clive's praises. More important, Berg's 1943 OSS application makes no reference to prior clandestine work.

Why, then, did Kaufman and others conclude that Moe was a spy in the 1934 All American tour of Japan? The only evidence is circumstantial and comes down to mysterious behavior. Proponents point to three supposedly unusual actions: Berg's inclusion on an all-star team, his letter of introduction from Secretary of State Cordell Hull, and his climb up St. Luke's tower.

With a .243 lifetime batting average and having appeared in just sixty-two games during the '34 season, Berg does not seem to have belonged on the All American roster, which contained six future Hall of Famers in addition to stars such as O'Doul, Miller, and Whitehill.[13] But Berg was better qualified for the trip than a number of his teammates. The 1934 team was more than just a baseball squad. They were goodwill ambassadors representing the United States. Berg had already been to Japan, made friends, and left a positive impression on the Japanese baseball world. After the poor behavior of the 1931 American team, Connie Mack and Lefty O'Doul wanted players who would behave like gentlemen. With his Ivy League education, proper manners, smattering of Japanese, and contacts in Japan, Berg was ideal. Although his Japanese was not as good as later biographers would claim, it was probably good enough to accomplish daily tasks and endeared him to his hosts. Furthermore, Berg was an outstanding defensive catcher, who had previously caught and was able to placate Earl Whitehill, the team's fiery pitcher. There is no mystery regarding his inclusion on the squad.

Kaufman and others regard the letter from Hull to "the American Diplomatic and Consular Officers" as evidence that the diplomatic corps should aid Berg in a clandestine mission. The letter states, "At the instance of the Honorable Chester C. Bolton, representative in the Congress of the United States from the State of Ohio, I take pleasure in introducing to you Mr. Morris Berg of Newark, New Jersey, who is about to proceed abroad. I cordially bespeak for Mr. Berg such courtesies and assistance as you may be able to render consistent with your official duties." Berg planned to continue his travels in Asia after the baseball tour finished. He would visit Korea and China, take the Trans-Siberian Railroad across Russia, arrive in Poland, and head home through Europe. As an American citizen traveling off the beaten path, he might, and it turns out would, have need of consular assistance. There is no reason to conclude that the document is anything other than a letter of introduction—a common practice in a time before easy telephone communication and fax machines. Moe had met numerous politicians during his time with the Washington Senators. Considering that he frequented political and diplomatic parties, it is likely that he knew Congressman Bolton and the representative penned it as a personal favor. Should Berg need official help during his travels, the letter would indicate his importance and help ensure better service.

Berg's visit to St. Luke's is not easily explained. Why would a professional athlete miss a game, dress in a disguise, use subterfuge to enter a hospital, secretly climb its tower, and take moving pictures of the city skyline? It was also not the first, or last, time on the trip Berg risked arrest to take photographs. He photographed both the Tsugaru and the Shimonoseki straits and took panoramic shots of Nagoya, Kobe, and Osaka. Later, he would be arrested in Korea for photographing the Yalu Bridge at the Korea-Chinese border. Police confiscated twenty-five feet of film before setting him free. In Moscow police stopped him from filming Lenin's tomb and took his film. Not long afterward he was stopped while filming the construction of a subway. A soldier took his camera and passport and told him to remain on the spot. Berg waited for five hours before the soldier returned with his passport and no further comment. His troubles with the police were not over. As he crossed the border to Poland he was searched again, and two more rolls were confiscated.[14] Berg was clearly filming sensitive areas.

Nicholas Dawidoff suggests that Moe did it for the thrill. Perhaps he began with the shots of the Tsugaru Strait just out of his perverse rebellion against authority, and enjoying the rush of defying the law, he continued. At first this explanation seems unsatisfactory, but Berg's behavior both during and after the trip indicates that he was not a spy. Berg seems to be untrained in clandestine operations. Although he managed to take pictures unnoticed in Japan, he was caught three times in his subsequent travels and had his film confiscated. One would expect a trained spy to do better. Berg also kept the film on his person, smuggling it through customs. If he had been taking pictures for the U.S. government, he would have handed it off to an American Embassy or consul. But most telling is what happened to his films after he returned to the United States— he kept them. Had Moe Berg been a government spy, he would have turned in his assignment. Even if he had kept copies, he would not have needed to screen his films for the OSS, the FBI, and other intelligence officers in 1942. The films would have been incorporated into intelligence data years before. The strongest evidence against Berg taking the films on government orders, however, comes from his letter to Ethel when he wrote, "They wondered how I got them."

Finally, were Berg's movies used to plan the Doolittle raid of Tokyo? Both Dawidoff and Japanese journalist Jiro Hirano have examined the question through primary sources and interviewed men involved in planning the raid. Both conclude that if the Berg movies were used at all, they played a minor role in identifying targets of military importance. Better sources than Berg's twenty-two-second panorama of Tokyo existed in 1942. According to Doolittle, the targets were identified by Capt. Steve Jurika, a former assistant naval attaché who spent 1939 to 1941 in Tokyo, secretly identifying and mapping sites of military and industrial importance.[15]

The 1934 trip to Japan was a pivotal point in Berg's espionage career, not because it was his first mission, but because it sowed the seeds for his future career as a spy. It was while shooting clandestine pictures in Asia that Berg realized his true calling.

For the remainder of his life, Berg would reminisce about his trips to Japan, but he would never return to the Land of the Rising Sun. Perhaps the feeling of betrayal was too strong.

33

Babe Ruth had believed the hype. He was convinced that his visit to Japan had sealed the friendship between the two countries and forestalled any possible war. After all, the *Sporting News*, *New York Times*, *Washington Post*, and even Connie Mack had said so. On top of that, Ruth had seen the hundreds of thousands waving American flags, chanting his name, clamoring for an autograph or handshake. He could not believe that such a friendly people, who also shared a passion for the game of baseball, would ever attack the United States.

He learned of the attack in his luxurious fifteenth-floor, eleven-room apartment at 173 Riverside Drive. Unlike Horio and Berg, who were overwhelmed by sadness, Ruth was absolutely furious. For him, Pearl Harbor was a personal betrayal. Cursing the double-crossing sobs, he heaved open the living room window that looked out over Riverside Drive to the Hudson River. Claire had decorated the room with souvenirs from the Asian tour—porcelain vases and plates, exquisite dolls, the bronze vases the Babe won as the tour's top batter, and various sundries. The Babe stormed to the mantle, grabbed a vase, and tossed it out the window. It crashed on the street below. Other souvenirs followed as Ruth kept up a tirade about the Japanese. Claire rushed around the room, gathering up the most valuable items before they joined the pile on Riverside Drive. She managed to save the dolls and the bronze vases.[1]

The Sultan of Swat knew how to take revenge. Using the same charisma that made him an idol in Japan, he threw himself into the war effort, raising money to defeat the Japanese and their allies. Ruth worked closely with the Red Cross, making celebrity appearances, playing in old-timer games, visiting hospitals, and even going door-to-door seeking donations. He became a spokesman for war bonds, doing radio commercials, print advertisements, and public appearances to boost sales, and even bought one hundred thousand dollars worth himself. Perhaps the Babe's most publicized event came on August 23, 1943, when 69,136 fans packed Yankee Stadium to watch Ruth play for the first time in seven years. The forty-seven-year-old Babe faced fifty-four-year-old Walter Johnson, regarded by most as the greatest pitcher of all time, in a demonstration before an old-timers game. Johnson threw fifteen pitches, and the Bambino hit the fifth one into the right-field stands. In the hyperbolic style of the time, sports columnist James Dawson wrote, "Babe Ruth hit one of his greatest home runs yesterday in the interest of freedom and the democratic way of living." The event raised eighty thousand dollars for the U.S. Army-Navy relief fund.[2]

Ruth's biographer Marshall Smelser later concluded, "Ruth in his late forties had become a patriotic symbol, ranking not far below the flag and the bald eagle." But Ruth's role as a symbol was not limited to the United States. In Japan the jovial, overweight, self-indulgent demigod of baseball, so welcomed in 1934, had become a symbol of American decadence. On March 3, 1944, the *New York Times* published Jeremiah O'Leary's description of the Japanese infantry screaming "To hell with Babe Ruth!" as they charged to their deaths across the mangrove swamps of the South Pacific. The Babe's response to O'Leary's report was classic Ruth: "I hope every Jap that mentions my name gets shot—and to hell with all Japs anyway!" The day after the *Times* article, Ruth took to the streets to raise money for the Red Cross, telling reporters that he was spurred on by the Japanese war cry.[3]

Understanding Ruth's notoriety in Japan, the American military even considered using the Babe to undermine Japanese morale. Just as Berg and others had been broadcast across Japanese airways to influence its population, a navy acquaintance submitted a plan to bring Ruth off the coast of Japan to make a series of radio broadcasts calling the Japanese to surrender. The plan, however, was rejected.[4]

Just before his death from cancer in 1948, Ruth reflected on the 1934 tour in *The Babe Ruth Story* with Bob Considine. "Despite the treacherous attack the Japanese made on us only seven years later, I cannot help but feel that the reception which millions of Japanese gave us was genuine. . . . No doubt there were plenty of stinkers among them; but looking back at the visit I feel it is another example of how a crackpot government can lead a friendly people to war."[5]

34

The attack on Pearl Harbor did not surprise or upset Eiji Sawamura. On December 7, 1941, Sawamura sat in a staging area on the Micronesian island of Palau, awaiting orders. Soon he would board a crowded transport as part of a massive assault group. He did not know where he would land, but he hoped that he would get to fight the Americans, whom at this point he considered to be little more than animals.

Like most Japanese Sawamura supported his country's military expansion and did not question the decision to go to war. Since 1890 when the Meiji government announced the Imperial Rescript on Education, all Japanese schoolchildren had been trained to obey the emperor and state. Joseph Grew told readers of his 1942 book *Report from Tokyo*:

> In Japan the training of youth for war is not simply military training. It is a shaping . . . of the mind of youth from the earliest years. Every Japanese school child on national holidays . . . takes part in a ritual intended to impress on him his duties to the state and to the Emperor. Several times each year every child is taken with the rest of his schoolmates to a place where the spirits of dead soldiers are enshrined. . . . Of his obligation to serve the state, especially through military service, he hears every day. . . . The whole concept of Japanese education has been built upon the military formula of obeying commands.[1]

As a result of this education, most Japanese believed that the Western powers were not only thwarting Japan's right to control Asia through the so-called Greater East Asian Co-Prosperity Sphere but also unfairly strangling the nation through oil and material embargoes. When Japanese radio announced the attack on Pearl Harbor, "the attitudes of the ordinary people," according to literary critic Takao Okuan, were "a sense of euphoria that we'd done it at last; we'd landed a punch on those arrogant great powers Britain and America, on those white fellows. . . . All the feelings of inferiority of a colored people from a backward country, towards white people from the developed world, disappeared in that one blow. . . . Never in our history had we Japanese felt such pride in ourselves as a race as we did then."[2]

Whereas most of the All Americans finished the 1934 goodwill tour with warm feelings toward Japan, Sawamura had grown to hate Americans. His loathing began during the Yomiuri Giants' first visit to the United States in 1935. Just before returning to America in 1936, a piece by Sawamura titled "My Worry" appeared in the January issue of *Shinseinen*. He wrote:

> As a professional baseball player, I would love to pitch against the Major Leaguers, not just in an exhibition game like I pitched against Babe Ruth, but in a serious game. However, what I am concerned about is that I hate America, and I cannot possibly like American people, so I cannot live in America. Firstly, I would have a language problem. Secondly, American food does not include much rice so it does not satisfy me, so I cannot pitch as powerfully as I do in Japan. Last time I went to America, I could not pitch as well as I do in Japan. I cannot stand to be where formal customs exist, such as a man is not allowed to tie a shoelace when a woman is around. American women are arrogant.[3]

Sawamura's dislike grew during his first tour in the Imperial Army. After leading the league in strikeouts in the fall of 1937, Eiji received a draft notice in January 1938. On the tenth he reported to Tsu City, Mie Prefecture, to join the Thirty-Third Infantry Regiment of the Sixteenth Division to begin basic training. Most of the regiment was currently in Nanking, becoming notorious as "the most savage killing machine among the Japanese military units."[4] The Japanese capture of Nanking in December 1937, commonly known as the "Rape of Nanking," is well known as one of the most brutal war atrocities in modern history. For six weeks victorious Japanese troops pillaged the city, raped tens of thousands of women and children, and murdered for sport. More than 260,000 Chinese civilians and 57,000 Chinese soldiers died. The Japanese army systematically killed all prisoners. The Sixteenth Division commander, Kesago Nakajima, reportedly practiced his swordsmanship by beheading kneeling Chinese prisoners. Sawamura's Thirty-Third Regiment was at the center of the atrocities against both civilians and prisoners of war. The regiment executed 3,096 prisoners and was rumored to have murdered hundreds by rolling train cars filled with Chinese prisoners into the Yangtze River.

Eiji completed his training and shipped out from Hiroshima on April 3, joining his regiment three days later in Shanghai. Soon after his arrival the Thirty-Third joined other Japanese forces at Xuzhou to face 600,000 Chinese in a monthlong battle. Relying on his baseball skills, Sawamura became renowned for his grenade throwing and was often given the task of cleaning out strong Chinese positions with a difficult toss. After a month of fighting the Chinese withdrew to the city of Wuhan to set up the largest battle of the war. Chiang Kai-shek commanded more than 1 million Chinese national troops to protect China's second-largest city, while the Japanese countered with 350,000 ground troops and five hundred aircraft in an attempt to end the war with a knockout blow. The battle raged for more than four months, as the Japanese attempted to surround Wuhan. Sawamura and the Thirty-Third attacked from the north through the Dabie Mountains in late August. A month later, on September 23, Sawamura took a bullet in his left hand. He spent an undisclosed amount of time in a military hospital and probably returned to his unit before being discharged the following year on October 8, 1939.

Sawamura took the mound again for the Tokyo Giants during the 1940 season, but throwing the heavy grenades had damaged his arm, and he could pitch only with a sidearm motion. He no longer had the velocity of his preservice years, but he remained a crafty hurler, tossing a no-hitter against the Nagoya team on July 6. It was the third no-hitter of his career, but it lacked the luster of his first two, as the war in China had depleted the pro baseball rosters. Five no-hitters were thrown in 1940, more than any other season in Japanese pro baseball. Eiji finished the 1940 season with a seemingly strong 2.59 ERA, but in truth it fell well above the league ERA of 2.12.

As the military furthered its control of Japan in the late 1930s, the movement to cleanse the country of Western influence and trappings strengthened. Pulitzer Prize–winning historian John Dower has shown that Japanese of the 1930s and '40s did not necessarily see themselves as a physically or intellectually superior race, but they did view themselves as more spiritually virtuous than others. Propaganda of the time focused on the development of a pure Japanese spirit, *Yamato Damashii*. This entailed a return to traditional Japanese lifeways, emphasis on self-denial and self-control, and reverence for the emperor. Western influences were viewed as corrupting, as they emphasized individuality and undermined Japanese culture and spirit. Gen. Sadao Araki proclaimed, "Frivolous thinking is due to foreign thought."[5] Imported amusements fell out of fashion. By the mid-1930s military marches had replaced jazz as the most popular music. During the war jazz would be outlawed, and even musical instruments used in the genre, such as electric guitars and banjos, would be banned. In the late 1930s the Ministry of Education decreed that scholastic sports should be stripped of "liberal influences" and replaced with traditional Japanese values and physical activities designed to enhance national defense. In 1940 Nippon Professional Baseball's board of directors followed suit. They declared that all games would be played following "the Japanese spirit" and banned English terms. Henceforth, the game would be known only as *yakyu* (field ball) and not *besuboru*. *Strike* would now be *yoshi* (good), and *ball* became *dame* (bad). Other English terms were also replaced with Japanese equivalents. Team nicknames, such as Giants and Tigers, were abandoned. Tokyo became known as Kyojin Gun (Giants Troop) and the Osaka Tigers became Moko Gun (the Fiery Tiger Troop). Two years later, in 1942, uniforms were changed to khaki, the color of national defense, and baseball caps were replaced with military caps.[6]

Although still hampered by his damaged arm, a continuing bout with malaria, and difficulty sleeping, Sawamura threw 153 innings for Yomiuri during the 1941 season. He was no longer a top pitcher.

His 2.04 ERA was the highest of the team's five regular pitchers and was .20 points above the league average. Just before the end of the season, Eiji married his longtime girlfriend, Yuko, but marital bliss was short-lived. Only three days later Sawamura received a second draft notice. He was to report immediately to the Thirty-Third Regimental headquarters. Units across Japan were being mobilized on the double.

The Thirty-Third left Nagoya on November 20 (the seventh anniversary of his near win against the All Americans) and headed by transport to the island of Palau in Micronesia, where they joined a 130,000-strong invasion force. In early December the Thirty-Third split. The Second and Third battalions left with the majority of the assembled troops, while Sawamura and his First Battalion remained on Palau. On the night of December 16–17 Sawamura and his comrades boarded a transport and set sail toward the Philippines.

As the main body of the invasion force attacked the island of Luzon and pushed toward Manila, Sawamura's force invaded the city of Davao on the island of Mindanao. They occupied the city without a fight, as the outnumbered American and Filipino garrison withdrew. Davao was the only area in the Philippines with a significant Japanese population, as thousands had immigrated to work on the area's hemp plantations. By 1941 the city contained a stable Japanese community of 20,000, with eleven Japanese-language schools.[7] With Davao secured the Japanese pushed into the surrounding jungles in pursuit of the American and Filipino troops. The Allies retreated before the superior Japanese force, only to mount swift counterattacks when they spotted a weakness. Sawamura found such behavior dishonorable and cowardly. "When we were strong and solid, the western devils got quiet as a cat. But, when they saw that we were not prepared, they would attack like a cruel evil." To Sawamura's shock, the outnumbered Americans soon surrendered. "They surrendered immediately even if they had enough bullets and guns," he later wrote with disgust. "While Japanese put their hands up in the sky in a banzai cheer at victory, Americans put their hands up in a halfway manner shamelessly as soon as they realized that they could not win and there was no way out."[8]

As Sawamura's First Battalion fought in Mindanao, the rest of his regiment and division had just defeated the main American force at the battle of Bataan. The Japanese took 75,000 American and Filipino prisoners and force-marched them sixty miles through tropical jungles without water or food. Stragglers were killed. Escorting Japanese (including members of Sawamura's regiment) beat, shot, and beheaded prisoners for sport as they traveled by the winding column. More than a quarter of the prisoners died before they reached an internment camp at Capas. Known as the Bataan Death March, the incident became one of the most notorious atrocities committed by the Japanese army.

Sawamura stayed in the Philippines for just over a year, returning to Japan with his regiment in January 1943. He rejoined the Tokyo Giants for the 1943 season, but three years in the Imperial Army had taken a toll. His famous control was gone. Eiji pitched in four games, logging eleven innings, but gave up seventeen hits and walked twelve. He finished out the season as a pinch hitter.

In November 1943 Sawamura published a nine-page article about his combat experiences in the baseball magazine *Yakyukai*. Articles supporting the war effort were common in Japanese magazines. Unlike the Nazis or Soviets, who had centralized bureaus responsible for all propaganda, in both Japan and the United States private enterprises willingly created propaganda to boost morale on the home front. The piece includes themes common in most Japanese propaganda. Sawamura depicts both the suffering and the daily toil of military life to remind readers that self-sacrifice is the moral obligation of all Japanese to support the war effort. Civilians were expected to bear their difficulties without complaint, as the military faced the true hardships. He praises the uniqueness of the Japanese spirit, emphasizing the virtues of self-sacrifice, respect, and duty. Following a universal theme of wartime propaganda, Sawamura depicts the enemy as cruel, demonic savages. One particularly unbelievable story has the American garrison of Davao gathering the entire Japanese population of 20,000 in basements rigged with mines. The Americans, according to Sawamura, were planning to blow up the prisoners before the Imperial Army entered the city, but the speed of the Japanese advance startled the Americans and caused them to retreat before setting off the explosives. Another story, which Sawamura admits he did not witness, has American soldiers executing prisoners by pouring boiling water over their heads. With Sawamura's popularity and *Yakyukai*'s wide circulation, thousands, if not millions, read the article. Just as Babe Ruth was using his popularity to support the American war effort, Japan's great diamond hero did what he could to support his nation. Sawamura, however, would ultimately give more than the Bambino.

Before the start of the 1944 season the Giants decided not to renew Sawamura's contract. Although he must have known it was coming, he was devastated. All he wanted to do was play ball. Eiji began to contact other teams, but Sotaro Suzuki advised him to retire, telling him, "You should remain 'Sawamura of the Tokyo Giants' and not tarnish your legacy by clinging to a career with another team."[9] Understanding Suzuki's wisdom, Eiji announced his retirement.

The 1944 season turned out to be a disappointment. The league faced shortages in materials and players. Many of the top players had been drafted by the military. Shigeru Mizuhara was serving in China, would be captured by the Russians the following year, and would spend the next four years in a Siberian prisoner-of-war camp. His rival, Osamu Mihara, served as a private in the infantry. The remainder of All Nippon's infield, first baseman Minoru Yamashita and shortstop Hisanori Karita, were also fighting in China. Sixty-nine professional players never came home. Among the casualties were three former All Nippon players: the young pitcher Kenichi Aoshiba, who died in the Pyongyang Military Hospital of disease; catcher Nobuo Kura, who died in the battle of Okinawa; and the young third baseman from Kokura, Usaburo Shintomi, who was killed in Burma.

Despite growing up in Japan and being fluent in the language, Victor Starffin was not a Japanese citizen. At first this had its advantages, as he did not have to serve in the military. He was able to stay in professional baseball and become the Tokyo Giants' top pitcher. The Russian led the league in wins and ERA in every season from the fall of 1937 through 1940 and again in 1942. He also won the MVP awards in 1939 and '40. But as the war progressed, the disadvantages became evident. As part of the purification process, the league made Starffin change his name in 1940. "Victor Starffin" was too Western, so he would thenceforth be known as Hiroshi Suda. In private protest Starffin wrote a large *V* for Victor on his undershirt and wore it beneath his uniform when he took the mound. In 1944 as bombs fell on Tokyo, the Giants, under pressure from the government, released Starffin, despite his 6–0 record and 0.68 ERA. Victor was then arrested on trumped-up charges of espionage and sent to the Karuizawa detention camp for the remainder of the conflict.[10]

As the summer of '44 progressed, Allied air raids became more frequent. In August, after each team had played just thirty-five games, the league was shut down. Sawamura spent the first year of his retirement with his wife, Ryoko, and his infant daughter, but in October another letter arrived from the Imperial Army. The Thirty-Third was being reactivated and sent into combat. By the fall of 1944 the tide of the war had turned against the Japanese. The battle of Midway in June 1942 had crippled the Japanese navy, allowing the Allies to begin their offensive. In the spring and summer of '44, Americans captured Saipan, Guam, and Palau and readied to retake the Philippines. On October 20, 1944, 200,000 American forces commanded by Gen. Douglas MacArthur landed on Leyte to begin the campaign. The Imperial Army's Sixteenth Division, Sawamura's old combat group, defended the islands. Heavily outnumbered, the Japanese rushed reinforcements to the area.

The Thirty-Third left Japan on November 27 and steamed toward the Philippines. But Sawamura never reached his destination. On December 2 an American submarine intercepted his transport off the coast of Taiwan and sank it. The hero of the 1934 goodwill tour was dead, killed by the creators of the game he loved.

Despite being a dominant pitcher for only a couple of seasons, Sawamura would become one of the icons of Japanese baseball. In 1947 the magazine *Nekkyu* created the Sawamura Award to honor the best pitcher in Nippon Professional Baseball. Incidentally, this award predates the Major League Cy Young Award by nine years. Twelve years later he became one of nine initial members of the Japan Baseball Hall of Fame. Later, statues of the pitcher would be raised outside of Shizuoka Kusanagi Stadium and his old high school in Kyoto. Sawamura's image would also be used on a Japanese postal stamp. His lasting popularity came not from outstanding charisma (he seems to have had little) or a long career, but from his role as a symbol of Japan.

In his short life Sawamura personified the trials of his country. In 1934, as Japan strove to be recognized as an equal to the United States and Britain, he nearly overcame the more powerful American ball club. Many viewed his performance as an analogy of Japan's struggles against the West—with the proper fighting spirit, Japan could overcome its rivals. In the late 1930s and early 1940s, Japan and Sawamura went to war. Eiji typified the millions of Japanese soldiers and civilians who dutifully sacrificed their livelihoods, families, and lives for their country. After the war Sawamura's life took on a different meaning. Recast as a victim of militarism rather than an active participant, he became a symbol of a nation and an entire generation whose dreams and lives had been shattered by war.

35

Lefty O'Doul waved from the backseat of the open limousine as it drove through the streets of Ginza. Tens of thousands lined the five-mile parade route. Many waved American flags and shouted, "Refty Odurru!" Confetti and streamers fell from the windows of the taller buildings as the line of cars passed a large banner reading, "Welcome San Francisco Seals." It was October 12, 1949; fifteen years had passed since the 1934 welcoming parade for the All Americans and four since the end of World War II.

American bombers had leveled Tokyo, Nagoya, and Kobe and obliterated Hiroshima and Nagasaki. Almost three million Japanese had died during the war, millions of civilians were displaced, and another million soldiers were stranded overseas. As the war had cut communication with Japan, O'Doul had not corresponded with his Japanese friends throughout the conflict, leaving him unsure of their whereabouts or fates. In early 1946 Lefty went to Japan to find them.

Arriving in Tokyo O'Doul drove through block after block of flattened debris. The former splendor and wealth of Tokyo was gone. Survivors, dressed in worn, patched clothing, struggled to rebuild their lives. Food, water, and fuel were scarce and electricity nonexistent in most areas. The trip was filled with sadness. Many of his friends had died.

O'Doul located Victor Starffin. He had learned English at the Karuizawa detention camp and after his release worked briefly for the Allies as an interpreter before returning to baseball. Starffin would pitch for ten more seasons, retiring in 1955 as the first player to win three hundred games. Two years later, just after his fortieth birthday, he would die in a car crash. O'Doul was unable to pay his respects to *Yomiuri Shimbun* owner Matsutaro Shoriki. The Allies had arrested

Shoriki in December 1945 for his role in disseminating war propaganda through his newspapers. He sat in Sugamo Prison, awaiting trial as a war criminal. He would remain incarcerated for two years before the charges would be dropped.

With the help of the occupying forces, O'Doul had already located Sotaro Suzuki. At the beginning of the war Suzuki had stayed with *Yomiuri* as a sportswriter and had served on the committee overseeing professional baseball. He argued against the league's rules for cleansing the game of English elements and, when overruled, refused to attend the board meetings. His protest drew the attention of the secret police, but somehow Suzuki escaped prosecution for unpatriotic acts. As the war progressed Suzuki became disillusioned with the Japanese military. Working at the newspaper gave him access to overseas reports that were not released to the public. He soon realized that Japan could never win. He cursed as the ballplayers were drafted and sent overseas and watched the troopships leave Yokohama Harbor with sadness, knowing that few of the men would return. When the professional league shut down in 1944, Suzuki left *Yomiuri* and tried, unsuccessfully, to reenter the silk industry.[1]

At noon on August 15, 1945, Emperor Hirohito read a prepared statement over Japanese radio. It was the first time he had addressed his people. He spoke in formal court Japanese in a high-pitched voice, making his message almost unintelligible to many of his subjects. "After pondering deeply the general trends of the world and the actual conditions obtaining to our empire today, we have decided to effect a settlement of the present situation by resorting to an extraordinary measure. . . . We have resolved to pave the way for a grand peace for all the generations to come by enduring the unendurable and suffering the insufferable."[2] The war was over. Two weeks later the American fleet arrived in Tokyo Bay, and the unconditional surrender was signed on the deck of the battleship *Missouri*. Immediately, Suzuki began to rebuild Japanese baseball. Luckily, the Supreme Commander of the Allied Powers, Gen. Douglas MacArthur, and Gen. William F. Marquat, the head of the occupation's section on economics and science, were baseball fans who understood the importance of the game to the Japanese and to international relations.

MacArthur's administration, known as SCAP, not only had to pacify and administer the former enemy but also convert the country to a democracy. Communism had replaced fascism as the ideological enemy, and Japan was crucial to America's plan to contain the "Red Menace." Whereas baseball diplomacy prior to the war had been limited to unofficial exchanges, encouraged but not sanctioned by either government, SCAP would now use baseball as a diplomatic tool to "Americanize" and "democratize" Japan. They banned traditional Japanese sports associated with militarism, such as kendo, archery, and martial arts. In their place they promoted the American pastime. SCAP restored baseball stadiums that had been used by the Japanese to store munitions and were now filled with rubble, unexploded ordinance, and fuel. They renovated parks, helped organize amateur and youth leagues, and supplied bats and balls.[3] They encouraged the Japanese to restart scholastic baseball programs, and on January 21, 1946, the *Asahi Shimbun* announced that the high school championship tournament at Koshien would be held later that year to "help mend young souls twisted by war, and contribute to the development of democratic spirit and the reconstruction of Japan."[4] SCAP also worked closely with Sotaro Suzuki and league president Ryuji Suzuki to reestablish professional baseball.

Ryuji Suzuki understood that the sport was more than just entertainment. "America is occupying Japan. We are wondering what will happen to our people's life if we fail to get along with America." "Baseball is the national sport of America. That's why we need to reorganize the game here. We have to use diplomacy, not weapons." "Baseball will build a bridge." On November 23, 1945, only three months after Japan surrendered, Nippon Pro Baseball held an all-star game at Meiji Jingu Stadium. Despite pervasive poverty and shortages in food, electricity, and housing, nearly 6,000 fans watched stars from eastern Japan beat those from the west, 13–9. The all-star squads played three more times that fall. The *Sporting News* and other American baseball writers applauded their efforts. Frederick Lieb, who had helped organize the 1931 tour, wrote, "It may take America a long time to forget the treachery of Pearl Harbor, the march from Bataan, the horror of the prison camps, but the baseball field may furnish some future meeting ground with our erstwhile foe."[5]

League play restarted the following spring, as eight pro teams played out a 105-game schedule. Marginal players, who would fade away once former stars returned from the war, filled out many rosters, but at least baseball was back. Japan was still in ruins, its economy devastated, yet 1,558,615 fans plopped down five yen each to attend the games. Sotaro Suzuki, now the league's vice president, vowed to make the league more exciting and financially stable by Americanizing the game. "Our league slogan this year is 'Follow the American ball,'" he told a *Collier's* reporter in 1947. In that spirit, the Japanese joined the Major Leagues by honoring a dying Babe Ruth by celebrating Babe Ruth Day on April 27, 1947. With the war over the Bambino was once again in the good graces of the Japanese fans.

Attendance rose over the next three seasons as a crop of young stars joined returning veterans, but the passion of prewar baseball was missing. *Collier's* writer Weldon James observed, "A couple hundred G.I.s, munching peanuts and sipping Army-ration beer . . . make more noise than the 50,000 Japanese overflowing Korakuen Stadium." Lefty O'Doul felt that he could help.[6]

After taking over the San Francisco Seals in 1935, he had been working with Sotaro Suzuki to bring the team to Japan, but the invasion of China in the summer of 1937 put an end to their plans. His visit in 1946 spurred O'Doul to try again. He later wrote, "I knew if we took a baseball team over there it would cement friendship between their people and ours."[7] Working closely with Suzuki, Moe Berg's old friend Takizo "Frank" Matsumoto, who was now a member of the Japanese Diet, and Lt. Tsuneo "Cappy" Harada from MacArthur's staff, O'Doul brought the Seals in October 1949.

The welcoming parade for the Seals rivaled the famous 1934 trek through Ginza. Pitcher Con Dempsey remembers, "A hundred thousand people waving American flags lined the streets of Tokyo when we arrived." The *Sporting News* reported that it was "a thunderous welcome—the biggest demonstration by the populace during the post-war period."[8] Despite the spectacle something was missing. O'Doul tried to stir them up. "*Banzai!*" he yelled. No response. "*Banzai!*" he tried again. Still no response. Lefty turned to Cappy Harada and asked, "Usually before the War when you yelled *banzai*, they would yell *banzai* back. How come they don't yell *banzai*?"

"That's the reason you're here, Lefty," responded Harada. "To build up the morale so that they will yell *banzai* again."

And that is exactly what the Seals did.

For four weeks the Seals traveled through Japan, playing eleven games—seven against Japanese teams and four against American military squads. Fans lined up outside Korakuen Stadium for two days to buy tickets for the opening game against the Yomiuri Giants. Tens of thousands went home empty-handed, and tickets were resold at 300 percent profit on the black market. With two spectators sharing single seats and squeezing "into every nook and cranny," fifty-five thousand crammed into the stadium, making it the largest crowd in the stadium's history. Prior to the game, the American and Japanese flags were raised together in a symbolic gesture of unity as both national anthems were played. It was the first time since the war that the flags were raised simultaneously, and it caught many Japanese by surprise. The gesture moved many to tears.

Other games sold out at a similar rate. More than sixty thousand watched Victor Starffin hold the Seals scoreless for six innings at Meiji Jingu Stadium on October 17 before the Seals scored four off a relief pitcher. An estimated five hundred thousand attended the eleven contests. To create more goodwill, the Seals donated one hundred thousand dollars of their income to local charities and spent their off days visiting with Japanese and American fans. But the final game was the true diplomatic coup de grâce. Declaring it Lefty O'Doul Day, all of Korakuen Stadium's fifty thousand seats were available only to children fifteen years old and under, and admission was free. O'Doul himself pitched three innings against a team of Japanese college all-stars and nearly lost the game. After the game ended O'Doul was brought to the Imperial Palace for a personal audience with Emperor Hirohito. The emperor praised Lefty's work, telling him, "I certainly am appreciative and proud of the good work the Seals have done on this tour and very happy it has been successful. It is by means of sports that our countries can be brought closer together."[9]

Nearly every observer agreed that the Seals' visit had somehow revitalized Japanese morale and helped spread American values. "The Seals are the biggest things to hit Japan since the atom bomb," shouted a Sporting News headline. Sgt. Dick Harn, a member of the occupying force, wrote a letter to the Sporting News explaining, "You have to be in Japan even to start to visualize the goodwill which was created in Japan for Americans through the six games played against Japanese professional teams and the single game played before 55,000 children who were all admitted free." Seals coach Del Young explained, "When we got there the Communists were on soapboxes on almost every street-corner. But we hadn't been there long before they disappeared in the crowds." An editorial in the same issue of the *Sporting News* concluded, "Let's stress the fact that the Seals did much to advance democracy in Japan; they did much to dim the satellites of the Communists; they did much towards spreading good will here; and they did much for the betterment of Japanese baseball." Even Supreme Commander Douglas MacArthur proclaimed, "This is the greatest piece of diplomacy ever." But Lefty said it best: "When I arrived it was terrible. . . . The people . . . were so depressed that when I hollered '*Banzai*' they didn't respond at all. No reaction at all. Nothing. But when I left there, a few months [*sic*] later, all Japan was cheering and shouting '*Banzai*' again."[10]

O'Doul and Suzuki had learned from 1934 that a single tour was not enough to cement international goodwill. They followed up the Seals' visit by bringing Joe DiMaggio in 1950 and teams of Major League all-stars in 1951 and '53—establishing what would become a fifty-five-year tradition of a Major League team coming to Japan about every two years. They arranged for the Yomiuri Giants to have spring training in the United States in 1953 and were instrumental in helping Wally Yonamine become the first American player to join the Japanese leagues since the end of the war. O'Doul's commitment to baseball diplomacy drew accolades from prime ministers, diplomats, and baseball commissioners. At his 1969 funeral Monsignor Vincent Breen proclaimed, "No single man did more to reestablish faith and friendship between our great nations than did Lefty O'Doul." Thirty-three years after his death, Lefty would join Sotaro Suzuki in the Japan Baseball Hall of Fame. Their lifelong friendship, cemented during the 1934 All American tour, and their shared belief in the ability of baseball to promote international understanding helped heal the wounds of the war and bind the countries together into the next century.

Appendix 1: THE ALL AMERICAN TOURING PARTY

Averill, Earl	Outfielder, Cleveland Indians
Averill, Gladys Loette Hyatt	Wife of Earl
Bell, Stuart	Newspaper writer, *Cleveland Press*
Berg, Morris (Moe)	Catcher, Cleveland Indians
Brown, Clinton	Pitcher, Cleveland Indians
Brown, Mary	Wife of Clint
Cascarella, Joe	Pitcher, Philadelphia Athletics
Ebling, Edward "Doc"	Trainer, Philadelphia Athletics
Foxx, Helen Heite	Wife of James
Foxx, James	Infielder, Philadelphia Athletics
Gehrig, Eleanor Twitchell	Wife of Louis
Gehrig, Louis	First baseman, New York Yankees
Gehringer, Charles	Second baseman, Detroit Tigers
Gomez, June O'Dea	Wife of Vernon and Broadway actress
Gomez, Vernon "Lefty"	Pitcher, New York Yankees
Hayes, Frank	Catcher, Philadelphia Athletics
Hillerich, John Andrew "Bud"	Partner of Hillerich & Bradsby, maker of the Louisville Slugger
Hillerich, Rose S. Ratterman	Wife of John
Macfarland, Elfreda	Daughter of Ben Shibe, part-owner of the Philadelphia Athletics, sister of Mary Reach
McGillicuddy, Cornelius "Connie Mack"	Manager, Philadelphia Athletics
McNair, Eric "Rabbit"	Shortstop, Philadelphia Athletics
McNair, Mildred	Wife of Eric
Miller, Edmund "Bing"	Outfielder, Philadelphia Athletics
Miller, Helen Fetrow	Wife of Edmund
O'Doul, Abigail	Wife of Frank
O'Doul, Frank "Lefty"	Outfielder, New York Giants
Quinn, John	Umpire

Reach, Mary	Daughter of Ben Shibe, part-owner of the Philadelphia Athletics, sister of Elfreda Macfarland
Ruth, Claire	Wife of George
Ruth, George "Babe"	Outfielder, New York Yankees
Ruth, Julia	Daughter of Claire, stepdaughter of George
Schroeder, Madeline	Wife of Robert
Schroeder, Robert	Traveling secretary, Philadelphia Athletics
Suzuki, Sotaro	Employee of *Yomiuri Shimbun* and traveling secretary of the All American team
Warren, Walter M.	Friend of Cornelius McGillicuddy
Warstler, Grace Mohler	Wife of Harold
Warstler, Harold "Rabbit"	Infielder, Philadelphia Athletics
Whitehill, Earl	Pitcher, Washington Senators
Whitehill, Violet Geissinger	Wife of Earl, model and correspondent for *Washington Herald*

Appendix 2: TOUR BATTING AND PITCHING STATISTICS

TABLE 1   All American batting statistics (40 or more ABs)

	BA	G	AB	R	H	2B	3B	HR	RBI	SO	BB	SB
Babe Ruth	.408	18	76	27	31	3	0	13	33	7	13	1
Earl Averill	.378	18	74	23	28	4	0	8	29	7	15	1
Bing Miller	.375	18	72	18	27	5	0	4	18	2	7	0
Eric McNair	.354	18	82	22	29	9	0	0	11	5	5	1
Lou Gehrig	.310	18	71	25	22	5	1	6	18	4	13	2
Charlie Gehringer	.288	18	80	24	23	3	1	4	21	1	13	1
Jimmie Foxx	.286	17	63	19	18	2	0	7	14	15	11	1
Frank Hayes	.226	14	53	12	12	2	0	1	8	10	10	1

TABLE 2   All American batting statistics (fewer than 40 ABs)

	BA	G	AB	R	H	2B	3B	HR	RBI	SO	BB	SB
Earl Whitehill	.458	9	24	9	11	1	0	3	11	6	2	0
Lefty Gomez	.412	6	17	3	7	1	0	0	2	2	3	0
Harold Warstler	.267	12	30	6	8	0	0	1	2	8	6	1
Clint Brown	.250	5	12	0	3	0	0	0	1	3	0	0
Joe Cascarella	.200	6	15	1	3	0	0	0	0	3	0	0
Moe Berg	.111	6	18	4	2	1	0	0	3	1	1	0

TABLE 3   All Nippon batting statistics (20 or more ABs)

	BA	G	AB	R	H	2B	3B	HR	RBI	SO	BB	SB
Toshiharu Inokawa	.348	11	23	3	8	1	0	1	1	1	0	0
Kumeyasu Yajima	.295	14	44	4	13	2	1	0	2	8	4	1
Isamu Fuma	.294	11	34	2	10	1	3	0	5	9	3	0
Hisanori Karita	.276	16	58	6	16	3	0	0	2	1	5	3
Fujio Nagasawa	.226	11	31	1	7	0	0	0	2	1	5	3
Mamoru Sugitaya	.222	12	36	2	8	2	0	0	3	3	1	0
Jimmy Horio	.195	15	41	4	8	0	0	1	1	6	4	0
Usaburo Shintomi	.167	13	36	6	6	1	1	1	5	3	4	0
Osamu Mihara	.158	11	38	4	6	1	0	0	2	8	2	5
Shigeru Mizuhara	.095	10	21	2	2	1	0	0	3	3	1	0
Haruyasu Nakajima	.222	12	36	2	8	2	0	0	3	3	1	0

TABLE 4   All Nippon batting statistics (fewer than 20 ABs)

	BA	G	AB	R	H	2B	3B	HR	RBI	SO	BB	SB
Masao Date	.444	5	9	0	4	1	1	0	0	2	1	0
Tokue Ihara	.429	4	7	0	3	0	0	0	0	2	0	0
Hisashi Asakura	.400	2	5	0	2	0	0	0	1	2	0	0
Tokio Tominaga	.333	4	12	1	4	0	0	0	1	2	1	0
Takenosuke Murai	.333	3	6	2	0	0	0	0	0	1	0	0
Shinji Hamazaki	.273	9	11	0	3	1	0	0	0	2	0	0
Eibin Ri	.200	6	5	1	0	0	0	0	0	2	1	0
Nobuo Kura	.182	4	8	1	1	0	0	0	0	1	0	0
Kenichi Aoshiba	.167	6	12	1	2	0	0	0	0	2	2	0
Minoru Yamashita	.158	7	19	3	3	1	0	0	1	2	0	0
Eichiro Yamamoto	.100	7	10	1	1	0	1	0	1	2	0	0
Jiro Kuji	.056	7	18	0	1	0	0	0	0	1	1	0
Eiji Sawamura	.000	5	7	0	0	0	0	0	0	5	2	0
Motonobu Makino	.000	4	10	0	0	0	0	0	0	3	2	0
Kaichi Takeda	.000	3	7	1	0	0	0	0	0	2	1	0
Nobuaki Nidegawa	.000	3	7	0	0	0	0	0	0	2	0	0
Yukio Eguchi	.000	1	2	0	0	0	0	0	0	2	1	0
Victor Starffin	.000	1	0	0	0	0	0	0	0	0	0	0

TABLE 5   All American pitching statistics

	ERA	G	GS	W	L	IP	H	HR	SO	BB	R	ER
Earl Whitehill	1.41	6	5	6	0	51	32	1	30	10	9	8
Lefty Gomez	1.47	6	4	5	0	43	29	1	34	21	8	7
Joe Cascarella	4.62	5	2	3	1	39	49	4	26	8	21	20
Clint Brown	2.73	5	3	4	0	33	18	0	7	9	12	10
Jimmie Foxx	1.50	3	0	0	0	6	6	0	5	1	2	1

TABLE 6   All Nippon pitching statistics

	ERA	G	GS	W	L	IP	H	HR	SO	BB	R	ER
Kenichi Aoshiba	7.83	6	1	0	3	33.1	49	8	17	25	39	29
Eiji Sawamura	7.85	6	2	0	4	28.2	33	8	25	25	34	25
Shinji Hamazaki	9.23	7	1	0	2	26.1	33	9	10	14	37	27
Kaichi Takeda	13.73	3	1	0	3	19.2	41	13	5	11	32	30
Masao Date	7.00	3	1	0	3	18	27	4	6	11	16	14
Shigeru Mizuhara	30.00	1	0	0	1	3	8	2	2	3	10	7
Victor Starffin	0.00	1	0	0	0	1	0	0	1	2	0	0

Appendix 3: TOUR GAME LINE SCORES

11/3	Meiji Jingu Stadium, Tokyo										
Tokyo	0	0	0	0	1	0	0	0	0		1
All Americans	2	3	1	2	4	0	2	3	X		17

WP Whitehill; LP Takahashi

11/4	Meiji Jingu Stadium, Tokyo										
All Nippon	0	0	0	1	0	0	0	0	0		1
All Americans	0	3	1	0	0	0	1	0	X		5

WP Cascarella; LP Date; HR Averill 2, Foxx, Gehrig

11/8	Hakodate										
All Nippon	0	0	0	1	0	0	1	0	0		2
All Americans	4	0	0	0	1	0	0	0	X		5

WP Gomez; LP Aoshiba; HR Averill

11/9	Sendai										
All Nippon	0	0	0	0	0	0	0	0	0		0
All Americans	2	0	2	0	0	0	0	3	X		7

WP Whitehill; LP Takeda; HR Ruth 2, Gehrig, Foxx, Miller

11/10	Meiji Jingu Stadium, Tokyo										
All Nippon	0	0	0	0	0	0	0	0	0		0
All Americans	1	2	0	1	2	0	4	0	X		10

WP Gomez; LP Sawamura; HR Ruth, Warstler, Averill

11/11	Meiji Jingu Stadium, Tokyo										
Ruth's Team	2	0	6	0	0	1	0	2	2		13
Miller's Team	0	0	0	0	2	0	0	0	0		2

WP Brown; LP Cascarella; HR Ruth 2, Foxx, Averill

11/13	Toyama										
All Nippon	0	0	0	0	0	0	0	0	0		0
All Americans	0	9	1	1	0	0	0	3	X		14

WP Whitehill; LP Mizuhara; HR Ruth, Whitehill, Foxx

11/17   Meiji Jingu Stadium, Tokyo

	1	2	3	4	5	6	7	8	9	R
All Nippon	0	3	1	0	0	0	0	1	1	6
All Americans	0	6	1	1	0	2	0	5	X	15

WP Brown; LP Hamazaki; HR Gehrig, Foxx, Ruth 2

11/18   Yokohama

	1	2	3	4	5	6	7	8	9	R
All Nippon	2	0	0	0	0	1	0	0	1	4
All Americans	2	4	1	2	0	3	8	1	X	21

WP Gomez; LP Aoshiba; HR Inokawa, Ruth 2, Gehrig, Foxx, Averill

11/20   Shizuoka

	1	2	3	4	5	6	7	8	9	R
All Nippon	0	0	0	0	0	0	0	0	0	0
All Americans	0	0	0	0	0	0	1	0	X	1

WP Whitehill; LP Sawamura; HR Gehrig

11/22   Nagoya

	1	2	3	4	5	6	7	8	9	R
All Nippon	2	0	0	0	1	0	1	1	0	5
All Americans	3	0	0	0	0	0	0	3	X	6

WP Cascarella; LP Date

11/23   Nagoya

	1	2	3	4	5	6	7	8	9	R
All Nippon	0	0	0	0	0	2	0	0	0	2
All Americans	1	0	2	0	1	0	2	0	X	6

WP Gomez; LP Takeda

11/24   Koshien Stadium, Osaka

	1	2	3	4	5	6	7	8	9	R
All Nippon	0	0	0	0	0	3	0	0	0	3
All Americans	0	0	0	5	2	4	0	4	X	15

WP Whitehill; LP Date

11/25   Koshien Stadium, Osaka

	1	2	3	4	5	6	7	8	9	R
Miller's Team	0	0	1	2	0	0	1	1	0	5
Ruth's Team	0	0	0	0	1	0	0	0	0	1

WP Brown; LP Aoshiba; HR Shintomi

11/26   Kokura

	1	2	3	4	5	6	7	8	9	R
All Nippon	0	0	0	0	0	0	1	0	0	1
All Americans	0	0	0	3	0	1	4	0	X	8

WP Cascarella; LP Hamazaki; HR Averill, Ruth

11/28	Kyoto										
All Nippon		0	0	0	0	0	1	0	0	0	1
All Americans		2	0	5	3	0	1	3	0	X	14

WP Gomez; LP Sawamura; HR Miller

11/29	Omiya										
All Nippon		0	0	0	1	0	4	0	0	0	5
All Americans		10	0	1	1	1	8	2	0	X	23

WP Whitehill; LP Takeda;
HR Horio, Gehringer 3, Ruth 2, Whitehill 2, Gehrig, Foxx, Hayes

12/1	Utsunomiya										
All Nippon		3	0	0	0	0	0	1	0	1	5
All Americans		2	3	2	2	1	0	4	0	X	14

WP Brown; LP Sawamura; HR Miller 2, Gehringer, Averill

12/5	Shanghai, China										
All Americans		0	0	0	2	11	4	0	5	0	22
Shanghai		0	0	0	0	0	0	0	0	1	1

WP Cascarella; LP Morris

12/9	Manila, Philippines										
All Americans		2	0	2	1	1	3	2	1	1	13
Manila Bay		1	0	0	0	0	0	0	0	0	1

WP Whitehill; LP Nelson; HR Gehrig, Ruth

12/9	Manila, Philippines										
All Americans		0	2	2	0	0	0	3	0	0	7
Olympics		0	0	0	0	2	1	0	0	0	3

WP Gomez; LP Armando; HR Averill 2, Gehringer

12/10	Manila, Philippines										
All Americans		3	0	0	0	3	2	0	1	0	9
Olympics		0	0	0	0	0	0	0	0	1	1

WP Brown; LP Bautista; HR Gehrig

Acknowledgments

There are many good restaurants in Tokyo. One can get delicious traditional Japanese fare, exquisite European fine dining, or exotic tastes from around the world, but the idea for this book was born in one of the worst. It served vegetarian meals favored by Buddhist monks and the rock-hard, tasteless dishes must have been part of their penance. I gathered there with members of the Tokyo Chapter of the Society of American Baseball Research (SABR) in October 2003 to discuss a groupwide research project for the Asian Baseball Research Committee. After much discussion, little actual eating, and not enough beer, the group decided to focus on the 1934 All American tour of Japan—an event that changed Japanese baseball and achieved legendary status among baseball fans in the United States. Personally, I had little enthusiasm for the project, as my interests lay in the postwar period. Several members investigated the topic for a few weeks, but their interest soon died and the project was scrapped. But the initial newspaper articles collected by SABR members Takao Hanyu and Hiroo Maki started me thinking.

Four years later, I decided to revisit the topic. I soon discovered that the 1934 tour was about more than baseball. The story contained diplomacy, espionage, infidelity, attempted murder, and an attempt to overthrow the Japanese government. Now hooked, I decided to recount the tale for American baseball fans. Many people on both sides of the Pacific helped me complete this project. I would like to thank them here.

To begin with, I need to thank the SABR members present at the initial meeting in 2003 and Ann Fabian, who spurred me to begin the book and also introduced me to my agent, Wendy Strothman. Wendy patiently guided me through several proposal drafts and pushed me to define my topic and focus my writing. I'd also like to thank her Strothman Agency partner, Lauren MacLeod, for her help as well as my publicist, Marty Appel.

Numerous SABR members, baseball writers, and baseball enthusiasts shared their expertise, enabling me to improve my work. In particular, I would like to thank Frank R. Ardolino, Bill Burgess, Harrington "Kit" Crissey, Will Dahlberg, Nicholas Dawidoff, Rob Elias, Gerald Gems, Wayne Graczyk, Masaru Hatano, Michael J. Haupert, Frank Holman, Izumi Ishii, William Kelly, Robert Klevens, Tara Krieger, Marty Kuehnert, Jeff Kusumoto, Bob Lapides, Larry Lester, Richard Leutzinger, Kerry Yo Nakagawa, Dennis Pajot, Chris Rainey, Tom Walsh, and Michael Westbay. I especially want to single out Ralph Pearce and Bill Staples for sharing their unpublished manuscripts and other primary sources with me. The Society of American Baseball Research also directly aided my research by awarding a SABR-Yoseloff Baseball Research Grant to fund some of the translating of Japanese sources.

To tell the story of the 1934 tour, I needed a fuller understanding of Japanese history. Many historians graciously answered my questions and pointed me in the right direction for further research. I would like to thank Susanna Fessler, Theodore J. Gilman, Carol Gluck, Barak Kushner, Michael Lewis, Michael Norman, Jennifer Robertson, Ben-Ami Shillony, and Henry Smith. Two scholars took extra time to help me with my research. I would especially like to thank John Dower, who provided numerous leads to valuable sources, and Christopher Szpilman, who tracked down several sources on the elusive War Gods Society. Their help was invaluable.

I would like to thank the staffs of the Arthur W. Diamond Law Library at the Columbia University School of Law, Cleveland Public Library, C. V. Starr East Asian Library at Columbia University, Diet Library in Tokyo, Houghton Reading Room at Harvard University, Library of Congress, National Baseball Hall of Fame Library at Cooperstown, New York Public Library, New York Society Library, and the Hamilton Library at the University of Hawaii for making their collections available and aiding my research.

A special thank-you is needed for Ryuichi Suzuki, Akiko Ogawa

Taku Chinone, Miwako Atarashi, and Takahiro Sekiguchi of the Japan Baseball Hall of Fame Library for their expertise, friendliness, and valiant efforts to understand my Japanese. It's always a pleasure to visit them.

It took a number of dedicated people to transform my manuscript into a publishable book. Thanks to Takamitsu "Taka" Tanaka for help translating Japanese sources and Adam Berenbak, Gary Engel, and Yoichi Nagata for commenting on the drafts. A special thanks goes out to Martin Beiser for his detailed and insightful comments. The University of Nebraska Press did a wonderful job. Thanks to Courtney Ochsner, Annette Wenda, Joeth Zucco, and especially my editor, Rob Taylor, who worked closely with me through the entire project.

Selecting images to reproduce in this book was a difficult task. Thank you to Aimee Scillieri of Sotheby's, Gwen Battad Ishikawa of the *Hawaii Herald*, Mike Henson, Karin Johnsrud of the Arthur W. Diamond Law Library, and Tomoaki Kawauchi of the *Yomiuri Shimbun* for their aid. I would like to thank the Arthur W. Diamond Law Library at the Columbia University School of Law, the *Hawaii Herald*, Kondansha, William Sear, Sotheby's, Yoko Suzuki, and the *Yomiuri Shimbun* for allowing me to reproduce their images.

I would also like to thank Carl Finstrom, Charles Pinck (president of the oss Society, Inc.), and Linda McCarthy for teaching me about Moe Berg; Tom Stevens for introducing me to Julia Ruth Stevens; Benjamin Shibe Macfarland III for his insight on the Philadelphia Athletics; and Sheila and Joe Buff for their advice on the publishing process and their encouragement.

I especially need to thank those who shared their memories or personal collections with me. The details these people provided were invaluable. William H. Amos, who spent a cold afternoon in the All Americans' dugout, provided me with an account of his experience. James Horio shared information about his father, Jimmy Horio. Virginia McCallum read me the tour diary of her parents, Harold and Grace Warstler. Bill Sear allowed me to view his amazing collection of tour artifacts and primary papers. Takashi Watanabe, executive director of the America-Japan Society, sent documents concerning the event organized by the society on November 14, 1934. Finally, but in no means least, I would like to thank Julia Ruth Stevens, the last surviving member of the All American entourage, for sharing her diary and memories of what she called a "trip of a lifetime."

A special thank-you is owed to four people. Robert Whiting responded to my numerous questions with detailed answers, recommended sources, and provided encouragement throughout the project. Yoko Suzuki, the stepdaughter of Sotaro Suzuki, invited me to her home to browse Sotaro's personal papers and photos and also provided me with copies of Sotaro's letters. Keiko Nishi translated most of the Japanese sources, did invaluable primary research in various Japanese archives, and handled Japanese-language interviews and requests. Finally, I would have been lost without Yoichi Nagata. Yoichi patiently answered dozens of difficult questions over the past four years, researched arcane topics of Japanese baseball history, read and commented on the manuscript, and pushed me to become a better historian. I want to thank each of you for your contributions and friendship.

The most important thank-you goes to my family: my parents, Donald and Beverly Fitts; my brother, Bill; and especially Sarah, Ben, Simon, and d'Artagnan for their enthusiastic support, helpful suggestions, and general tolerance of my insanity.

Notes

PROLOGUE

1. *New York Times*, November 3, 1934, 9, January 6, 1935, S7.

CHAPTER 1

1. Biographical details about Shoriki come from Uhlan and Thomas, *Shoriki*.
2. Uhlan and Thomas, *Shoriki*, 83.
3. Robertson, "Blood Talks."
4. Details of this conversation are from Izumino, *Matsutaro Shoriki*. Translated for the author by Takamitsu Tanaka.
5. Kiku, "Japanese Baseball Spirit," 38–39.
6. Elfers, *Tour to End All Tours*, 10.
7. Elfers, *Tour to End All Tours*, 108–22.
8. *Sporting News*, October 20, 1932.
9. *Sporting News*, January 14, 1923, 4.
10. Richter, *Reach Official American League Guide*, 495–98.
11. Michael J. Haupert, personal communication, September 18, 2008.
12. *Sporting News*, January 24, 1923, 4.
13. Sayama, "Their Throws."
14. Izumino, *Matsutaro Shoriki*, 11–13.

CHAPTER 2

1. Montville, *The Big Bam*; Ruth and Slocom, *The Babe and I*.
2. Details of Sotaro Suzuki's life prior to 1930 come from an interview conducted on June 7, 2009, with Masaru Hatano, who is writing a Japanese-language biography of Suzuki.
3. LaFeber, *The Clash*, 147–59.
4. *Sporting News*, February 16, 1922, 1.
5. Telegram of November 20, 1930, reprinted in Ikei, *Hakkyu Taiheiyo o Wataru*, 108–9.
6. *Sporting News*, January 1, 1931, 3.
7. Lieb, *Baseball as I Have Known It*, 198.
8. Izumino, *Matsutaro Shoriki*, 23–33.
9. Lieb, *Baseball as I Have Known It*, 198.
10. Considine and Ruth, *The Babe Ruth Story*, 185–86.
11. Although Fred Lieb states that the admiral was a member of the Japanese

delegation to the London Naval Treaty, no evidence corroborates this story, and there is no evidence of the delegation meeting or traveling in October 1931. The identity of this admiral is unknown.

12. Lieb, *Baseball as I Have Known It*, 199–200.

13. *New York Times*, December 23, 1931, 26.

14. Lieb, *Baseball as I Have Known It*, 203.

15. Lieb, *Baseball as I Have Known It*, 205; Whiting, *You Gotta Have Wa*, 41; Sayama, "Their Throws," 85–88.

16. Lieb, *Baseball as I Have Known It*.

17. Figures from 1931 gate receipts come from Sotaro Suzuki to Lefty O'Doul, August 31, 1933, Suzuki Papers.

18. O'Doul to Suzuki, August 9, 1933, Suzuki Papers.

CHAPTER 3

1. Lefty O'Doul in Ritter, *Glory of Their Times*, 276.

2. Leutzinger, *Lefty O'Doul*, 26.

3. O'Doul to Suzuki, January 19, 1932, Suzuki Papers.

4. Kiku, "Japanese Baseball Spirit," 44–45.

5. Suzuki to O'Doul, February 8, 1932, Suzuki Papers.

6. O'Doul to Suzuki, April 24, 1933, Suzuki Papers.

7. Suzuki to O'Doul, June 5, 1933, Suzuki Papers.

8. Suzuki to O'Doul, July 4, 1933, Suzuki Papers.

9. O'Doul to Suzuki, August 9, 1933, Suzuki Papers.

10. O'Doul to Suzuki, August 9, 1933, Suzuki Papers.

11. Suzuki to O'Doul, September 14, 1933, Suzuki Papers.

12. Suzuki to O'Doul, September 14, 1933, Suzuki Papers.

13. Suzuki to O'Doul, September 1, 14, 21, 1933, Suzuki Papers.

14. Izumino, *Matsutaro Shoriki*, 59–61.

15. *Sporting News*, December 28, 1933, 1.

16. Suzuki to O'Doul, April 28, 1934, Suzuki Papers.

17. Julia Ruth Stevens, interview by author, October 29, 2007.

18. *Yomiuri Shimbun*, July 20, 1934, 5.

19. *Sporting News*, August 16, 1934, 1.

CHAPTER 4

1. Details of Suzuki's trip from Suzuki Papers.

2. *Tokyo Nichi Nichi*, September 22, 1934, 1, September 23, 1934, 1.

CHAPTER 5

1. Montville, *The Big Bam*, 293; Considine and Ruth, *The Babe Ruth Story*, 176–78.

2. Creamer, *Babe*, 351–52.

3. Creamer, *Babe*, 373; Montville, *The Big Bam*, 323–24; Smelser, *Life That Ruth Built*, 461.

4. Creamer, *Babe*, 376–77.

CHAPTER 6

1. Details on Horio's life from Nagata, *Jimmy Horio*; and James Horio, interview by author, October 2009.

CHAPTER 7

1. Dawidoff, *Catcher Was a Spy*, 69.
2. Dawidoff, *Catcher Was a Spy*, 69.
3. Dawidoff, *Catcher Was a Spy*, 78; Berg Papers.
4. Berg to family, November 9, 1932, Berg Collection.
5. Berg to family, November 9, 1932, Berg Collection.
6. Staples, "Matsumoto and Zenimura."
7. Dawidoff, *Catcher Was a Spy*, 80–81; Berg to family, November 26, 1932, Berg Collection.
8. Dawidoff, *Catcher Was a Spy*, 88.
9. Quoted in Kaufman, Fitzgerald, and Sewell, *Moe Berg*, 3.
10. Berg to family, October 19, 1934, Berg Collection.
11. Berg to family, October 19, 1934, Berg Collection.
12. Berg to family, October 19, 1934, Berg Collection.
13. *New York Herald Tribune*, October 16, 1934; Suzuki, *Unofficial History*, 179; Daniel, *Jimmie Foxx*, 79; Mah, "Barney Brown."
14. *Winnipeg Free Press*, October 20, 1934, 2, 8.
15. Len Corben, "When the Babe Came Calling," *Vancouver Courier*, October 20, 2004, http://archive.vancourier.com/issues04/103204/news/103204nn1.html.
16. Corben, "When Babe Came."
17. Suzuki, *Unofficial History*, 180–81.
18. *Cleveland Press*, October 20, 1934.

CHAPTER 8

1. Victoria, *Zen War Stories*, 51; Dogen, *Omori Sogen*, 44.
2. Nishida's first name, Mitsugu, is often misread as Zei or Chikara in English sources.
3. This simplified summary of Ikki Kita's position is based on Delmer Brown, *Nationalism in Japan*; Shillony, *Revolt in Japan*; Wald, *Young Officers*; and Szpilman, "Kita Ikki."
4. Ikki Kita in Morris, *Japan, 1931–1945*, 22.
5. Roshi Omori quoted in Victoria, *Zen War Stories*, 45.
6. Quoted in Shillony, *Revolt in Japan*, 74.

7. Quoted in Wald, *Young Officers*, 31–32.

8. Shillony, *Revolt in Japan*, 17.

9. Wald, *Young Officers*, 119–20.

10. Victoria, *Zen War Stories*, 41.

11. Victoria, *Zen War Stories*, 51.

12. Hosokawa, *Omori Sogen*.

13. Quoted in Victoria, *Zen War Stories*, 51.

14. Bix, *Hirohito*, 302.

15. Isobe, "Prison Diary."

16. Quoted in Victoria, *Zen War Stories*, 52.

CHAPTER 9

1. Read, "Major Windstorm."

2. *Cleveland Press*, November 5, 1934, 28.

3. Sansom, *Living in Tokyo*, 1.

4. *Cleveland Press*, November 5, 1934, 28.

5. Montville, *The Big Bam*, 331–32; Pirone with Martens, *My Dad, the Babe*, 90–91, 109–10; *New York Times*, October 26, 1934, 29.

6. *New York Times*, October 26, 1934, 29.

7. *Cleveland Press*, November 6, 1934, 20.

8. Dawidoff, *Catcher Was a Spy*, 90.

9. *Cleveland Press*, November 7, 1934, 26.

10. Suzuki, *Unofficial History*.

11. *Cleveland Press*, November 8, 1934, 28.

12. *Cleveland Press*, November 9, 1934, 44.

13. *Cleveland Press*, November 9, 1934, 44.

14. Information on Cartwright and baseball in nineteenth-century Hawaii from Nucciarone, *Alexander Cartwright*; Ardolino, "Missionaries"; and Franks, *Asian Pacific Americans*.

15. http://www.census.gov/population/www/documentation/twps0056/tab26 .pdf.

16. *Sporting News*, December 24, 1934, 5.

17. *Honolulu Star Bulletin*, October 24, 1934.

18. *Honolulu Star Bulletin*, October 24, 1934.

19. Suehiro, *Honolulu Stadium*, 1–4, 46–47.

20. *Honolulu Star Bulletin*, October 20, 1934.

21. *Honolulu Star Bulletin*, October 26, 1934, 11.

22. *Hawaii Hochi*, October 26, 1934, 3.

23. *Honolulu Star Bulletin*, October 26, 1934, 11.

24. *Honolulu Star Bulletin*, October 26, 1934, 11.

25. *Hawaii Hochi*, October 26, 1934, 3.

26. Franks, *Asian Pacific Americans*, 91.

27. *Honolulu Star Bulletin*, October 26, 1934, 11.

28. *Cleveland Press*, November 10, 1934, 8.

29. Montville, *The Big Bam*, 333; Creamer, *Babe*, 380; Wagenheim, *Babe Ruth*, 251.

30. *Cleveland Press*, November 10, 1934, 8.

31. Gehrig and Durso, *My Luke and I*.

32. Montville, *The Big Bam*, 332.

33. *Washington Post*, November 2, 1934, 23.

34. LaFeber, *The Clash*, 141, 158–59.

35. *New York Times*, October 28, 1934, 5, October 30, 1935, 6.

CHAPTER 10

1. Grew, *Turbulent Era*, 948 49.

2. Grew, *Ten Years in Japan*, 143.

3. Grew to Hull, February 23, 1933, quoted in Grew, *Turbulent Era*, 939–40.

4. Grew, *Ten Years in Japan*, 115, 121.

5. Grew quoted in Henrichs, *American Ambassador*, 199.

6. Kesaris, *Confidential U.S. Diplomatic Post Records*.

7. Grew, *Ten Years in Japan*, 27.

CHAPTER 11

1. Steele, "History of the Tama River," 223.

2. *New York Times*, November 3, 1934, 2.

3. *Cleveland Press*, November 23, 1934, 44.

4. *Cleveland Press*, November 23, 1934, 44.

5. *Japan Times*, November 2, 1934, 1–2.

6. Gehrig and Durso, *My Luke and I*, 151.

7. *Cleveland Press*, November 23, 1934, 44.

8. Kaufman, Fitzgerald, and Sewell, *Moe Berg*, 15.

9. Thomas and Barton, *Seeing Japan*, 36.

10. Garis, *Their Japan*, 15.

11. *Hawaii Hochi*, November 3, 1934, 3; Stevens, interview by author, August 13, 2008.

12. The term *maiko* is used to refer to apprentice geisha in the Kyoto and Osaka region. In Tokyo apprentice geisha were called *hangyoku* or *oshaku*. Nonetheless, I will use *maiko* in this book, as it is more familiar to English-speaking readers.

13. Dawidoff, *Catcher Was a Spy*, 90.

14. *Chicago Daily Tribune*, November 3, 1934, 23; Quinn, "American League Stars," 264–65.

CHAPTER 12

1. *Cleveland Press*, November 24, 1934, 8.
2. Garis, *Their Japan*, 8–9.
3. Garis, *Their Japan*, 9.
4. Nagata, *Jimmy Horio*, 133–40.
5. *Cleveland Press*, November 24, 1934, 8.
6. Inahara, *The Japan Yearbook, 1935*.
7. *Yakyukai* 24, no. 14 (1934): 185.
8. *Cleveland Press*, November 26, 1934, 24.
9. *Cleveland Press*, November 26, 1934, 24.

CHAPTER 13

1. *Yomiuri Shimbun*, November 6, 1934, 6.
2. *Yomiuri Shimbun*, November 5, 1934.
3. Macht, *Connie Mack*, 24, 244.
4. *Yakyukai* 25, no. 3 (1935): 184.
5. *Yakyukai* 25, no. 3 (1935): 184; Grew, Diaries and Scrapbooks, 2092.
6. *Yakyukai* 25, no. 3 (1935).
7. *Japan Times*, November 5, 1934, 6.
8. McAuley, "Veteran Whitehill."
9. Johnson, "Earl Whitehill."
10. *New York Times*, June 12, 1920, 5.
11. Description of the November 4 game is drawn from *Japan Times*, November 5, 1934, 6.
12. Mamoru Sugitaya interviewed in *Yakyukai* 25, no. 1 (1935).
13. *Japan Times*, November 5, 1934, 6.
14. *Yomiuri Shimbun*, November 5, 1934.
15. Stevens, interview by author, October 29, 2007.

CHAPTER 14

1. *Cleveland Press*, November 27, 1934, 18.
2. *Cleveland Press*, November 27, 1934, 18.
3. Fuma interviewed in *Yakyukai* 25, no. 1 (1935).
4. *Japan Times*, November 6, 1934, 6.
5. *Osaka Mainichi*, November 6, 1934; *Tokyo Nichi Nichi*, November 6, 1934.
6. Biographical information on Joe Cascarella drawn from various unsourced newspaper clippings in his file at the National Baseball Hall of Fame.
7. *Japan Times*, November 6, 1934, 6.
8. *Washington Post*, November 6, 1934, 17.
9. *Cleveland Press*, November 27, 1934, 18.

CHAPTER 15

1. Grew, Diaries and Scrapbooks, June 26–December 31, 1934.
2. *Osaka Mainichi*, November 7, 1934.
3. *Sporting News*, October 18, 1934, 3.
4. Wildes, *Japan in Crisis*, 87–93; *Japan Weekly Chronicle*, November 1, 1934, 610, November 8, 1934, 642; *Japan Times*, November 13, 24, 1934; Nippon Dampo News Agency, *Japan Illustrated, 1934*, 234–35; *Japan Times*, November 27, 1934, 1.
5. Quinn, 1934 Tour Scrapbook.
6. Dawidoff, *Catcher Was a Spy*, 93 but no primary source is referenced.
7. *Cleveland Press*, December 3, 1934, 22.
8. *Time*, April 2, 1934; *Japan Times*, March 23, 1934.
9. *Cleveland Press*, December 3, 1934.
10. Wildes, *Japan in Crisis*, 133–36.
11. *Cleveland Press*, December 3, 1934.
12. *Washington Herald*, October 21, 1934, 2.
13. *Cleveland Press*, November 28, 1934, 14.
14. *Yakyukai* 25, no. 1 (1935): 120–35; Warstler, Tour of Japan Diary, November 8, 1934.
15. Lieb, *Baseball as I Have Known It*, 206–7.

CHAPTER 16

1. C. James, *Frank Lloyd Wright's Imperial Hotel*, 35–46.
2. Whymant, *Stalin's Spy*, 181.
3. *Cleveland Press*, December 6, 1934, 26.
4. Smith, "Chûshingura in the 1980s."
5. *Cleveland Press*, December 6, 1934, 26.
6. *Cleveland Press*, December 6, 1934, 26.
7. *Cleveland Press*, December 4, 1934; *Yomiuri Shimbun*, November 7, 1934, 7.
8. Gehrig and Durso, *My Luke and I*, 154.
9. *Cleveland Press*, November 29, 1934; Sansom, *Living in Tokyo*, 52.
10. *Cleveland Press*, December 4, 1934; Sansom, *Living in Tokyo*, 52.
11. Grew, *Ten Years in Japan*, 61.
12. Lieb, *Connie Mack*, 253; Suzuki, *Unofficial History*, 289.

CHAPTER 17

1. *Kyoka*, November 15, 1934, 1.
2. Byas, *Government by Assassination*, 163, 164–65.
3. Wildes, *Japan in Crisis*, 41.

4. Details on Atsuta, Nagasaki, and the War Gods are drawn from Sano, *Kyokaiden*; *New York Times*, February 22, 1935, 1; *Osaka Mainichi*, February 23, 1935; *Japan Times*, February 23, 1935, 2; and *Yomiuri Shimbun*, February 23, 1935.

CHAPTER 18

1. *Hawaii Hochi*, November 10, 1934, 3.
2. Suzuki, *Unofficial History*, 220.
3. Quinn, 1934 Tour Scrapbook.
4. Speech delivered by Moe Berg over Radio Tokyo to United States, November 1934, Berg Collection.
5. *Japan Times*, November 10, 1934, 2; *Japan Weekly Chronicle*, November 15, 1934, 683.
6. *Japan Times*, November 10, 1934, 1.
7. Amos, "I Remember."
8. *Yakyukai* 25, no. 1 (1935): 120–35; Amos, "I Remember."
9. *Yakyukai* 25, no. 1 (1935).
10. *Japan Times*, November 11, 1934, 1.
11. *Hawaii Hochi*, November 11, 1934, 3.
12. *Japan Times*, November 11, 1934, 1.
13. Why the team was named after Miller, one of the lesser-known stars on the squad, is unknown.
14. *Japan Times*, November 11, 1934, 2.
15. Thomas and Barton, *Seeing Japan*, 81–87.
16. Berg, speech to Meiji University students, November 1934, Berg Papers.
17. *Osaka Mainichi*, November 14, 1934.
18. Grew, Diaries and Scrapbooks, 2120–22.
19. *Japan Times*, November 16, 1934, 2; *New York Times*, November 16, 1934, 29; *Japan Advertiser*, November 16, 1934.

CHAPTER 19

1. *Osaka Mainichi*, November 13, 1934; *Japan Times*, November 14, 1934; *New York Times*, November 10, 1934.
2. Details of Muranaka's plans are based on accounts written after World War II. Some members of Mitsugu Nishida's Young Officers, interviewed after the war, denied that Muranaka actually outlined this plan. Most historians point out that the alleged plan of November 1934 is consistent with the plan Muranaka actually put into action on February 26, 1936. For a discussion of the 1934 plan, see Schenck, *Brocade Banner*, 67–68; Shillony, *Revolt in Japan*, 45–46; and Wald, *Young Officers*, 168–69.

CHAPTER 20

1. *Yakyukai* 25, no. 3 (1935): 161.
2. *Japan Times*, November 18, 1934, 1.
3. *Osaka Mainichi*, November 18, 1934; *Japan Times*, November 18, 1934.
4. *Yomiuri Shimbun*, November 20, 1934, 5.
5. *Yomiuri Shimbun*, November 19, 1934, 5.
6. *Japan Weekly Chronicle*, November 29, 1934, 755.
7. Tokyo Yomiuri Giants 50th Anniversary Editorial Room, *50-Year History*, 139–40.
8. *Yakyukai* 25, no. 1 (1935): 118–19.
9. *Yakyukai* 25, no. 1 (1935): 117–38.
10. *Cleveland Press*, December 10, 1934; *Yakyukai* 25, no. 3 (1935): 180; Grew, Diaries and Scrapbooks, 2120.
11. Tokyo Yomiuri Giants 50th Anniversary Editorial Room, *50-Year History*, 116.
12. *Cleveland Press*, December 10, 1934.
13. Guthrie-Shimizu, "For Love of the Game."
14. There is a lively, if somewhat misguided, debate on the origins and meaning of "samurai baseball." See Blackwood, "Bushido Baseball?"; Hayford, "Samurai Baseball" and "Response"; Kelly, "Blood and Guts" and "Is Baseball a Global Sport?"; Kiku, "Bushido"; and Whiting, "Samurai Baseball" and "Samurai Way of Baseball."
15. From the introduction of *Yakyu Bushi Fukisoku Dai Ichi Koto Gakko Koyukai* (Tokyo, 1903), translated by Robert Whiting and reprinted in Whiting, *Samurai Way of Baseball*, 6.
16. Ikegami, *Taming of the Samurai*.
17. Carr, "Making War."
18. Kano quoted in Carr, "Making War," 183.
19. Shin Hashido quoted in Whiting, *Samurai Way of Baseball*, 57.
20. Marasco, "Not a Typical College Road Trip."
21. Suishu Tobita quoted in Whiting, *You Gotta Have Wa*, 37–38.
22. *Yakyukai* 25, no. 1 (1935): 138.

CHAPTER 21

1. Harries and Harries, *Soldiers of the Sun*, 170–75.
2. Quoted in Harries and Harries, *Soldiers of the Sun*, 173.

CHAPTER 22

1. This narrative on the November 20, 1934, game is based on *Japan Times*, November 21, 1934, 5; *Osaka Mainichi*, November 21, 1934; Suzuki, *Sawamura*

Eiji, 75–77; *Yakyukai* 25, no. 1 (1935): 160–61; and *Yomiuri Shimbun*, November 20, 1934, 5.

2. Many American newspapers mistakenly reported that Ruth hit the winning home run.

CHAPTER 23

1. Harries and Harries, *Soldiers of the Sun*, 342–43.
2. Details of how the plot was discovered are fragmentary and sometimes contradictory. See Schenck, *Brocade Banner*, 67–68; Shillony, *Revolt in Japan*, 45–46; and Wald, *Young Officers*, 168–69.

CHAPTER 24

1. *Yakyukai* 25, no. 3 (1935): 180; Stevens, interview, November 18, 2007.
2. Akimoto, *The Lure of Japan*.
3. Stevens, interview, November 18, 2007.
4. *Osaka Mainichi*, November 24, 1934, 24.
5. Suzuki, *Sawamura Eiji*, 93–94.
6. Suzuki, *Sawamura Eiji*, 93–94.
7. *Osaka Mainichi*, November 24, 1934; *Japan Times*, November 25, 1934.
8. *Yakyukai* 25, no. 1 (1935): 120–35; Mihara, *My Baseball Life*.
9. *Osaka Mainichi*, November 25, 1934; *Japan Weekly Chronicle*, November 29, 1934, 754.
10. *Japan Weekly Chronicle*, November 29, 1934, 755.
11. *Cleveland Press*, December 17, 1934, 26.
12. Quinn, "American League Stars," 264–65; Suzuki, *Unofficial History*.
13. Mihara, *My Baseball Life*.
14. *Osaka Mainichi*, November 28, 1934; *Japan Times*, November 28, 1934; Mihara, *My Baseball Life*.

CHAPTER 25

1. *Osaka Mainichi*, November 24, 1934, 3.
2. *Yakyukai* 25, no. 1 (1935): 180.
3. Details of Maria Stokanova's murder are found in the *Hokkai Times* from January 25 to 27, 1933.
4. The following narrative of how Starffin signed with the All Nippon is a simplified version of events related in Starffin, *Glory and Dream*. The full story with its large cast of participants is beyond the scope of this book.
5. *Yomiuri Shimbun*, October 8, 1934.
6. *Yakyukai* 25, no. 3 (1935).
7. Suzuki, *Sawamura Eiji*, 100–102.

8. *Osaka Mainichi*, November 29, 1934; *Japan Times*, November 30, 1934.

9. Warstler, Tour of Japan Diary, November 28, 1934.

10. Suzuki, *Sawamura Eiji*, 102–5.

11. *Yakyukai* 25, no. 1 (1935): 180.

12. Exactly when Berg decided to visit Lyon at St. Luke's is unknown, but considering that the birth announcement was contained in the afternoon edition of the November 26 issue of the *Japan Advertiser*, he probably read the announcement on the trip from Kokura to Kyoto or during the two-day stay in Kyoto.

CHAPTER 26

1. Shay, "Level of Living in Japan."

2. Grew to Hull, December 26, 1933, in Kesaris, *Confidential U.S. Diplomatic Post Records*, 3.

3. The description of Berg's visit to St. Luke's is taken from Dawidoff, *Catcher Was a Spy*, 94–95.

4. Kaufman, Fitzgerald, and Sewell, *Moe Berg*, 83.

5. Grew to Hull, December 26, 1934, in Kesaris, *Confidential U.S. Diplomatic Post Records*.

6. Kesaris, *Confidential U.S. Diplomatic Post Records*, reel 17, 437–89.

7. *New York Times*, October 27, 1932, 6.

8. "Report of Conditions in Japan during the Month of November, 1934," in Kesaris, *Confidential U.S. Diplomatic Post Records*, 14; *Japan Weekly Chronicle*, December 13, 1934, 823.

9. Dawidoff, *Catcher Was a Spy*, 259.

10. *Washington Herald*, January 3, 1935.

CHAPTER 27

1. Warstler, Tour of Japan Diary, November 30, 1934.

2. Details of this game come from Suzuki, *Unofficial History*, 258.

3. *Yomiuri Shimbun*, December 7, 1934.

4. *Manila Daily Bulletin*, December 10, 1934, 3–4.

5. *Yomiuri Shimbun*, December 2, 1934.

6. *Washington Herald*, December 18, 1934, 35.

7. *Yomiuri Shimbun*, December 2, 1934.

CHAPTER 28

1. *Cleveland Press*, December 20, 1934, 26, December 23, 1934, 8.

2. Warstler, Tour of Japan Diary, December 5, 1934.

3. Willing, "Chinese Fan," 6c.

4. *Manila Daily Bulletin*, December 6, 1934, 1; Willing, "Chinese Fan," 6c.
5. The widely disseminated Associated Press report mistakenly credits Ruth with hitting three home runs in the game.
6. *North-China Herald*, December 12, 1934, 422.
7. Information on the All Americans' stop in Manila comes from Walsh's excellent article "When Babe Ruth Came to Manila" as well as a variety of Manila newspapers.
8. Reaves, *Taking in a Game*, 96.
9. *Tribune* (Manila), December 9, 1934, 24, December 6, 1934, 9.
10. *Manila Daily Bulletin*, December 11, 1934, 3.
11. *Manila Daily Bulletin*, December 11, 1934, 9, quoted in Walsh, "When Babe Ruth Came to Manila," 28.
12. *Tribune* (Manila), December 11, 1934, 1, 9.

CHAPTER 29

1. *Sporting News*, March 2, 1935, 1.
2. *Japan Times*, December 26, 1934, 5.
3. *Sporting News*, January 17, 1935, 4.
4. Elias, *The Empire Strikes Out*, 21–22.
5. Adachi, "Attaboy Japan," 68.
6. *Sporting News*, November 1, 1934, 4.
7. For academic discussions of the link between diplomacy and the 1934 All American tour, see Crepeau, "Pearl Harbor"; Sinclair, "Baseball's Rising Sun"; and especially Gripentrog, "Transnational Pastime."
8. *Sporting News*, January 24, 1935, 4, January 3, 1935, 4.
9. *Philadelphia Inquirer*, January 8, 1935, 15; Berg, letter to family, November 9, 1932, Berg Collection; Kushner, *The Thought War*, 34.
10. *Chicago Tribune*, November 12, 1934, 14.
11. R. Lee, *Orientals*.
12. *Washington Post*, November 13, 1934, 17; *Sporting News*, November 15, 1934, 3; *Washington Herald*, November 13, 1934.
13. *Sporting News*, February 7, 1935, 1; Quinn, "American League Stars," 264; *Time*, November 12, 1934.
14. Grew, Diaries and Scrapbooks.

CHAPTER 30

1. Details from Nagasaki's attack on Shoriki are drawn from *Japan Times*, February 23, 1935, 2; *New York Times*, February 22, 1935, 1; *Osaka Mainichi*, February 23, 1935; Sano, *Kyokaiden*; and *Yomiuri Shimbun*, February 23, 1935.
2. *Time*, March 4, 1935.

CHAPTER 31

1. Nagata, *Tokyo Giants*; Pajot, "Almost an International Incident."
2. Nagata, *Tokyo Giants*, 176–77, 208–9.
3. Quoted in Shillony, *Revolt in Japan*, 147–48.

CHAPTER 32

1. Dawidoff in *The Catcher Was a Spy* interprets Berg's writing to read, "I predicted in the year 1922 . . ." (128), but Berg's katakana reads "nainden tarude shi," or 1933.
2. Berg Papers.
3. Berg quoted in Kaufman, Fitzgerald, and Sewell, *Moe Berg*, 141–46.
4. *Sporting News*, December 18, 1941, 4. For a discussion of the *Sporting News*'s attitudes toward the Japanese, see Crepeau, "Pearl Harbor: A Failure of Baseball?"; Elias, *The Empire Strikes Out*; Gems, *Athletic Crusade*; and Sinclair, "Baseball's Rising Sun."
5. *Sporting News*, December 25, 1941, 4.
6. *Sporting News*, February 3, 1944, 11, February 4, 1943, 1.
7. *Sporting News*, January 1, 1942, 1.
8. Berg in Dawidoff, *Catcher Was a Spy*, 134.
9. Dawidoff, *Catcher Was a Spy*, 153.
10. Kaufman, Fitzgerald, and Sewell, *Moe Berg*, 14–15, 28, 122.
11. Item number 4616894628 offered for sale on eBay, December 5, 2009.
12. Kaufman, Fitzgerald, and Sewell, *Moe Berg*, 122; Grew, Diaries and Scrapbooks, November 2, 1934, 2089.
13. Lewis, "Reflections."
14. Dawidoff, *Catcher Was a Spy*, 96.
15. Dawidoff, *Catcher Was a Spy*, 135.

CHAPTER 33

1. Stevens, interview, November 7, 2007.
2. Smelser, *Life That Ruth Built*, 525–27; Bedingfield, "Babe Ruth in World War II"; Dawson quote from Elias, *The Empire Strikes Out*, 137.
3. Smelser, *Life That Ruth Built*, 526; *New York Times*, March 3, 1944, 2, March 5, 1944, 37.
4. Considine and Ruth, *The Babe Ruth Story*, 229–30.
5. Considine and Ruth, *The Babe Ruth Story*, 204–5.

CHAPTER 34

1. Grew, *Report from Tokyo*, 51.
2. Quoted in Buruma, *Inventing Japan, 1853–1964*, 111.

3. Sawamura, "My Worry."

4. Yamamoto, *Nanking*, 92.

5. Wildes, *Japan in Crisis*, 52.

6. *Sporting News*, November 7, 1940, 10; Reaves, *Taking in a Game*, 78–79; Dower, *War without Mercy*, 203–33; Buruma, *Inventing Japan, 1853–1964*, 93; Abe, Kiyohara, and Nakajima, "Sport and Physical Education"; Ikei, *Hakkyu Taiheiyo o Wataru*; Shillony, *Politics and Culture*.

7. Furiya, "Japanese Community Abroad."

8. Sawamura, "Memoirs."

9. Sawamura, *Sawamura Eiji*.

10. Berry, *Gaijin Pitcher*, 99–103.

CHAPTER 35

1. Hatano, personal communication.

2. Kennedy, *The Flowers of Edo*, 528–29.

3. Dahlberg, "Tool for Diplomacy."

4. Quoted in Guttman and Thompson, *Japanese Sports: A History*, 163–64.

5. Suzuki quoted in Reaves, *Taking in a Game*, 82–83; *Sporting News*, September 6, 1945.

6. W. James, "Japan's at Batto Again."

7. Leutzinger, *Lefty O'Doul*, 62.

8. Kelley, *San Francisco Seals*, 114; Leutzinger, "Diamond Diplomacy," 3.

9. *New York Times*, October 31, 1949, 28; Leutzinger, *Lefty O'Doul*, 64–65; *Sporting News*, October 19, 26, 1949.

10. *Sporting News*, December 14, 1949; MacArthur quoted in Leutzinger, *Lefty O'Doul*, 65; O'Doul quoted in Ritter, *Glory of Their Times*, 278.

Bibliography

PRIMARY SOURCES

Manuscript Collections

Berg, Moe. Collection. Arthur W. Diamond Law Library, Columbia University, New York.

————. Papers. New York Public Library.

Grew, Joseph. Diaries and Scrapbooks. Houghton Library, Harvard University, Cambridge MA.

National Baseball Hall of Fame Library Player File Collection. National Baseball Hall of Fame Library, Cooperstown NY.

Quinn, John. 1934 Tour Scrapbook. Private Collection. Collection owner and contact on request to author.

Suzuki, Sotaro. Papers. Private Collection of Yoko Suzuki, Yokohama, Japan.

Warstler, Harold and Grace. Tour of Japan Diary. Private Collection of Virginia McCallum.

SECONDARY SOURCES

Abe, Ikuo, Yasuharu Kiyohara, and Ken Nakajima. "Sport and Physical Education under Fascism in Japan." *Yo: Journal of Alternative Perspectives* (June 2000).

Adachi, Kinnosuke. "Attaboy Japan." *Everybody's* 40 (May 1919): 68.

Akimoto, Shukichi. *The Lure of Japan*. Tokyo: Board of Tourist Industry, 1934.

Allyn, John. *The 47 Ronin Story*. Rutland VT: Charles Tuttle, 1970.

Amos, William H. "I Remember Baybu-Rutu and Me." *Yankee Magazine* 59, no. 11 (1995).

Andryszewski, Tricia. *The Amazing Life of Moe Berg*. Brookfield CT: Millbrook, 1996.

Ardolino, Frank. "Missionaries, Cartwright, and Spalding: The Development of Baseball in Nineteenth-Century Hawaii." *Nine* 10, no. 2 (2002): 27–45.

Baldassaro, Lawrence, and Richard A. Johnson, eds. *The American Game: Baseball and Ethnicity*. Carbondale: Southern Illinois University Press, 2002.

Bedingfield, Gary. "Babe Ruth in World War II." *Baseball in Wartime*. http://www.baseballinwartime.com.

Beim, George, with Julia Ruth Stevens. *Babe Ruth: A Daughter's Portrait*. Dallas: Taylor, 1998.

Berg, Ethel. *My Brother Morris Berg: The Real Moe*. Newark NJ: Ethel Berg, 1976.

Berry, John. *The Gaijin Pitcher: The Life and Times of Victor Starffin*. LaVergne TN: CreateSpace, 2010.

Bix, Herbert. *Hirohito and the Making of Modern Japan*. New York: Harper Collins, 2000.

Blackwood, Thomas. "Bushido Baseball? Three Fathers and the Invention of a Tradition." *Social Science Japan Journal* 11, no. 2 (2008): 223–40.

Board of Tourist Industry, Japanese Government Railways. *Pocket Guide to Japan*. Tokyo: Toppan, 1934.

———. *Pocket Guide to Japan*. Tokyo: Toppan, 1935.

Brown, Delmer. *Nationalism in Japan*. Berkeley: University of California Press, 1955.

Brown, DeSoto. *Aloha Waikiki*. Honolulu: Editions, 1985.

Buruma, Ian. *Inventing Japan, 1853–1964*. New York: Modern Library, 2003.

Byas, Hugh. *Government by Assassination*. New York: Alfred A. Knopf, 1942.

Caiger, George. *Tell Me about Tokyo*. Tokyo: Hokuseido, 1939.

Carr, Kevin Gray. "Making War: War, Philosophy, and Sport in Japanese Judo." *Journal of Sport History* 20, no. 2 (1993).

Considine, Bob, and Babe Ruth. *The Babe Ruth Story*. New York: Scholastic, 1948.

Creamer, Robert. *Babe*. New York: Simon & Schuster, 1992.

Crepeau, Richard C. *Baseball: America's Diamond Mind*. Lincoln: University of Nebraska Press, 1980.

———. "Pearl Harbor: A Failure of Baseball?" *Journal of Popular Culture* 15, no. 4 (1982): 67–74.

Crowley, James B. "Japanese Army Factionalism in the Early 1930s." *Journal of Asian Studies* 21, no. 3 (1962): 309–26.

Dahlberg, William N. "A Tool for Diplomacy: Baseball in Occupied Japan, 1945–1952." Paper presented on August 6, 2010, at SABR 40, Atlanta.

Dalby, Liza. *Geisha*. Berkeley: University of California Press, 1983.

Daniel, W. Harrison. *Jimmie Foxx*. Jefferson NC: McFarland, 2004.

Dawidoff, Nicholas. *The Catcher Was a Spy*. New York: Vintage Books, 1995.

Dower, John. *War without Mercy*. New York: Pantheon Books, 1986.

Elfers, James. *The Tour to End All Tours*. Lincoln: University of Nebraska Press, 2003.

Elias, Robert, ed. *Baseball and the American Dream*. Armonk NY: M. E. Sharpe, 2001.

———. *The Empire Strikes Out*. New York: New Press, 2010.

Fitts, Robert K. *Remembering Japanese Baseball: An Oral History of the Game*. Carbondale: Southern Illinois University Press, 2005.

Franks, Joel. *Asian Pacific Americans and Baseball: A History*. Jefferson NC: McFarland, 2008.

Friday, Karl F. "Bushido or Bull? A Medieval Historian's Perspective on the

Imperial Army and the Japanese Warrior Tradition." *History Teacher* 27, no. 3 (1994): 339–49.

Fujimoto, T. *The Nightside of Japan*. London: T. Werner Laurie, 1927.

Furiya, Reiko. "The Japanese Community Abroad: The Case of Prewar Davao in the Philippines." In *The Japanese in Colonial Southeast Asia*, ed. George Kahin, 155–72. Ithaca NY: Cornell University Press, 1993.

Garis, Frederic de. *Their Japan*. Yokohama: Yoshikawa, 1936.

Gehrig, Eleanor, and Joseph Durso. *My Luke and I*. New York: Signet, 1976.

Gems, Gerald. *The Athletic Crusade*. Lincoln: University of Nebraska Press, 2006.

Gluck, Carol. *Japan's Modern Myths*. Princeton NJ: Princeton University Press, 1985.

Golden, Arthur. *Memoirs of a Geisha*. New York: Vintage, 1997.

Gordon, Andrew. *The Evolution of Labor Relations in Japan*. Cambridge MA: Council on East Asian Studies, Harvard University, 1988.

Grew, Joseph. *Report from Tokyo*. New York: Simon & Schuster, 1942.

——. *Ten Years in Japan*. New York: Simon & Schuster, 1944.

——. *Turbulent Era: A Diplomatic Record of Forty Years*. New York: Houghton Mifflin, 1952.

Gripentrog, John. "The Transnational Pastime: Baseball and American Perceptions of Japan in the 1930s." *Diplomatic History* 34, no. 2 (2010): 247–73.

Guthrie-Shimizu, Sayuri. "For Love of the Game: Baseball in Early U.S.-Japanese Encounters and the Rise of a Transnational Sporting Fraternity." *Diplomatic History* 28, no. 5 (2004): 637–62.

Guttmann, Allen, and Lee Thompson. *Japanese Sports: A History*. Honolulu: University of Hawaii Press, 2001.

Harries, Meiron, and Susie Harries. *Soldiers of the Sun*. New York: Random House, 1991.

Hayford, Charles W. "Response to 'Samurai Baseball vs. Baseball in Japan'— Revisited." *Asian-Pacific Journal: Japan Focus* (May 2008). http://japanfocus .org/products/topdf/2765.

——. "Samurai Baseball vs. Baseball in Japan." *Asian-Pacific Journal: Japan Focus* (April 2007). http://japanfocus.org/products/topdf/2398.

Henrichs, Waldo H., Jr. *American Ambassador: Joseph C. Grew and the Development of the United States Diplomatic Tradition*. New York: Oxford University Press, 1966.

Hibbard, Don, and David Franzen. *The View from Diamond Head*. Honolulu: Editions, 1986.

Hirano, Jiro, et al. *The Spy Who Loved Japan*. Tokyo: NHK, 1979.

Hori, Yukio. *Right Wing Dictionary* [in Japanese]. Tokyo: Sanrei Shobo, 1991.

Hosokawa, Dogen. *Omori Sogen: The Art of a Zen Master*. New York: Kegan Paul International, 1999.

Hurst, G. Cameron, III. "Death, Honor, and Loyalty: The Bushido Ideal." *Philosophy East and West* 40, no. 4 (1990): 511–28.

Ikegami, Eiko. *The Taming of the Samurai.* Cambridge MA: Harvard University Press, 1995.

Ikei, Suguro. *Hakkyu Taiheiyo o Wataru* [White ball over the Pacific] [in Japanese]. Tokyo: Chuokoron, 1976.

Ikki, Kita. "Plan for the Reorganization of Japan." In *Japan, 1931–1945: Militarism, Fascism, Japanism?*, ed. Ivan Morris. Lexington MA: D. C. Heath, 1967.

Inahara, K., ed. *The Japan Yearbook, 1935.* Tokyo: Kenkyusha Press, 1935.

Inoue, Shun. "Budo: Invented Tradition in the Martial Arts." In *The Culture of Japan as Seen through Its Leisure*, ed. Sepp Linhart and Sabine Fruhstuck, 83–93. Albany: SUNY Press, 1998.

Isobe, Asaichi. "Prison Diary." In *The February 22 Incident* [in Japanese], ed. Tsukasa Kono, 168–84. Tokyo: Nihon Shuhosha, 1957.

Izumino, Seiichi. *Matsutaro Shoriki* [in Japanese]. Tokyo: Tsuru Shobo, 1966.

James, Cary. *Frank Lloyd Wright's Imperial Hotel.* New York: Dover, 1968.

James, Weldon. "Japan's at Batto Again." *Collier's*, August 2, 1947, 44–47.

Johnson, William. "Earl Whitehill." Baseball Biography Project. http://bioproj.sabr.org/bioproj.cfm?a=v&v=l&bid=3374&pid=15127.

Kasza, Gregory. "Fascism from Below? A Comparative Perspective on the Japanese Right, 1931–1936." *Journal of Contemporary History* 19, no. 4 (1984): 607–30.

Kaufman, Louis, Barbara Fitzgerald, and Tom Sewell. *Moe Berg: Athlete, Scholar, Spy.* Boston: Little, Brown, 1974.

Kelley, Brent P. *The San Francisco Seals, 1946–1957.* Jefferson NC: McFarland, 2002.

Kelly, William. "The Blood and Guts of Japanese Professional Baseball." In *The Culture of Japan as Seen through Its Leisure*, ed. Sepp Linhart and Sabine Frühstück, 95–112. Albany: SUNY Press.

———. "Is Baseball a Global Sport? America's 'National Pastime' as Global Field and International Sport." *Global Networks* 7, no. 2 (2007): 187–201.

Kelly, William, and Atsuo Sugimoto. *This Sporting Life: Sports and Body Culture in Modern Japan*, ed. William Kelly and Atsuo Sugimoto. New Haven CT: Yale CEAS Occasional Publications, 2007.

Kennedy, Michael Dana. *The Flowers of Edo.* New York: Vertical, 2010.

Kesaris, Paul, ed. *Confidential U.S. Diplomatic Post Records: Japan, Part 3, 1930–1941.* Frederick MD: University Publications of America, 1984.

Kiku, Koichi. "Bushido and the Modernization of Japanese Sports." In *This Sporting Life: Sports and Body Culture in Modern Japan*, ed. William Kelly and Atsuo Sugimoto, 39–54. New Haven CT: Yale CEAS Occasional Publications, 2007.

————. "The Japanese Baseball Spirit and Professional Ideology." In *Japan, Sport, and Society*, ed. Joseph Maguire and Masayoshi Nakayama, 35–54. New York: Routledge, 2006.

Kusaka, Yuko. "The Development of Baseball Organizations in Japan." *International Review for the Sociology of Sport* 22 (1987): 263–78.

Kushner, Barak. *The Thought War*. Honolulu: University of Hawaii Press, 2007.

LaFeber, Walter. *The Clash*. New York: Norton, 1997.

Lamster, Mark. *Spalding's World Tour*. New York: Public Affairs, 2006.

Lee, Frank H. *Tokyo Calendar*. Tokyo: Hokuseido, 1934.

Lee, Robert G. *Orientals*. Philadelphia: Temple University Press, 1999.

Leutzinger, Richard. "Diamond Diplomacy." Unpublished manuscript in author's possession.

————. *Lefty O'Doul: The Legend That Baseball Nearly Forgot*. Carmel CA: Carmel Bay Publishing Group, 1997.

Lewis, Michael. "Reflections on Moe Berg's Japanese Reflections." *Studies on Asia*, 3rd ser., 3, no. 2 (2006). http://studiesonasia.illinoisstate.edu/seriesIII/vol3-2 .shtml.

Lieb, Frederick. *Baseball as I Have Known It*. New York: Coward, McCann & Geoghegan.

————. *Connie Mack*. New York: Putnam, 1945.

Macht, Norman. *Connie Mack and the Early Years of Baseball*. Lincoln: University of Nebraska Press, 2007.

Mah, Jay-Dell. "Barney Brown." Western Canadian Baseball. http://www.atthe plate.com/wcbl/brown_barney.htm.

Marasco, David. "Not a Typical College Road Trip." Baseball Fever.com, March 12, 2005. http://www.baseball-fever.com/showthread.php?25550-Early-Japanese -Baseball./page2.

Matsubayshi, Yoshikazu, ed. *Baseball Game History: Japan vs. U.S.A.* [in Japanese]. Tokyo: Baseball Magazine, 2004.

Matsumoto, Takizo. *The American Ventures in East Asia*. Tokyo: Meiji University Press, 1943.

McAuley, Ed. "Veteran Whitehill Always Ready to Pitch or Fight, Joins Tribe." December 10, 1935. National Baseball Hall of Fame Library Player File Collection, Earl Whitehill File.

Mihara, Osamu. *My Baseball Life* [in Japanese]. Tokyo: Toashuppan, 1947.

Mitchell, Richard H. *Thought Control in Prewar Japan*. Ithaca NY: Cornell University Press, 1976.

Miyasaki, Gail. Jimmy Horio. *Hawaii Herald* 29, no. 20 (2008).

Montville, Leigh. *The Big Bam*. New York: Doubleday, 2006.

Morris, Ivan. *Japan, 1931–1945*. Boston: D. C. Heath, 1963.

Murakami, Hyoe. *Japan: The Years of Trials, 1919–52*. Tokyo: Kodansha, 1983.

Nagata, Yoichi. *Jimmy Horio and U.S./Japan Baseball: A Social History of Baseball* [in Japanese]. Osaka: Toho Shuppan, 1994.

——— . *The Tokyo Giants North American Tour of 1935* [in Japanese]. Osaka: Toho Shuppan, 2007.

——— . "The Tokyo Giants North American Tour of 1935." Paper presented at the 38th Annual Conference for the Society of American Baseball Research, Cleveland, July 27, 2008.

Nakagawa, Kerry Yo. *Through a Diamond: 100 Years of Japanese American Baseball*. San Francisco: Rudi, 2001.

Nippon Dampo News Agency. *Japan Illustrated, 1934*. Tokyo: Nippon Dampo News Agency, 1934.

Nucciarone, Monica. *Alexander Cartwright: The Life behind the Baseball Legend*. Lincoln: University of Nebraska Press, 2009.

Ogawa, Dennis. *From Japs to Japanese: The Evolution of Japanese-American Stereotypes*. Berkeley CA: McCutchan, 1971.

Pajot, Dennis. "Almost an International Incident in Milwaukee." Seamheads.com, March 5, 2009. http://www.seamheads.com/2009/03/05/almost-an-inter national-incident-in-milwaukee.

Palmer, Albert. *Orientals in American Life*. New York: Friendship, 1934.

Pirone, Dorothy Ruth, with Chris Martens. *My Dad, the Babe*. Boston: Quinlan Press, 1988.

Police Bureau of the Japanese Home Ministry. *Report on Social Movements* [in Japanese]. Tokyo: Police Bureau of the Japanese Home Ministry, 1935.

——— . *Report on Social Movements* [in Japanese]. Tokyo: Police Bureau of the Japanese Home Ministry, 1936.

Quinn, John. "American League Stars Tour Far East." In *Spalding Official Base Ball Guide, 1935*, ed. A. G. Spalding & Bros., 264–65. Chicago: A. G. Spalding & Bros., 1935.

Read, Wolf. "The Major Windstorm of October 21, 1934." Storm King, February 24, 2003. http://www.climate.washington.edu/stormking/October1834.html.

Reaves, Joseph. *Taking in a Game: A History of Baseball in Asia*. Lincoln: University of Nebraska Press, 2004.

Richter, Francis C. *The Reach Official American League Guide, 1923*. Philadelphia: A. J. Reach, 1923.

Ritter, Lawrence. *Glory of Their Times*. New York: Quill, 1966.

Robertson, Jennifer. "Blood Talks: Eugenic Modernity and the Creation of New Japanese." *History and Anthropology* 13, no. 2 (2002): 191–216.

Roden, Donald F. "Baseball and the Quest for National Dignity in Meiji, Japan." *American Historical Review* 85, no. 3 (1980): 511–34.

Ruth, Mrs. Babe [Claire], and Bill Slocom. *The Babe and I.* New York: Avon, 1959.

Sano, Shinichi. *Kyokaiden: A Century of Matsutaro Shoriki and His Kagemushas* [in Japanese]. Tokyo: Bungei Shunju, 1994.

Sansom, Katharine. *Living in Tokyo.* London: Chatto & Windus, 1936.

Sawamura, Eiji. "Memoirs of Fighting Baseball Player" [in Japanese]. *Yakyukai* 33, no. 11 (1943): 92–100.

———. "My Worry" [in Japanese]. *Shinseinen* (January 11, 1936): 258–59.

Sayama, Kazuo. "The Impact of Babe Ruth on Japan and Japanese Culture." In *Baseball and the "Sultan of Swat,"* ed. Robert N. Keane. New York: AMS Press, 2008.

———. "Their Throws Were Like Arrows: How a Black Team Spurred Pro Ball in Japan." *Baseball Research Journal* 16 (1987): 85–88.

Schenck, H. G. *The Brocade Banner: The Story of Japanese Nationalism.* Washington DC: General HQ Far East Command Military Intelligence Section, General Staff, 1946.

Seidensticker, Edward. *Tokyo Rising.* New York: Alfred A. Knopf, 1990.

Shay, Ted. "The Level of Living in Japan, 1885–1938." In *Stature, Living Standards, and Economic Development,* ed. John Komlos, 173–204. Chicago: University of Chicago Press, 1994.

Shillony, Ben-Ami. *Politics and Culture in Wartime Japan.* Oxford: Clarendon Press, 1981.

———. *Revolt in Japan.* Princeton NJ: Princeton University Press, 1973.

Sinclair, Robert. "Baseball's Rising Sun: American Interwar Baseball Diplomacy." *Sports History Review* 16, no. 2 (1985): 44–53.

Smelser, Marshall. *The Life That Ruth Built.* Lincoln: University of Nebraska Press, 1975.

Smith, Henry D., II. "Chûshingura in the 1980s: Rethinking the Story of the 47 Ronin." Paper presented at the Modern Japan Seminar, Columbia University, 2003.

Spalding, A. G., & Bros. *Spalding Official Base Ball Guide, 1935.* Chicago: A. G. Spalding & Bros., 1935.

Staples, Bill, Jr. "Matsumoto and Zenimura: Unsung Ambassadors of U.S. and Japanese Baseball." Unpublished manuscript.

Starffin, Natasha. *Glory and Dream on a White Ball: My Father V. Starffin* [in Japanese]. Tokyo: Baseball Magazine, 1979.

Steele, M. W. "The History of the Tama River: Social Reconstructions." In *A History of Water,* ed. Terje Tvedt and Eva Jakobsson, 217–38. London: I. B. Tauris, 2006.

Steiner, Jesse. *Behind the Japanese Mask.* New York: Macmillan, 1943.

Stevens, Julia Ruth. *Major League Dad.* Chicago: Triumph, 2001.

Storry, Richard. *The Double Patriots*. Westport CT: Greenwood, 1957.

———. *A History of Modern Japan*. New York: Penguin, 1984.

Suehiro, Arthur. *Honolulu Stadium*. Honolulu: Watermark, 1995.

Suzuki, Sotaro. *Sawamura Eiji: The Eternal Great Pitcher* [in Japanese]. Tokyo: Kobunsha, 1982.

———. *Unofficial History of Japanese Professional Baseball* [in Japanese]. Tokyo: Baseball Magazine, 1976.

Szpilman, Christopher W. A. "Kita Ikki and the Politics of Coercion." *Modern Asian Studies* 36, no. 2 (2002): 467–90.

Tankha, Brian. *A Vision of Empire: Kita Ikki and the Making of Modern Japan*. New Delhi: Sampark, 2003.

Thomas, Lowell, and Rex Barton. *Seeing Japan with Lowell Thomas*. Akron OH: Saalfield, 1937.

Thompson, Stephen, and Masaru Ikei. "Victor Starffin: The Blue-Eyed Japanese." *Baseball History* 2, no. 4 (1988): 4–19.

Tokyo Yomiuri Giants 50th Anniversary Editorial Room, ed. *Tokyo Yomiuri Giants 50-Year History* [in Japanese]. Tokyo: Tokyo Yomiuri Giants, 1985.

Uhlan, Edward, and Dana L. Thomas. *Shoriki: Miracle Man of Japan*. New York: Exposition Press, 1957.

Victoria, Brian Daizen. *Zen at War*. New York: Rowman & Littlefield, 2006.

———. *Zen War Stories*. New York: Routledge, 2003.

Vlastos, Stephen. *Mirror of Modernity: Invented Traditions of Japan*. Berkeley: University of California Press, 1998.

Wagenheim, Kal. *Babe Ruth*. City: e-reads.com, 2001.

Wald, Royal Jules. *The Young Officers Movement in Japan, ca. 1925–1937: Ideology and Actions*. Ann Arbor MI: University Microfilms, 1949.

Walsh, Thomas P. "When Babe Ruth Came to Manila." *Bulletin of the American Historical Collection* 30, no. 3 (2002): 8–44.

Whiting, Robert. "Samurai Baseball vs. Baseball in Japan—Revisited." *Asian-Pacific Journal: Japan Focus* (May 2008). http://japanfocus.org/products /topdf/2764.

———. *The Samurai Way of Baseball*. New York: Warner Books, 2005.

———. "The Samurai Way of Baseball and the National Character Debate." *Asian-Pacific Journal: Japan Focus* (September 2006). http://japanfocus.org/products /topdf/2235.

———. *You Gotta Have Wa*. New York: Macmillan, 1989.

Whymant, Robert. *Stalin's Spy*. New York: St. Martin's Press, 1998.

Wildes, Harry Emerson. *Japan in Crisis*. New York: Macmillan, 1934.

———. *Social Currents in Japan*. Chicago: University of Chicago Press, 1927.

Willing, Richard. "Chinese Fan Plays Catch across an Ocean." *U.S.A. Today*, December 12, 1997.

Yamamoto, Masahiro. *Nanking*. New York: Praeger, 2000.

Yasuda, Daijiro. "One Aspect of Criminal Justice in Japan: Confessions." Paper presented at the Australian Network for Japanese Law International Conference in Japanese Law, Sydney, February 23, 2005.

Young, A. Morgan. *Imperial Japan, 1926–1938*. New York: William Morrow, 1938.

Zeiler, Thomas W. *Ambassadors in Pinstripes*. Lanham MD: Rowman & Littlefield, 2006.

Index

Abe, Iso, 168

Ainu, 124

Akimoto, Motoo, 199–200

All American tour of Japan: arrival in Japan, xiii–xv, 88–96; departure from Japan, 212–13; and entertainment stipend controversy, 195, 200, 201–2; and establishment of Japanese pro ball, 27, 223–24; finances of, 27; food, 96, 102, 113, 207; as goodwill ambassadors, 120, 150–51, 202, 227–28, 229–30; home run contests during, 157, 189; hostility toward, 146; and player conduct, 53, 252; popular enthusiasm for, 91, 93, 94, 99, 103, 106, 107–8, 142–43, 212; post-tour evaluations, 225–31; recruitment of players for, 24–30; sightseeing by, 71, 98–99, 131, 132, 133–34, 147–48, 185, 214; Suzuki U.S. trip for, 31–38; U.S.-Canada barnstorming by, 51–53; U.S. media coverage of, 97, 119, 227, 228–29; voyages to and from, 53–54, 65–71, 78, 79–80. *See also* baseball games (All American tour)

All American tour of Japan stops: Hakodate, 122–29; Honolulu, 70–71, 74–77; Kokura, 190–92; Kyoto, 195, 200–202; Manila, 218–22; Nagoya, 184–87; Omiya, 207; Osaka, 187–92; Sendai, 129–30; Shanghai, 214, 216–17; Shizuoka, 172–81; Tokyo, xii–xv, 90–93, 95–96, 99, 104–5, 109–12,

115–19, 131–36, 142–47, 157–58; Toyama, 149–50; Yokohama, 88–90, 158–60

All Nippon team roster, 100–102, 107, 114–15, 275–76

America-Japan Society, 150, 151, 152

The American Ventures in East Asia (Matsumoto), 246

Amos, Billy, 143–44, 145

anti-Japanese prejudice, 28–29, 40–41, 226, 229

anti-Semitism, 44

Aoshiba, Kenichi, 211, 224, 276; in tour ballgames, 128, 189, 201, 210; during war, 264

Arai, Gyoji, 13

Araki, Sadao, 58, 137, 155, 261

Asahi Shimbun, 141, 177, 269

Asahi Sports, xiii

Asakura, Hisashi, 209, 276

Asano, Naganori, 132–33

assassination: attempt on Hirohito, 4; attempt on Shigenobu Okuma, 100, 138; attempt on Shoriki, 141, 236–37, 238–39; of Osachi Hamaguchi, 81; of Queen Min of Korea, 138

Atsuta, Sukeyasu, 137, 140, 235, 236

Averill, Earl, xiv, 30, 75, 126–27, 157, 212; aboard *Empress,* 66, 68; alcohol drinking by, 184, 209, 210, 212; in tour ballgames, 111, 116, 118, 128, 147, 150, 159, 175, 186, 191, 207, 209, 210, 212, 220; tour statistics, 210, 275

Axelson, G. W., 226

The Babe Ruth Story (Considine), 256–57
Barrow, Ed, 35, 36, 68
Bartlett, Charlie, 41
Baseball as I Knew It (Lieb), 129
baseball diplomacy, 15, 143, 152, 248–49,
   255; baseball as "civilizing" force, 226;
   and 1934 tour, xv, 143, 227–28, 255;
   postwar, 269, 272
baseball games (All American tour),
   277–79; Hakodate (11/8), 128–29;
   Honolulu (10/25), 75–77; Kokura
   (11/26), 191–92; Kyoto (11/28),
   200–201; Manila (12/9, first), 219–20;
   Manila (12/9, second), 220–21; Manila (12/10), 221–22; Nagoya (11/22),
   185–87; Nagoya (11/23), 187; Omiya
   (11/29), 207; Osaka (11/24), 188–89;
   Osaka (11/25), 189; Sendai (11/9),
   129–30; Shanghai (12/5), 217; Shizuoka (11/20), 172–81; Tokyo (11/3),
   109–12; Tokyo (11/4), 115–19; Tokyo
   (11/10), 144–46; Tokyo (11/11), 146–
   47; Tokyo (11/17), 157–58; Toyama
   (11/13), 149–50; Utsunomiya (12/1),
   208–10; Yokohama (11/18), 159–60
baseball tours of Japan: in 1907 (St.
   Louis School of Honolulu), 7; in 1908
   (Major and Minor League), 7; in
   1913–14 (Major League), 7; in 1920
   (Minor League), 7–8; in 1922 (Major
   League), 8–9; in 1927 (Negro League),
   9–10; in 1931 (Major League), 16–21,
   252; in 1932 (instructional), 24, 46–47;
   in 1949 (San Francisco Seals), 270–72;
   in 1950 (Joe DiMaggio), 272; in 1953
   (Major League), 272. *See also* All
   American tour of Japan
baseball, Japanese: American players in,
   272; attendance, 270; creation of professional league, 23–24, 27, 121, 223–
   25, 242, 243–44; differences with U.S.

game, 160–62; history, 6–7, 162–69;
   hitting in, 161; as national sport, 6,
   152, 167; pitching and fielding in, 160;
   and samurai philosophy, 23, 165, 167,
   168, 169, 223; Sawamura as icon of,
   xv, 181, 265–66; strategy in, 161–62;
   university teams, 6–7, 8, 9, 13, 23,
   100, 115–16, 120–21, 130, 168–69; during World War II, 261–64, 265; after
   World War II, 268–70; Yomiuri Giants
   and, 224–25, 240–41, 243, 272
Bataan Death March, 263
Bates, Albert, 163
Bautista, Joe, 221
Bell, Stuart, 71, 91, 98, 102, 103, 113, 190,
   214; aboard *Empress*, 65–66, 68, 70; on
   Japanese baseball, 161–62; on Japanese life and culture, 127–28, 135–36;
   sightseeing by, 131, 132, 133–34
Berg, Moe, xiv, 50, 94, 143, 149, 223,
   228; aboard *Empress*, 66, 68–69; alleged spying by, xiv, 49, 250–54;
   background, 43–46; friendship with
   Suzuki and Matsumoto, 47, 228, 246;
   on geishas, 96, 97; inclusion on 1934
   tour, 48, 252; infatuation with Japan,
   46–47, 246; and Japanese language,
   46, 68–69, 245–46; Japanese people
   addressed, 149, 246–48; movie filming by, 49, 123, 190, 249, 253–55;
   newspaper reading by, 46, 184; on
   1932 instructional trip, 24, 46–49,
   125–26; and oss, xiv, 49, 249–50; on
   Pearl Harbor, 245; tour statistics, 210,
   275; visit to St. Luke's Hospital, 202,
   203–5, 206–7, 253, 295n12
Berry, Charlie, 30, 50–51
Bix, Herbert, 62–63
Black Dragon Society, 138–39
Bolton, Chester C., 49, 252–53
Bolton, Peggy, 69

Nobriga, Ted, 76–77
nudity, 127–28

O'Doul, Abigail, 29
O'Doul, Frank "Lefty," xiv, 67, 120, 143, 201, 252; career, 22; and creation of Japanese pro baseball, 223, 224, 225; eulogy for, 272; Hirohito audience with, 271; on Japanese ballplayers, 161; in Japanese Hall of Fame, 20, 272; recruitment of players for tour, 28–30, 33, 34, 38; as San Francisco Seals manager, 78, 225, 270, 271–72; and Shoriki, 27–28, 267; and Suzuki, 14, 22–30, 223, 228, 268; visit to Japan (1931), 17, 20–21; visit to Japan (1932), 46, 206; visit to Japan (1949), 267–68, 270–71
Okada, Keisuke, 156, 242
Okuan, Takao, 259
Okuma, Marquis Nobutsune, 95–96, 97, 100, 108–9, 150, 224
Okuma, Shigenobu, 100, 138
O'Leary, Jeremiah, xiii
Oliver, Tom, 249
Omiya, 207
Omori, Roshi, 57, 60–61
Oncinian, Armando, 220
Ono, Michimaro, 9
Osaka, 187–88; All American tour in, 187–92
Osaka Mainichi, 150, 192
An Outline of Measures for the Reorganization of Japan (Kita), 56

Pacific Coast League, 25, 31, 211, 240–41
Pearl Harbor, 240; Japanese reactions to, 258, 259; U.S. reactions to, 240, 244, 245, 254
Pennock, Herb, 8
Perry, Matthew, 56

Philadelphia Athletics, 67
Philadelphia Record, 227–28
Philippines: All American tour in, 218–22; history of baseball in, 218–19; Japanese troops in, 262–63
Principles of National Defense and Proposals for Strengthening It, 137
prostitution, 122, 125
Pullen, Neil, 101

Quigley, Ernie, 16
Quinn, John, 67, 159–60, 162, 209, 221; on Japanese fans, 97, 143, 225; on tour's results, 228, 230

Reach, Mary A., 67
Reardon, John, 162
Report from Tokyo (Grew), 258
Ri (Lee), Eibin, 130, 276
Richer, Francis, 226
Ritter, Lawrence, 22
Roosevelt, Teddy, 109
Ruppert, Jacob, Jr., 35–36, 37, 68
Ruth, Babe, 53, 71, 103–4, 151, 152, 217, 222; assessment of tour by, 256–57; autographs sought of, 90, 98, 112; baseball card of, 113–14; Berg and, 50; convinced to participate in tour, 13, 24–25, 26, 29, 33, 34, 37–38; death of first wife and remarriage, 12–13; Eleanor Gehrig and, 79–80; and entertainment stipend controversy, 195, 202; feud with Gehrig, 66, 80; as focus of fan cheers, 91, 93, 94, 103, 106, 107–8, 212; and geishas, 96, 97; as goodwill ambassador, 120, 229–30; on Japanese baseball and fans, 95, 142, 161; Japanese day of tribute to (1947), 270; and Japanese food and drink, 96, 102, 184; as manager of All American team, 67, 123–24, 186;

manager prospects of, 35–37, 67–68, 78–79; on Philippines ballplayers, 220–21; Shoriki and, 5–6, 10, 13–14, 15–16, 17–18, 26, 239; Suzuki and, 26, 34, 37–39, 69, 123, 201, 208, 212; as symbol in Japan, xiii, xv, 256; in tour ballgames, 75, 77, 110–11, 116–18, 128, 130, 145, 147, 149, 150, 157, 158, 159, 172–74, 179, 180, 189, 191–92, 207, 219, 220, 221; tour statistics, 210, 275; and U.S. war effort, 255–56; voyage to Japan, 30, 66, 67, 68, 69–70; in welcoming parade and ceremony, xiii, xiv–xv, 88, 89, 91, 93, 94; work to get in shape by, 69–70

Ruth, Claire Hodgson, 29, 50, 78–79, 201; and Gehrigs, 66, 79, 80; marriage to Babe, 12–13

Ruth, Dorothy, 66

Ruth, Helen Woodford, 12

Ruth (Stevens), Julia, 29, 50, 67, 89, 228; aboard *Empress*, 69, 70; on Japanese food and drink, 96, 184; sightseeing by, 132, 147–48

samurai, 93–94, 165–67, 171. *See also* Bushido

San Francisco Seals, 78, 225; tour of Japan by, 270–72

Santa Rosa, Johnny, 222

Satsuma Rebellion (1877), 138

Sawada, Renzo, 15

Sawamura, Eiji: on All Nippon team roster, 100–101, 107; almost defeats All Americans, 172–76, 179–81; background, 176–79; death of, 264; expulsion from school, 101, 120–21; hatred of America by, 259; in Japanese army, 259–60, 262–63, 264; in Japanese professional league, 224, 243–44, 260–62,

263, 264; as Japan national hero, xv, 181, 265–66; seen as potential Major Leaguer, 160, 180, 211; support to Japanese war effort by, 258, 263–64; in tour ballgames, 145, 146, 172–76, 179–81, 200–201, 208, 209–10, 276; tour of U.S. by, 240–41

Schroeder, Robert, 67

Sendai, 129–30

Sewell, Tom, 250

Shanghai: All American tour of, 214, 216–17; Japanese attack on, 86, 215–16

Shawkey, Bob, 16, 35

Sheely, Earl, 45

Shibata, Hidetoshi, 89, 94

Shibe, John D., 28

Shimbashi Athletic Club, 6, 164

Shimpeitai (Sacred Soldiers), 60

Shintomi, Usaburo, 189, 190, 264, 275

Shiobe, Shinazo, 199

Shiratori, Toshio, 14

Shizuoka, 172–81; Kusanagi Stadium in, 172, 173–74, 180

Shoriki, Matsutaro, 95–96, 97, 150, 163, 212; assassination attempt against, 141, 236–39; biographical information, 3–4; and creation of Japanese pro league, 23, 27, 121, 224, 242; efforts to arrange 1934 tour, 5–6, 10–11, 13–18, 25–30, 26; incarcerated as war criminal, 267–68; and tour of Japan in 1931, 16–17, 21

Showa Restoration, 57, 58, 61, 63–64, 141; Young Officers and, 155, 182–83, 243

Simmons, Al, 17, 20, 74

Smelser, Marshall, 256

So This Is Africa, 31

Spalding, A. G., 226

Spink, J. G. Taylor, 249